BALLADS AND STORIES
FROM TUN-HUANG

by Arthur Waley

THE OPIUM WAR THROUGH CHINESE EYES

THE NINE SONGS

THE REAL TRIPITAKA

THE POETRY AND CAREER OF LI PO

THE LIFE AND TIMES OF PO CHÜ-I

CHINESE POEMS

MONKEY

THREE WAYS OF THOUGHT IN ANCIENT CHINA

THE ANALECTS OF CONFUCIUS

THE BOOK OF SONGS

THE WAY AND ITS POWER

THE TALE OF GENJI

THE NŌ PLAYS OF JAPAN

THE TEMPLE AND OTHER POEMS

MORE TRANSLATIONS FROM THE CHINESE

THE PILLOW-BOOK OF SEI SHŌNAGON

YUAN MEI

ARTHUR WALEY

BALLADS AND STORIES FROM TUN-HUANG

AN ANTHOLOGY

THE MACMILLAN COMPANY
NEW YORK
1960

To Alberto de Lacerda

PREFACE

This is merely a routine preface. Most of what usually goes into a preface or introduction I have put into the Afterword. That is because I want the reader to plunge straight into the ballads and stories themselves, rather than be confronted at the start with information that will mean little to him till he is acquainted with the texts that it concerns.

The main part of the book is meant for the lover of stories and ballads, irrespective of where they come from. Only the appendices, the references given in the notes and some of the notes themselves are meant for specialists.

I want in a conspicuous place to thank Wang Chung-min and his collaborators who in 1956, having collated about 190 MSS, furnished for the first time a readable text of the seventy-eight pieces of popular literature which they included in the 992 pages of their great work *Tun-huang Pien-wen Chi*. I have sometimes disagreed with their readings; but without the aid of the essential spade-work which they have done I should never have ventured to attempt this anthology.

I have not as a rule tried to relate the legends to the facts of history. In most cases this has already been done in articles listed at the end of the *Pien-wen Chi*.

I am also deeply grateful to Dr Liu Tsun-yan of Hongkong for sending me a recent book, Chiang Li-hung's *Tun-huang Pien-wen Tzu-i T'ung-shih* ('Explanations of expressions used in the Tun-huang *pien-wen*') which put me right on several points, and to the Warburg Institute which allowed me to reprint the Swan-maiden story from the pages of its *Journal*. The editor supplied me with several references. For information on Hindu marriage I am indebted to

7

Dr Ganesh Gaur. Professor Hatto called my attention to Aucassin et Nicolette and Denis Sinor helped me with regard to Turkish plant-names.

References such as that on page 27, line 22 are to the *Pien-wen Chi*.

CONTENTS

9

CHAPTER ONE

THE SWALLOW AND THE
SPARROW

Iɴ the middle of spring, in the second month,
Two swallows circled in the air,
Intending to build a home.
Husband and wife consulted together,
East and west they paced the measurements,
North and south they took the omens,
Avoiding offence to the General and the Year Star[1]
So as to be sure of blessing and free from harm.
They took a tall-headed compass
And piling mud made their nest.
They hauled the beams up into place
And spread straw to make their beds.
They provided against every danger,
They would not nest on feather curtains.[2]
They found a first-rate place to live in
Before they put up their broad beams.
When all the arrangements were complete
They went off to the Embankment for a while.
There came some brown sparrows
With head tapering to a point,
Going down alley and lane
Beating up those weaker than themselves.
Seeing that the swallows were not at home
They went in, meaning to rob the house,
But finding that it was so new and clean
Instead of that, they took possession of it.
Mrs Sparrow and the boys and girls

Were all delighted with these new premises,
Boasting uproariously:
'See we have got for our own
What another took pains to build!
"It is the ploughman who starts the hare,
But those that follow him who drink the broth."
The old proverb puts it neatly;
That is really what happens!
Brandish your fists fiercely,
Swing your arms around,
And if the swallow succeeds in getting in,
Hit at his legs with a stick.
He is quite unsupported,
And after such a gnawing(3) and hacking as he'll get from us
And the talking-to we'll give him
He'll be yours to piss upon in the end!'
While Sparrow was still talking,
The swallows came back.
Swallow stamped on the ground and called out,
And Sparrow came to the door.
Without more ado
Sparrow bared his fists and pounded him;
Pushed him this way, hoisted him that,
Slit his ear and slapped his cheek.
The little sparrows pulled him by the leg,
Mrs Sparrow stooped over him and pecked him.
Swallow thus belaboured
Was no better than a corpse.
He could not lift his head,
He could not open his eyes.
He and his wife, a sad pair,
Lamented gasping and sobbing:
'We never once crossed the path of the Leopard's Tail;(4)
Why have we got into this cursèd scrape?'
Then Swallow went to King Phoenix's Court
To file his petition and explain his case:
'I, the swallow, alone and needy

12

Managed to build myself a house.
But it was seized by the sparrow,
Who not content with this violence
Sought to intimidate me with threats.
"There was a Decree",[5] he said, "that all strangers from afar,
Were to be subject to the usual *corvées* and taxes.
You, Swallow, fled from your place of origin,
Yet were never once seen to do service to the King.
Finally an official was told to beat you on the back
And you were banished to Tan, Yai, Hsiang and Po.[6]
I, on the contrary, am well-connected;
The kite is my maternal uncle, the hawk is my father's
    brother.
Governors and Prefects
Form one long line in my family.
If you file a complaint against me
You not I will suffer in the end.
You had better both of you, swift as fire,
Leave my door, or in a moment
You'll be in for a thrashing."
I, the swallow, was indignant
And pressed my rightful claims.
Whereupon Sparrow dragged me by the head,
Caught hold of my coat and tore it,
Pummelled me pell-mell with naked fists,
Recklessly flinging himself into the fray.
Then all the sparrows, father and sons,
Threw themselves upon me and belaboured me.
I, the swallow, was flogged,
My plumage tattered, my feathers scattered on the ground.
I could neither stand up nor sit down;
I thought each moment was my last.
I humbly ask you to verify my charge;
See for yourself that I am red and blue.
Such wrongs I cannot endure;
I beg your Majesty to give a verdict
In accordance with the gravity of this crime.'

The Phoenix said,
'The indictment laid by Swallow
Is couched in convincing terms.
That Sparrow's conduct was high-handed
Is beyond all dispute.
But the two must be confronted and each state his case.
I must know the rights and wrongs
Before I can give my verdict.
I hereby charge the wren
To go and make the arrest.'
The wren, hearing the King's command,
Not daring an instant to delay
Half walking, half running
Shot swift as a falling star.
When he arrived at Sparrow's door
He stood listening for a while.
He could hear sparrow-talk inside the nest
And a voice was saying
'Last night I had a bad dream;
This morning my eyelids twitched.
That means either a private quarrel
Or else some trouble with the law.
The *corvées* allotted to me of late
I have each time fulfilled.
It can only be that the swallow
Has filed a petition against me at Court.
Now, boys and girls, whatever you do,
Be sure not to open the door!
If anyone asks for me, you are to say
I am at the village to the east!'
The wren, from outside the door,
Said 'It's no use your trying to hide.
I heard everything you said just now.
Come out at once and get this straight.
How came you to seize this house
And then proceed to knock him about?
I have here a warrant from the Court

Instructing me to arrest you.
You must answer in person for what your own hands have
    done.
You are in a hole from which there is no escape,
Plot and scheme as you will.'
This put Sparrow in a great fright;
His heart fluttered and he trembled.
All his family, big and little,
Were scared out of their wits.
In the end he went and knelt before the wren,
Calling him Eldest Son, Second Son.
'You have come with your message a long way in the heat.
Wouldn't you like to cool yourself in my nest?
They say "A guest may be in a hurry;[7]
But there is no such thing as hurry for a host."
Come and sit down for a minute
While we prepare our family meal.'[8]
'This fellow must be quite mad', said the wren,
'So to misjudge his situation.
Finding me easy-going
He tries by hook or crook to gain time.
It's no use your talking about food;
I don't happen to be hungry.
I must be off, swift as fire;
The King will be cross if I am late.'
The Sparrow, though very depressed,
Still hoped to profit by delay.
Again and again he refused to go,
On the chance of somehow escaping his fate.
With empty pretences and far-fetched arguments
A thousand times he entreated,
Ten thousand times he besought:
'Couldn't it, as a compromise, be put off till tomorrow
When we can really cook you something good?'
The wren's patience was exhausted,
He grasped Sparrow by the waist and dragged him away.
Sparrow was worried. How he puckered[9] his brows!

Crestfallen he was carried away,
And they were soon at the district Court.
The Phoenix seeing them from afar
Asked 'Who is this?'
At once Sparrow bowed his head
And knelt before the throne,
Doing homage to the King.
'I, your subject Sparrow,' he said,
'Am by the swallow slanderously accused
Of seizing his house.
Yesterday I was summoned by the King's warrant
And have scuttled here with dutiful haste,
Lest I should be charged with delay.
Swallow's affidavit
Is all a pack of lies,
Designed to hoodwink this Court.
I beg your Majesty to be allowed to confront him.'
The King said, 'This good-for-nothing scamp!
Maggots must have damaged his brain.
A vile creature(10) indeed!
Leave all this for me to deal with.
Stick out your left leg, expose your behind
And hold your brain-cap high.'
Sparrow, his spirit broken by these threats,
Cried out that, though he deserved death,
He hoped Swallow would be sent for to confront him.
Swallow bustled forward
And with a low bow made his plea.
'Sparrow', he said, 'seized my house
And is now openly residing there.
As regards the wounds he inflicted
I have in no way exaggerated;
A glance will verify what I have said.'
Sparrow, seeing himself thus worsted,
Put a solemn expression on his face
And asked to be allowed to speak on oath.
He then began a long rigmarole:

'If it is true that I seized Swallow's house
May I and my whole generation be destitute.
May I in the morning meet the hawk and be seized,
In the evening meet the kite and be grabbed;
When I go out, be caught in the net,
When I stay at home, be hit by a pellet,
May my business go to bits
And my leisure be without peace.
May I bury a relative each day
Till of my whole family none is left!'
But though he swore and swore again
The swallow said:
' "A man in straits burns incense;
A dog in straits jumps over the wall."
But with a scabby, leprous creature like this
Nothing remains but to bury the corpse.
The oaths that he has rattled off in such profusion
Were only meant to mislead our great King.'
The Phoenix was very angry.
After a time he gave judgment, saying
'Sparrow's misdemeanour
Was of incalculable gravity,
And when put under interrogation
He showed obstinate resistance—
As penalty I condemn him at once
To five bouts(11) of flogging;
He is to wear a cangue on his neck and go to gaol;
Such is my judgment.'
Swallow shouted his delight,
Pleased and gratified beyond measure:
'You seized my house and heaped abuse upon me,
Thinking your luck would hold.
But on the contrary, to your surprise,
Heaven has paid you out,
Bringing you to such a state as this
When "five beats" is the tune!'(12)
The wagtail was at hand,

Who being Sparrow's younger cousin
Wanted to help in any way he could,
And had remained in constant attendance.
Seeing Swallow's exultation
He now stepped forward and burst out angrily: (12b)
'Sir, that my own brother has offended you
Reflects shame on your humble servant.
I have heard that when the fox dies
Even the hare is sad
At the fate of his own species.
"All are brothers within the Four Seas"
And the more so if they are of one breed.
Today you secured a decision in your favour
And you must leave it to the Court to give their judgment
　　due effect.
"One does not aim pellets at a dead sparrow",
Still less should one follow them up with abuse.'
When Mrs Sparrow heard that her husband had been
　　flogged
She sank into a state of utter collapse.
She could only hammer her bosom and beat her breast,
Into such anxiety about him did she fall.
Somehow making one stride out of two
She ran to the prison to look after him.
There was Sparrow lying on the ground,
IIis face the colour of dust,
And on his back there stood out a lump
That seemed a foot and a half high.
Sparrow was in great distress;
Tears fell from his eyes like rain.
She at once sprinkled urine(13) on his wounds
And then plastered them with old paper:
'I firmly remonstrated at the time;
But you were too obstinate to follow my advice.
All your jabberings and twitterings were no use,
And in the end you were dealt with in Court,
Put into a cangue and held in gaol,

And in fact made thoroughly uncomfortable!
All these troubles are your own doing;
Don't blame the God of the Stove.'(14)
'I, the sparrow, was obstinate, went my own way
And let fall some rude remarks.
But a man that is worthy of the name
If, because he handles matters badly,
His back is knocked to bits,
Has no need to be dismayed.
"In life things repeat themselves;
Death can only happen once."
And does not the proverb say
"Better brave ten wolves or nine tigers
Than the anger of a fool"?
All the slanders that have been breathed against me
That black crone(15) set going.
Now that I am in prison
I would rather die than be humiliated.
Go at once and call for the myna-bird;
He has his wits about him.
Get him to "gnaw" at those in authority
So that they may put in a word for me with the King.
If he can get me off another beating,
Give him a bundle of sesamum.'
When Sparrow had been in prison several days
He begged the gaoler to take off his cangue,
But again and again the gaoler refused.
Then with tempting words Sparrow cajoled him:
' "Where officially a needle will not pass
Privately there is room for a coach."
I implore you to take it off!
Do please, till the evening session,
Not demanding too heavy a bribe.
The person who comes with my food(16)
Will be sure to give you a silver hairpin.'
The gaoler said:
'The reason you are now in the Yellow Sands(17)

Is that you failed to rebut Swallow's charge.
I have the honour to serve as the King's officer;
I cannot accept bribes to protect you.
If by any chance the King found out
He would pound me like hemp-seed crushed for oil.
I would rather you should be uncomfortable
Than that my conduct should be impugned.'
The sparrow sighed. 'In ancient days', he said,
'High Ministers were tormented by their gaolers
Just as now is happening to me.
I see nothing for it but to pray to Buddha
And inwardly to make this vow:
"If I succeed in escaping from this trouble with officials
I will collate and copy the whole of the *Heart Sūtra*".'[18]
Next he said coaxingly to the Clerk:[19]
'Can't you cut out the interrogation?
To the Court Assessors high and low
I will put my case fairly and without flinching;
Just for today be a little accommodating.
However, I could do with paper and a brush;
"Never speak with cold face and empty hand".'
The Clerk said,
'Your wits must be very dull,
Or is it that your eyesight is dim?
Having seized his house
You had not the sense to apologize and withdraw.
But instead resorted to violence
Struck him and got into trouble.
You have broken the King's law
And the Phoenix sent me to question you.
Tomorrow when you rise early and appear before the
    Court
You will certainly be in for another bout,
And by the time you've had ten strokes and more
It will depend on Heaven whether you only come
To within half an inch of expiring.
Just prepare your back for humble reception;[20]

We need no documents to frame our sentence.'
Sparrow thus ticked off
Almost choked with anger.
But when the questioning began
He became even more distressed.
Question: 'The swallow built his house
Meaning to live there himself.
How came it that you so high-handedly
Dared to seize it by force?'
Respectful answer: 'My famous brain[21]
Tempted the crow to pursue me.
I had to run for it, however difficult the way;
Where I found a hole, I had to shelter in it.
I did for a time take Swallow's house
Merely to avoid being caught.
The fact is, I was a refugee.
I did it in an emergency;
It was no case of forcible seizure,
I hope the King will appreciate this.'
Further question:
'Granted that you are a refugee
How came it that you used intimidation,
Went so far as to trip him up and strike him
And caused his feathers to fall out?
According to the Law of the Land the proper penalty
Is a hundred with the bamboo.
If you have any argument to the contrary
State clearly what it is.'
Respectful reply:
'It was solely on account of my brain
That I became a refugee
And sheltered for a time in Swallow's house.
I saw that it was not inhabited
And pulled up there for a short rest.
Then Swallow arrived
And I was just coming out to apologize
When he, knowing nothing of the circumstances,

Began at random to abuse me.
Then he and his children in a band
Tried to drag me off to Court.
In a passion, not thinking what it would lead to,
I at once gave him a knock.
Swallow complains of losing feathers,
But I also am lamed in the leg.
The damage sustained by each side,
By him and by me, is much the same.
However, that my use of his house
May be put on a proper footing
Allow me to pay as compensation
Twice the real value of his premises.
If I am punished in strict accordance with the law
I shall not venture to complain.
In that case, the fact that I was decorated
As a Pillar of the State
Will, I hope, be regarded by the Court
As a mitigation of my crime.'
Further question:
'Your offence in seizing premises, with intimidation,
Is of a kind that cannot be overlooked.
But you claim to have been decorated;
On what occasion were your services performed?'
Respectful answer:
'In the nineteenth year of Chen-kuan[22]
During the great attack on Liao-tung
I, Sparrow, was called up
And took part in the campaign,
Being allotted to a place in the vanguard.
I did not ride on horseback, I had no bow in my hand,
But in my mouth held lighted tinder
Which I launched down the wind,
And the Koreans were destroyed.
Such were my services and, as precedent demanded,
I was made a Pillar of State,
As may be seen from the Honour List.

The Swallow and the Sparrow

But if you want to be quite sure,
I suggest that you should verify it
In the *Book of Hills and Seas*.[23]

At the trial the Phoenix gave judgment:
'Sparrow regardless of the consequences
Forcibly seized Swallow's house,
And when questioned about how it happened
Would not at first admit his guilt.
But the fact that he was decorated
As a Pillar of State
Must be set against his crime,
And he should not be imprisoned.
The case had for the present better be dismissed
Or the files will become unwieldy.'
Having got off like this
Sparrow could not contain himself for joy.
He called to Swallow
To come and drink two pints.
'Your recent blunder', said Swallow,
'I hope you now deplore
And will in future be particularly careful
To obey the King's commands,
Never hankering again
After places already occupied.'
Swallow and Sparrow, now reconciled,
Went back together to their village.
Here they found a busybody heron
Who took the two of them to account:
'In the dispute that has just occurred
You, Sparrow, would not "retire to the closet",
But "with open eyes wetted your bed"
By acting in defiance of the Law.
Fortunately for you the Phoenix was indulgent
And let you continue your paltry existence.
But at any moment the kite may pounce upon you,
And you will be finished for good and all.'

Then he scolded the swallow:
'You're a silly troublesome fellow!
Why make so much fuss over a trifle,
Putting another in danger of his life?
An inhuman way to carry on!
Neither of you has any sense
And by rights I ought not to consort with you.'
Swallow and Sparrow rejoined in chorus:
'Who would have thought
That, though Phoenix spared his anger,
The busybody heron would scold us?
It is not for you to pronounce judgment.
The case is over now, so why all this talk?
If you want to demonstrate your talents
Choose a subject on which to make a poem.'
The heron, nettled that despite his good intentions
The two were being sarcastic about him,
Recited a poem, to make them understand:
'The heron's heart has long been set on things far away,
Concerning which Swallow and Sparrow are quite
  uninformed.
In one morning he can sail away far above the blue clouds;
In three years he flies and sings just at this time'(?)[24]
Whereupon Swallow and Sparrow replied in chorus:
'The great rukh sets out on its journey to the South
While the little wren nests on its one bough.
Yet each finds contentment in its own haunts;
So why question (?) the knowledge of us two creatures?'[25]

CHAPTER TWO

WU TZU-HSÜ

ONCE upon a time there was a King of Ch'u so power-
ful that his dominions reached as far as the land
of Buddha. This King had a minister called Wu
She, whose two sons were in service in other kingdoms.
Tzu-shang, the elder, was at the Court of the land of Cheng;
Tzu-hsü, the younger, was serving in the land of Liang.

The Heir-Apparent of the King of Ch'u was old enough
to have a wife, but was not yet married. The King said to
his ministers, 'Who is there that has a daughter fit to be his
consort? I have heard that a kingdom without an Eastern
Palace[26] is like a land that is half wilderness. . . . Half the
majesty of a kingdom belongs to its Crown Prince, yet our
Prince has no bride. What should be done?'

'I have heard', said the Grand Minister Wei Ling, 'that the
Duke Mu of Ch'in has a daughter of sixteen whose beauty
surpasses that of all women. Her eyebrows are like the moon
at its waning, her cheeks are like frozen light (?), her eyes
are like falling stars, her face has the beauty of a flower,
her hair is seven feet long, her nose is straight and her forehead square, her ears are like hanging pearls, her hands fall
below her knees, her ten fingers are slender and long. I
would have your Majesty give orders that a marriage with
her should be negotiated for the Prince. For if arrangements
can be made that meet your wishes, it would bring glory to
all your domains and be a fine thing!'

So Wei Ling was sent to solicit the Duke of Ch'in's
daughter. When he came home with her, the King of Ch'u
sent for him and said, 'I am afraid you have had a hard
journey through wind and frost.'

When the King saw the girl, she was so beautiful that he suddenly felt a wolfish, a tigerish desire for her. Wei Ling was quick to play up to this feeling.

'Why don't you take her for a consort yourself?' he said. 'We can look elsewhere for a bride for the Crown Prince; there are plenty of pretty girls. Surely this would be no crime?'

When the King heard Wei Ling's words, he was beside himself with joy. He at once took the girl from Ch'in as a consort and for three days on end stayed in the inner palace, never once holding audience.

When Wu She heard this he was very angry, and not fearing the thunder and lightning of the King's might he let down his hair and went straight to the Palace. Here, braving his Majesty's displeasure, he bluntly reproved him for what he had done. The King was startled and dismayed.

'Have there been any unfavourable omens?' he asked.

'I look upon your Majesty as having committed such a crime', said Wu She, 'that I much fear you will lose your kingdom. If rebellion breaks out and ministers flee, it will certainly be because of this daughter of the Duke of Ch'in. You fetched a wife for your son and then took her as your own consort. What is this but to compete for a bride with your own son? Is not this to bring upon yourself the scorn of Heaven and Earth? By this deed you have confounded the Statutes and upset all usages and rights. What can I do but reprove you, when I see you put your realm in jeopardy?'

The King's face flushed with shame at being thus humiliated in the presence of his ministers.

'Chancellor of the Realm,' he said, 'have you not heard the saying: "Spilt water cannot be recovered; a plan that is in action cannot be called in question?" What I have done, I have done, and I can tolerate no reproof.'

But Wu She saw that the King, contrary to all right, had taken the girl from Ch'in as his own consort, and braving his displeasure he again bluntly reproved him.

'Your Majesty', he said, 'is lord of ten thousand men and you have the governance of many lands. How comes it that you have let yourself be guided by the words of Wei Ling?'

(At this point there is a gap in the text. It is evident that the King of Ch'u imprisons Wu She; but Wu She manages to get a letter through to the King of Cheng, where his elder son is serving at Court. The King of Cheng tells the elder son (Wu Tzu-shang) that it is his duty to rescue his father. Wu Tzu-shang therefore hastens to Liang, where the second son, Wu Tzu-hsü, is serving, to concert with him a plan for the rescue of their father. But Wu Tzu-hsü feels sure the letter does not really come from his father in prison, but was concocted by the wicked King of Ch'u in order to get the two sons into his power. He therefore tells the messenger who brought the letter to go back to Ch'u and tell him that he, Wu Tzu-hsü, is about to 'raise an army and take vengeance on his father's enemies'. The elder brother believes in the genuineness of his father's summons and goes back with the messenger to Ch'u, where he is promptly cast into prison along with his father.)

When (p. 3, l. 12) the sovereign of Ch'u heard the messenger's words, he smote the steps of his throne and called out angrily, 'A curse upon this paltry rebel! Can an inch of weed measure the vault of Heaven? Can a wisp of hair hope to resist the embers of the stove? These words of Wu Tzu-hsü are madness. They are not worth regarding. They are mere idle tittle-tattle, fit only to be ignored.'

The King of Ch'u then called for Wu She and his son Wu Tzu-shang to be taken out of gaol and executed. When Tzu-shang was about to die, he looked up towards Heaven and said sighing, 'Had I but listened to my younger brother's advice, I would not have come all this way only to share in my father's execution. But now it is too late to repent. I can only pray that after my death my brother will live on and, if

Heaven opens the way for him, will slay the King of Ch'u and so avenge our father.'

No sooner had he said these words than they slew him. Father and son, at the same time, were cruelly slaughtered.

The King of Ch'u issued a proclamation ordering the arrest of Wu Tzu-hsü. How does this passage go?[27] The proclamation said:

'A servant of the land of Liang, the rebel Wu Tzu-hsü, had a father who in his service to me, his lord, showed no loyalty or respect, who when he should have been planning the welfare of the realm showed the savage greed of a ravening tiger. Both this father and his son Tzu-shang, who was in service with the land of Cheng, I have duly executed. There only remains the other son, Wu Tzu-hsü, who fled and at present has not been caught. Anyone apprehending him and handing him over will receive a reward of a thousand catties of gold and a fief of a thousand families. Anyone sheltering him will be dealt with according to the full rigour of the Code. First he will be beheaded, and then his whole clan will be exterminated. Any undue lenience on the part of those concerned will entail loss of office and prosecution. It must be reported to me at once and the culprit sent to the capital under strict duress.'

No sooner had the proclamation been issued than the waterways were wedged with ships carrying notifications to every district, and placards appeared on every highway. All villages were searched, and no one dared give him shelter. Indeed, so greedy were they all for the high reward that the people scrambled to be first in catching him. . . .

When Wu Tzu-hsü reached the River Ying, the wind came brushing his ears, carrying the sound of silk being beaten. He was afraid to push straight on, and stood in hiding. . . .

The girl who was beating silk in the stream had looked up and seen a man approaching with wild stride, distraught in spirit, hungry of countenance, and with a sword at his waist. She knew at once it must be Wu Tzu-hsü, and said to herself sadly, 'I have heard that in return for a single meal given to him in the mulberry-grove Ling Che[28] propped the chariot; the yellow sparrow[29] that was given a salve for its wound brought white jade rings as a thank-offering. I am a chaste virgin, flawless and unspoilt. Now beating silk by the water-side I have had the good fortune to meet with a gentleman. True my home is ill-provided; but I do not grudge him a meal.'

So thinking she walked slowly along the bank, and called out, 'Wanderer, stop for a while! Gentleman with the sword, from what quarter do you come? Of what land are you the paragon? . . . What urgent business hurries you on your way, companionless, distraught and flustered? From the look on your face I can see that you are on some quest. If you are not a knight-errant carrying out a vendetta, then you are fleeing to escape arrest by King P'ing. I can offer you such fare as a poor home provides. How do you feel about that? Pray condescend to step this way.'

'I am a man of Ch'u,' he replied, 'employed as an envoy by the land of Yüeh. Recently it fell to my lot to bring tribute from Yüeh and I journeyed westward to the King of Ch'u. After having also collected contribution for military purposes in the lands of Liang and Cheng I was on my way back to Yüeh, richly laden, when coming to a small river I was attacked by fierce robbers, and was lucky to escape with my life. Today, climbing hills and crossing ridges, I ran short of provisions. Hearing in the air the sound of your silk-beating, I looked about everywhere to see where it came from. I fear that in my plight I cut an awkward figure. But I am indeed in a desperate hurry, for I must be back within the time appointed by the King. Tell me how I can get through to the road that leads to Kuei-chi. What I want of you is to point out the right way; I would not venture to expect food.'

'I have heard an old saying', the girl replied, 'which was not idly spoken: "It is easier to make whole a broken bow-string than to detain one who is determined to get away." As to the road you should take, that is easily known. But seeing you glancing over your shoulder and then gazing ahead, a sad look in your face, stained with the wind and dust of long travels over rivers and across the hills, I cannot but beg you to overlook the boldness of one so humble, and let me offer you a meal. . . .'

Wu Tzu-hsü (p. 6, l. 4) wanted to go on; but twice and again she urged him to stay and at last, for men's feelings are hard to understand, he squatted by the waterside, and began to eat. But after three mouthfuls he stopped; for he was ashamed to be indebted to a woman. He was on the point of setting out again, but the girl insisted that he must eat up all she had given him. Being now more deeply beholden to her than ever he at last told her what was on his mind:

'Your humble servant, if the truth be told, is Wu Tzu-hsü;
I am fleeing from Ch'u and making my way towards Wu
    in the south.
Because I am afraid that the King of Ch'u may follow me
    and catch me
I travel only in the starry night, choosing desolate ways.
The food you have given me amply suffices to stave off my
    hunger;
Indeed you have done for me far more than I can ever
    repay.
Strength and lightness have returned to my limbs, my eyes
    again are bright;
The time has come to say farewell and start on my long
    road.
I am an exile forced to leave the comfort of my royal home;
At this very moment by the King of Ch'u I know that I
    am sought and pursued.
If you wish me well, tell no one that I have been this way;
I beg and entreat you, lady, to respect and understand my
    feelings.'
When Tzu-hsü had said this, he set out on his way;
When she saw him go, she shouted to him, saying with
    doleful cry

'Traveller, how lonely you look! I am not happy about you.
You creep on like one that is dying and yet is greedy for
  life;
In giving you this one meal I have not done enough;
A mere woman cannot satisfy a hero's true need.
You, I know, would have much preferred to refuse what I
  offered;
But I, as I think, forced you to suffer no light shame.'
Saying this, she wept bitterly, and then wiping her tears:
'To think that once this haggard wreck was a lord of stately
  mien!
If afterwards, as well may happen, you are caught by your
  pursuers
You will certainly think "It was this woman that got me
  into trouble."
At the age of thirty I have never before talked with a
  grown man;
All the time I have stayed in my village living in my
  mother's house.

(This and the following three lines do not fit in well here
and properly belong to a Confucian, upper-class version of
the story, according to which the girl 'cannot bear' the
thought that after living alone with her mother up to the age
of thirty a life of the strictest propriety she has now infringed
the 'rites and usages' by giving food to a strange man (*Wu
Yüeh Ch'un Ch'iu*, fol. 16). In the early fourteenth-century
play *Wu Tzu-hsü Blows the Pipes* the Confucian motif is
dropped and the girl drowns herself solely in order that Wu
Tzu-hsü may 'go on his way with an easy mind', and not be
worried by the suspicion that the girl may be going to
denounce him to the Ch'u authorities.)

A face aglow with graceful charm, as you can see for your-
  self,
A virtuous woman, chaste and true, is cast away in vain.
Lord Wu,' she called to him, 'set your mind at rest!'

Then clasping a heavy stone she leapt into the stream and
    died.
Tzu-hsü, who had turned round to look at her once more,
For he had become fond of this lady and was feeling sad
    about her,
Saw her from afar clasp the stone and disappear in the river,
Letting slip (scarce knowing what she said) a last outraged
    cry:
'If you should chance in the days to come to get high rank
Spend a hundred pieces of gold on making me a tomb!'
Pitiless the waters of the Ying closed in upon her;
Tzu-hsü sighed and wept, sadder than before.

Tzu-hsü, when his lament was over, went on his way again.
. . . At last he came to a watered valley in which a house
stood. He knocked at the door and asked for food. The
woman who came to answer his knocking recognized at a
distance her brother's voice and knew from far away that it
was Tzu-hsü.

She did all she could to comfort him and condole with
him; but he kept his mouth shut and would not say a word.
She saw that for a long time he had been thirsty and in need,
so she took a gourd and filled it with rice and made, to go
with it, a salad of bitter herbs.

Tzu-hsü was wiser than most and guessed at once what she
meant. Carefully reflecting, he understood the meaning of
what she had done.

'A gourd filled with rice', he said to himself, 'means bitter-
ness without and sweetness within; a salad of bitter herbs
means bitter mixed with bitter. What she intends me to
understand is that I must go away at once, go away at once!
I must not stay here any longer', and so thinking he took his
leave.

'When you set out again,' she said, 'where do you intend
to betake yourself?'

'To the land of Yüeh,' he said. 'My father and brother have
been murdered, and I must avenge them.'

She clasped her brother's head, and moaned out in a voice choked with sobs, not daring to make a loud lament: 'Oh, the anguish of it, the misery!' Then, beating her breast: 'What sin can you and I have done in former lives, that we should be left orphaned and wretched?'

Tzu-hsü parting from his sister said, 'Farewell!
It is no use lamenting and weeping a thousand rows of tears.
Our father and brother by a wrongful sentence have been
    done to death;
To think of it sets my heart seething with fierce rage.
Only a coward would consent to live under the same sun!
In a brave man's heart the pain that gathers is too cruel a
    hurt.
If the day comes when Heaven's justice opens up my way
I swear that I will catch alive King P'ing of Ch'u,
    Scoop out his heart and chop him into bits,
    Exterminate his clan to the ninth degree.
    I swear that until all this is done
    I will not set foot again in my native place!'

When he had said these words he went off towards the south, but when he had gone some twenty leagues his eyes blinked and his ears felt hot. He at once drew a diagram on to ground in order to take the omens, and the signs told him that his sister's sons were pursuing him. He put water on his head to drive them off, thrust a piece of bamboo into his belt and put on his clogs back to front. And then again he drew the patterns called 'The Door of Earth' and 'The Gate of Heaven'. Having done so he lay down among the rushes and recited the spell:

      Death to those that catch up with me,
      Doom to those that catch hold of me
      Swift, swift as Lü ling.[30]

Now Tzu-hsü's two nephews, Tzu-an and Tzu-yung, came home and found that a man had been eating there. They knew

that it must have been their uncle Tzu-hsü, and caring nothing
for their mother's feelings they got a wicked idea into their
heads and set off in pursuit of him.

'When we see the Sovereign of Ch'u', they said, 'we shall
be given the reward and shall also certainly be promoted to
high rank. The rebel has been recently at these doors, and
we shall have no difficulty in catching him.'

When they had gone about ten leagues, they sat down by
the roadside to rest. One of the brothers, Tzu-yung, knew
something of *Yin-Yang* magic(31), so he drew a diagram on the
ground and took the omens. The signs revealed that Uncle
Tzu-hsü had 'water on his head', which could only mean that
he had fallen from the bank into the river; also that he had
a piece of bamboo stuck into his belt, meaning that his body
had not been recovered and a cenotaph had been built. Lastly,
that his wooden clogs were put on back to front must mean
going backwards and forwards and so getting nowhere.

'All these signs can only mean that he is dead. Let us go
home and not look for him any more!'

Tzu-hsü, on his side, bent over his magic text and saw that
his nephews were no longer pursuing him, so he hastened on
through the starry night, never once stopping.

In a watered valley he again came to a house. Its walls were
very beautifully built. It stood all alone, with no man living
on any side. Not ashamed to be a full-grown man and yet
play the beggar, he knocked at the gate and asked for food.

Tzu-hsü knocked at the gate and begged to be given food;
His wife (it was she) composed her countenance and came
out to answer.
As soon as she saw him she knew quite well that this was
her own husband,
And her first thought was to show by what she said that
she knew who he was.
But on second thoughts she hung back and thinking the
matter over

34

She felt she ought not to come forward and draw closer
    to him.
Instead she decided merely to meet him with a formal
    inclination,
Sadly and in a tearful voice she put to him the question:
'I, your handmaid, live all alone in the wild countryside,
Round about me are no neighbours; desolate my lodging,
What can it be that brings to such a place a gentleman like
    you?
There is great sadness in your face, and you look half-
    starved—
Cowering in the bushes haggard and wild, as though you
    were afraid of someone,
Doubled up, as though you wished to hide, and asking to
    be fed.
Although I spend my life shut up deep in my inner bower,
Something about you, in a vague way, seems faintly
    familiar.'
       Wu Tzu-hsü answered his wife, saying:
'Your servant is a man of Ch'u, sent on a distant mission;
Hill on hill, dale on dale I make my way home.
During my travels I lost my way, confused by failing light;
And not knowing where I was going I suddenly found
    myself here.
My native place is far away, at the western end of the lakes,
A long journey, and lying between are the waters of three
    rivers. . . .
Madam, you have judged too hastily, I am not what you
    suppose,
Nor do I, lady, remember ever meeting you before.
I want at once to set out on my way to the east of the river,
And beg of you as a great kindness to point where my road
    lies!'

(The wife then shows that she knows who he is and what
has been happening to him in a passage consisting largely of
the names of medicines, both vegetable and mineral, used

punningly. For example *tang-kuei* means a kind of angelica, but also 'you must go back'. *Tu-huo* means another kind of angelica, but also 'live alone'. Wu Tzu-hsü replies in the same vein. This passage is of course untranslatable, as the plays on words cannot be reproduced in English. The wife then complains, in straight language, of the lonely life she has been leading, explains that she recognized him owing to his two protruding teeth, and begs him to stay for a little and have something to eat. But Wu Tzu-hsü stolidly keeps up the pretence that she is mistaken):

'Lady (p. 11, l. 14), your husband's surname is Wu and he
  holds high office;
I am a person of humble birth and live in the grassy wilds.
If I ever chance to meet your husband I will give him news
  of you
And put it to him as strongly as I can that he ought to
  return home.
Now, as my business is very urgent, I must go east of the
  river
And go quickly, I cannot stay another day or night.'

His wife knew that he schemed great things and did not dare further play upon his feelings. She furnished him with what he needed and duly sent him on his way.

Wu Tzu-hsü, having been recognized by his wife, said no more. 'I, a grown man,' he thought, 'before reaching my goal have let myself be recognized by a woman. But I am not going to allow a small matter to prevent the achievement of a great duty.' So saying—for a hero wherever he goes always carries a stone in the folds of his dress—he knocked out his two protruding teeth. Then guided by the sun by day and by the stars at night he sped, never pausing till he came to the north bank of the River Wu. Here, fearing that someone might be pursuing him, he hid amongst the reeds. . . .

Presently he saw someone upon the waves, singing a folk-song while he plied his oar, line and hook in hand, evidently a fisherman. So he put his head out of the reeds and called, 'You in the boat, with the fishing-hook, I must trouble you to come to the bank and have a word with me. You will forgive me for bothering you. I would take it as a great favour if you could assist me.'

The fisherman, hearing some one call, looked about to see where the voice came from and suddenly noticed that there was someone among the reeds. He at once paddled his boat to the shore. He wound in his line, stopped paddling and drifting on the stream briskly chanted some unrhymed stanzas:

'Gentleman, where is it that you want to get to?
Why do you hide on the river bank beside this cove?
You do not seem to have travelled here aboard ship;
You have no comrade with you, but are all alone;
Or is to that you capsized and were washed ashore,
And now loiter, with no boat, by the river bank?
If you are looking for a boat to carry you to the other shore,
There is not here any ferry to take you across.
But if you will accept the service of a simple man
I beg you to tell me just what it is you have in mind.'

'I have heard', said Wu Tzu-hsü, 'that whereas fish forget one another in stream and lake, so men are brought together by the Arts of Tao. I, your humble servant, am a wanderer. I would not dare say so if it were not true. At present, in consequence of a trifling predicament, I want to make my way to the south of the river. I am not clever at expressing myself, and hope you will please understand. If you were good enough to take me across, my life would be at your disposal, so great would be my gratitude. But if you cannot consent to do this, I will give up the idea at once.'

'Sizing up your appearance just now and noting your expression,' said the fisherman, 'I saw that you were no ordinary man. I know what is in your thoughts and there is no need for you to explain any further. I have heard that just as he who can recognize precious stones need never be poor,

37

so too he who can distinguish between man and man will always rise in the world. Duke Mu of Ch'in won gratitude by a present of wine. . . .(32) I can see that you have been suffering hardship for many days, have been thirsty and ill-supplied for a long while. You cannot cross the river on an empty belly. I should like to serve you with a meal. My house, to get there and come back, is some ten leagues away. If I keep you waiting for a little while, you must not be impatient.'

'All I want is a boat to take me across,' said Wu Tzu-hsü. 'I do not dare expect food.'

'I have heard', said the fisherman, 'that when the unicorn gets food, it can go a thousand leagues in a day; when the phoenix gets food, it can soar round the four seas.' So saying he left his boat and went on foot towards his house to get food, while Wu Tzu-hsü minded the boat for him. But soon Wu Tzu-hsü thought to himself: 'He told me that he was going to his house to get food. But I shouldn't be surprised if he has really gone to inform against me and get people to arrest me.'

So he left the boat, ran towards the reeds and hid among them.

After a while the fisherman came back to his boat, bringing a jug of wine, five catties of fish, ten biscuits and a pot of rice. But when he got to the boat, the man whom he had found hiding in the rushes had disappeared. There was nothing to be seen but the empty boat, moored to the shore. He had begun to feel great affection for the stranger and was bitterly disappointed. The fisherman sang out, 'Man of the Reeds, why are you hiding? Come here at once and let me see you. You must not suspect me of having bad intentions against you. Don't make difficulty on difficulty. I have brought a meal for you. Why don't you come and eat it?'

When Wu Tzu-hsü heard him say this, he knew that he had no evil intentions, and came out of the reeds. But he felt humiliated at having given the fisherman the trouble of fetching food, and he apologized abjectly.

The fisherman then rowed him into the middle of the river, laid out the meal, and they both ate. When Wu Tzu-hsü had had his fill he thought to himself, 'There is a saying: "If from another you accept one dish only,(33) a look of gratitude is enough, but if you accept two dishes, you must bestir yourself on his behalf." '

He took a jade disc out of the folds of his dress and gave it to the fisherman . . . but he refused to accept it. Wu Tzu-hsü could only suppose that he thought the present was insufficient; so he unsheathed his jewelled sword and offered it. The fisherman stopped rowing and turning to him said, 'You had better think three times before doing that! You're in far too much of a hurry. To be treated to a single meal is of no such great account. . . . The King of Ch'u is after you and has promised a reward of a thousand pieces of gold to anyone who captures you, and anyone who gives you shelter is to be executed, together with all his family. I care nothing for the King's reward any more than I am afraid of the punishments he threatens. Why should you want to give me a jewelled sword, a possession of the King of Ch'u, a sword from a dragon's pool? You should use it to defend yourself. And as for the jade disc, that is a treasure of the land of Ching, which you should use in effecting what you set store by. If in time to come you rise to riches and honour, do not forget this day of meeting. I reproach myself that we should only have met so late, when my years are in decline. Do not insist on leaving the sword and jade. I am sure you will understand my feelings and not force me to decline a second time.'

Wu Tzu-hsü, seeing that he would not accept the presents, began to feel uncomfortable. He thought to himself, 'Probably the fisherman thinks my presents too few and poor. They were the treasured possessions of a King, true enough, but that can't be helped.'

So saying he threw the sword into the river. It flashed with a divine light; three times it leapt, three times it sank; then hovered over the water. The River God heard from afar the

39

bellowing of the sword . . . and holding it up in both hands in fear and trembling gave it back to Wu Tzu-hsü. . . .

He (p. 14, l. 12) asked the fisherman, 'What is your name and surname? To what commandery and to what district do you belong?'

'I have no name or surname', said the fisherman. 'My only comrade is the river. . . . Today two brigands meet, what need to mention names? You are the Man in the Reeds; I am the Man on the Boat. That describes me sufficiently; all that matters is that you should not forget me when you are rich and grand.'

'Even a wounded snake, if given medicine, finds a way to reward its benefactor', said Wu Tzu-hsü. 'I shall certainly never forget the help you have given me.'

'When you flee from here,' said the fisherman, 'to what land do you intend to betake yourself?'

'To the land of Yüeh', said Wu Tzu-hsü.

'Hm,' said the fisherman, 'the land of Yüeh? Yüeh is on friendly terms with Ch'u and there have never been hostilities between them. If you go there they will arrest you and send you back to Ch'u. That is not the way to effect the revenge on which your heart is set. Now if you were to place yourself at the disposition of the land of Wu, you would certainly do better business. The King of Wu is at constant enmity with Ch'u, and the two countries are on very bad terms. Wu and Ch'u are continually fighting, but in Wu there are no able ministers. You would be an important acquisition for them.'

'How can I get my services accepted by Wu?' asked Wu Tzu-hsü.

'When you get to Wu', said the fisherman, 'go into the market-place of the capital, smear your face with mud, let down your hair and rave, running about now to east now to west, and moan loudly three times.'

'Pray explain to me the meaning of this performance', said Wu Tzu-hsü.

'The smearing of your face with mud', said the fisherman,

'means that though dirty without you are clean within. The three loud moans and the running about now to east, now to west, mean that you are in search of an enlightened ruler. Let down your hair in the market, because it is the natural thing to do (?). I am not a sage; but I have had a lot of experience.'

Having received these instructions Wu Tzu-hsü bowed and took his leave. He was afraid he might meet envoys sent from Ch'u, and dared not stay any longer. The moment the boat reached the far shore, he disembarked and set out. . . . Turning (p. 15, l. 5) his head and looking into the distance he suddenly saw the fisherman capsize his boat and die.(34)

Humiliated by what the fisherman had done he sobbed and wept unceasingly, and then made a song of grief:

'The waters of the great river stretch on for ever,
Cloud joins to water and water to cloud.
Oh, the misery, the pain, hard indeed to endure!
From of old men's feelings have been difficult to sift,
Life and death, riches and poverty all depend on Heaven.
What grievance had my teacher against me
That he upset his boat in the middle of the river?
On the waves the boat now floats, now sinks—
I sing of a great wrong, very sharp and deep—
My heart is pierced by sorrow that cuts like a sword;
As I go on my way I cannot stop the tears that fall on my
    dress.
I look towards the land of Wu, but cannot get there;
I think of my native land and my grief is deep.
But if I meet with a good ruler and can rise high in his
    service
I will show at last of what stuff a hero's heart is made!'

Before (p. 17, l. 6) many days had passed he reached the kingdom of Wu and did all that the fisherman had told him to. He went into the market with his hair down and his face smeared with mud, and moaned aloud crazily three times, running now to the east, now to the west.

A minister of the land of Wu, happening to pass through the market on horseback, noted at once his unusual expression and build, for he was a man over six feet high, and knew that he would be valuable as a minister. He hastened back to the Palace and said to the King: 'After I left your Majesty I was going through the market, when I saw a gentleman from another land, who had smeared his face and was behaving crazily. He had let his hair down and with doleful cries was running now to east, now to west. From what as a mere onlooker, but one who closely studied his outward appearance, I was able to judge, I strongly recommend your Majesty to send some one to detain and question him. He is without any doubt a man who has been gravely wronged and is pursuing a vendetta.'

The King was delighted at this news, summoned all his ministers, opened his pearl-string curtains, and told them of his dream:

'Last night at the third watch I dreamt that I saw a man of singular worth enter my domains, and at once felt a lightness in my limbs and an added strength in my frame, so that I could not help skipping and jumping. I want you to take counsel together and interpret this dream for me. Is it a good dream or a bad?'

When the hundred ministers heard this they all performed the dance of homage and in chorus loudly cried: 'May your Majesty reign in peace for ten thousand years! This means that the tall gentleman in the market-place will give your Majesty continual satisfaction. All your ministers present today are delighted at your good fortune.'

So the King of Wu at once sent an express messenger to the market, to fetch this valuable minister.

'Inform him', said the King, 'that although I am not acquainted with him I am most anxious to see him and tell him face to face what I have at heart.'

The messenger, bringing this verbal mandate, galloped to the market-place and told Wu Tzu-hsü what the King had said. And Wu Tzu-hsü, on receiving the King's order, did not dare delay, but set out with the messenger at once. When he reached the King's Palace, he crawled with his face on the ground, sobbing and wailing, and did not rise for a long while. The King knew that it was Wu Tzu-hsü and said sorrowfully, 'The King of Ch'u, refusing to listen to loyal reproofs and blindly accepting the advice of flatterers, wrongfully slew your father and brother. I am unutterably sad that this should have happened, bitterly distressed! It is indeed an unbearable outrage. That you should have come over mountains and rivers, toiling through winds and clouds, all this long way to a kingdom so narrow and small as mine I take as a great compliment.'

Wu Tzu-hsü, after a long pause, clutched his hair in his hands and said: 'My father and brother failed in their duty to their lord and were executed by his Majesty of Ch'u. Instead of carrying on the family line, I abandoned my father and my prince and fled from the land. I have heard that when a tree is doomed to crack, wind and frost attack it together; when a kingdom is about to fall, calamities vie (?) to undo it. He who strives alone seldom succeeds. Witnessing these grievous happenings, in which black and white were not distinguished, the dragon and the snake were confounded, I would have cut my throat and died, had I not been ashamed to face my ancestors in the world below.

'That is why I have put myself at your Majesty's disposition, and I hope my intention is apparent to you. I am a man of rustic origin, accustomed to humble surroundings, and am unfit to hold office and serve your Majesty. I am indeed lucky to have received recognition from you.'

'My country is of small extent', said the King of Wu, 'and I am very short of faithful helpers. I propose to ask you so far to demean yourself as to become my minister. I hope you will not consider the offer insulting.'

'I am a person of no account', said Wu Tzu-hsü, 'and the

mere fact that, through no merit of my own, I have had the great good fortune to receive your Majesty's recognition is proof of your exceptional favour towards me. If in addition to this I accept office, I should be guilty of an act of presumption that would deserve the death penalty!'

The King of Wu then turned to those about him and said, 'What do you gentlemen think?'

From every row of the assembled ministers came the cry, 'It is your Majesty's reputation that has attracted to your service this adherent from another land. If he were to be made assistant Minister of State, all the people of our country would cry "Long live the King!"'

When (p. 18, l. 8) Wu Tzu-hsü had governed the land for a year there was so little wind that the branches scarcely rustled, the rain fell so gently that it did not break the clods. When he had governed the land for two years, the barns were brimful of grain, everywhere under Heaven there was peace, scribes were no longer greedy nor high officials tyrannous. When he had governed for three years, the six barbarians sent tokens of friendship, the ten thousand lands all offered their services. When he had governed for four years, such was the power of his virtues that the Dragon of Light appeared as a portent, and the Red Bird came with a book in its mouth. Magic herbs grew in rows, luck-bringing corn-shoots sprouted close together. Ploughmen yielded the boundary-lines, what was dropped on a path no one picked up, the three religions(35) flourished side by side, the city gates were never shut, there were no summonses or *corvées*; people worked for themselves. After five years, the sun and moon doubled their light, in the markets there was no haggling, cats and mice lived in the same hole, rice and corn were reckoned by fractions of a farthing. There were no prisoners in the gaols. Everyone declared that the ruler and his minister were at one in their ways and praise of them spread far and near.

The common people, ashamed to benefit by the deeds of Wu Tzu-hsü and do nothing in return, all went to his gate, crying, 'We want, on our Minister Wu Tzu-hsü's behalf, to go to war with the land of Ch'u.'

(In the attack on Ch'u that followed Wu Tzu-hsü 'fought ten battles and won nine victories without losing a single soldier'. King P'ing of Ch'u was dead and had been succeeded by his son King Chao. Wu Tzu-hsü executed King Chao and Wei Ling, the evil counsellor of the late King P'ing, and offered their hearts and livers as a sacrifice to the spirits of his father and brother. But he was unable to find their bones and could only set up a memorial to them: '120 odd leagues south-east of Po-chou, where it can still be seen, though no one in after ages remembered in whose honour it had been erected. It is at the place now called Ch'eng-fu *hsien*.'(36)

Wu Tzu-hsü's next act of vengeance was against the King of Cheng. This King, at a loss how to resist the all-conquering armies of Wu, offered half his kingdom and a thousand pieces of gold to anyone who could devise a scheme for halting the enemy.)

There (p. 21, l. 13) was a boatman's son who responded to this invitation by offering his services. 'I can halt the armies of Wu,' he said, 'and for that purpose I shall not need "an inch of soldier or a foot of sword". All I shall need is one small boat and a punting-pole, a pair of dried fish, a bowl of boiled wheat and a jug of good wine. The boat containing these must be placed on the moat to the east of the city walls, and I shall know how to turn them to account.'

The King of Cheng agreed, the boat and other things were found and brought to the moat. The fisherman plied his oar and, singing a long ballad, cruised about in his boat. The King of Cheng shut the western gate of the city and, standing on the walls, looked out afar to see by what stratagem the fisherman was going to halt the armies of Wu. When Wu Tzu-hsü's troops were about thirty leagues

45

away he sent scouts on ahead to find out what forces Cheng could put against him. When they reached the capital of Cheng they found the four city gates all tightly shut. When they got to the eastern gate, in the moat outside it they saw a boat with an awning, and on board it a solitary figure, chanting the words: 'That man in the reeds must surely be a gentleman in distress. I have a jug of good wine, five catties of fish, ten flat loaves and a bowl of cooked grain. Pray come to my boat and eat!

'Come as an enemy, and you must take the consequences,
Come as a friend and you will understand what I mean.
If I can do a service to my wise ruler
It will gain for me glory, riches and honour.
If by chance the thing is feasible,
I appeal to you not to cast me aside.'(37)

When the scouts heard the boatman's words they went back and repeated them to Wu Tzu-hsü. He knew at once that this must be the fisherman's son, and was delighted.

'When I had enemies that had to be destroyed,' he said, 'it was owing to this man's father that I came through alive. How can I fail to repay him? Those who, when rich and grand, forget the days of their poverty, Mighty Heaven does not help. Those who do not repay a kindness are unworthy of the name of men; to accept a kindness and repay it shows good breeding and distinction.'(38)

Wu Tzu-hsü rode to the moat, where he reined in his horse, put his whip in its case, and flung his arms round the young man. Then, weeping copiously, he condoled with him saying: 'Your father's having been drowned in that deep river was a terrible calamity, and an irreparable loss! I hope you do not feel that I was to blame.'

At this moment the King of Cheng, all of a tremble, came out from within the walls and, prostrating himself before Wu Tzu-hsü, said, 'I was delighted to hear, great General, that you have been able to revenge yourself on your enemies, and must hasten to congratulate you. I know that I have richly deserved death at your hands and can only entreat you to spare my worthless life.'

'My elder brother', said Wu Tzu-hsü, 'was in your service, and you ought to have sheltered him. Instead, in order to curry favour with the King of Ch'u, you sent him to his death. For that death, you must pay with your life.'

'The letter that the messenger brought from afar', said the King of Cheng, 'stated that your good father had been forgiven and released. I, of course, knew little about the matter, and thought your brother had better go and see for himself. I imagined he would be back in a few weeks. I had no idea that the King of Ch'u would execute him. I know that I deserve death for this, and am ready to die without complaint. That you, great General, have been able to take vengeance on your enemy and destroy his ancestral shrines is a joy to me that makes me hop and skip, and I cannot sufficiently congratulate you. I therefore implore you to deal leniently with me and find some way to preserve my life.'

Here the boatman's son interposed: 'Great General! I enlisted in the service of the King of Cheng on the understanding that I was in a position to halt the armies of Wu. In return for this I was to receive a thousand catties of gold and a fief of ten thousand families. I am anxious to get that great reward. What do you think about it?'

'As you are not demanding my life as payment for your father's, what can I do but enable you to claim the reward? How can I refuse to withdraw my troops?' said Wu Tzu-hsü.

Urged by the fisherman's son he at once set free the King of Cheng. The King was delighted and, getting together mountains of wine and food, regaled the armies of Wu for three days and three nights. Wu Tzu-hsü then set the fisherman's son on the throne, as Emperor of Ch'u, and the two countries of Ch'u and Cheng lived in peace.

(Wu Tzu-hsü then sets out to take revenge on the King of Liang, who 'slaughters a thousand cattle and roasts ten thousand sheep' in order to divert his rage. Wu absent-mindedly allows his troops to banquet on these provisions, whereupon the soldiers, of course, remind him of the often-quoted proverb (see above, p. 39): 'If you accept one dish only, a look of gratitude is enough; if you accept two dishes. . . .' Whereupon Wu Tzu-hsü pardons the King of Liang, and withdraws his troops.)

When (p. 23, l. 7) he reached the shores of the Ying river, he looked up into the sky and sighed, saying: 'When long ago during my flight I reached this place, I asked a girl to give me food and she did not refuse. But then, clasping a stone, she flung herself into the river and died. Today I have nothing else with which to repay what she did for me', and as she had asked him to do while she was alive, he took a hundred pieces of gold and flung them into the Ying river. Then he made this address to her soul:

'Long ago when I was fleeing southward and was entering the land of Wu
Going on my way I chanced to meet you, and asked you to give me food.
To you I was beholden for giving to me one midday meal;
But clasping a stone you leapt into the river and so your life closed.
Since the time when we said farewell many years have passed;
But day by day and dusk by dusk I remember you all the time.
I think of your soul-awareness carried where the waves will,
Of your roving spirit's dissolution among the brambles and thorns.'

So he spoke and with tears in his voice once again addressed her:

'Oh, that your dark potence might know the thoughts that lie within my heart!

48

After thus your flawless frame was cast upon the waters
   and lost,
In the Land of Death may you never have felt loneliness
   and sadness!
The Darkened and the Bright go separate ways and
   cannot know each other,
The Living and the Dead are set apart, each in his own
   course.
I have nothing else to give you in return and can only,
   as you once asked,
Take these hundred pieces of gold and fling them where
   you died.'

(Wu Tzu-hsü then goes to his sister's house, shaves the
heads of his two wicked nephews, cuts off their ears,
knocks out some of their front teeth, and condemns them
to perpetual slavery.

He next goes to fetch his wife. She refuses to admit him
to the house and he jumps to the conclusion that she has
fallen in love with someone else. But it turns out that she
is only cross because he has neglected her for so long, and
he in turn explains that he had felt shy of approaching her,
because of the 'heavy load of shame' her kindness to him
during his flight had laid upon him. These points having
been cleared up they became 'as affectionate as in old days',
and he took her back with him to Wu.

Here he gives to the King a long account of his recent
campaigns which to a large extent repeats what we have
already been told.)

Afterwards (p. 26, l. 2) the King of Yüeh took up arms
and moved his hosts, and came to attack the armies of Wu.
A wise minister in the land of Yüeh, called Fan Li, reproved
the King, saying, 'In Wu there is a wise minister called
Wu Tzu-hsü. He is well versed in astronomy and geography,
in the classics of literature and the rules of war, and has
thus risen to greatness. In appearance he is remarkable and

in spiritual powers outstanding. At present he is Chief Minister in Wu, and is at the summit of the State. If you now attack Wu, I am certain you will bring yourself to ruin.'

'My plans are already made,' said the King of Yüeh, 'and I cannot stop half-way.'

So he took up arms and moved his hosts and went to attack the armies of Wu.

When the soldiers of Yüeh came to attack him, the King of Wu sent his Chief Minister Wu Tzu-hsü to take his armies and attack Yüeh. He led his soldiers and fought with the armies of Yüeh. He slew the warriors of Yüeh, so that their corpses lay strewn all over the open lands, and so much blood was spilt that their wooden shields floated about in it.

The King of Yüeh, seeing that his soldiers were slain, took refuge along with his minister Fan Li in the hills of Kuei-chi. The King of Yüeh and Fan Li sent word to Wu Tzu-hsü, saying, 'Hearing that your Excellency had taken vengeance on your father's enemies, we came to see you. we had no intention of making war. . . .'

After the King of Yüeh had withdrawn his troops and returned to his capital the King of Wu fell ill, and when he was dying he gave these instructions to the Crown Prince, Fu-ch'a: 'When I am gone and it falls to you to bring quiet to the land and good rule to the people, follow at all times the advice of the Chief Minister, Wu Tzu-hsü!'

Soon the King of Wu died and the Crown Prince, Fu-ch'a, became King in his stead.

One night the new King dreamt first that a mysterious light shone above the hall; then that over the city walls thick verdure spread. Next, that under the southern room-wall there was a closed chest and under the northern room-wall there was an open basket. Then, that at the city gate warriors were locked in battle; and last, that blood was flowing to the south-east. The King sent for the Minister P'i to interpret these dreams. P'i said, 'A mysterious light shining above the hall means abundance of blessings. Thick verdure spreading over the city walls means dew like hoar-frost.(39) A closed chest under the southern room-wall and an open basket under the northern room-wall means that you will live a long time. Warriors locked in battle at the city gate means that your defences will be secure. Blood flowing to the south-east means that the armies of Yüeh will perish.'

The King of Wu then sent for Wu Tzu-hsü to interpret the dreams. Wu Tzu-hsü was well versed in astronomy and geography, in the feelings of men, in the classics of literature and in the rules of war. He was in close communication with every kind of demon and divinity. That was why the King of Wu sent for him to interpret his dreams.

'I look upon these dreams', said Wu Tzu-hsü, 'as very ill-omened. If your Majesty accepts the interpretation of the Minister P'i, I am certain that the kingdom of Wu will perish.'

'Why?' asked the King.

Wu Tzu-hsü then bluntly interpreted the dreams: 'Your seeing a mysterious light above the hall means that a great man will come. Thick verdure spread over the city walls means that they will be covered with thorns and brambles. A closed chest under the southern room-wall and an open basket under the northern room-wall means that the King will lose his throne. Warriors locked in battle at the city gate means the arrival of an army from Yüeh. Blood flowing to the south-east means corpses everywhere and the destruction of your armies and kingdom. All this, because of what P'i has told you.'

When the King of Wu heard him say this, he rolled his eyeballs and glared angrily. Then, striking his throne, he shouted, 'How dare this old minister pour out such a flood of imprecations against our land?'

When Wu Tzu-hsü saw that the King was angered by his interpretation of the dreams, he picked up his skirts and went down from the hall.

'Why do you pick up your skirts and go down from the hall?' the King asked.

'The thorns and brambles are already growing over your Majesty's hall', said Wu Tzu-hsü. 'They are pricking my feet. That is why I picked up my skirts and went down from the hall.'

The King then gave him the sword Candle-jade and ordered him to kill himself with it.

When the sword had been given to him, he said to the ministers and others who were there, 'When I am dead, cut off my head and hang it above the eastern gate of the walls, that I may see the army of Yüeh arrive, when it comes to conquer the land of Wu.'

(Yüeh destroyed Wu in 473 B.C., twelve years after the death of Wu Tzu-hsü. The MS goes on for another fifteen lines or so, telling of events after Wu Tzu-hsü's death, and then, after becoming fragmentary, breaks off in the middle of a sentence. I have thought it best to stop at Wu Tzu-hsü's death.)

CHAPTER THREE

THE CROWN PRINCE

LONG ago, at the end of the former Han dynasty, the Emperor suddenly fell ill. It was a very bad illness and he did not seem likely to get well. So he gave his Heir Apparent these last instructions:

'As you are so young, it may be that you will not be able to rule the land and that someone else will usurp your shrines and altars. If so, you must take refuge in the prefecture of Nan-yang. There lives in that place someone to whom I once did a kindness, and he certainly ought to help you.'

At that time (A.D. 3) there was a relation by marriage of the Han Emperor, called Wang Mang, who seeing that in the Palace the Emperor's grandson was young made a plot to seize the throne. When the Han Emperor suddenly died, without letting it be known in the Inner Palace, Wang Mang taught a boy out in the streets of the town to sing a boy's song:

'Sooner will copper horses grow on bamboo joints
Than Wang Mang seize the Empire.'

Then, without letting anyone outside the Palace know, he mounted the throne. The Crown Prince fled, meaning to take refuge at Nan-yang; but when he was some ten leagues to the north of the walls, not knowing exactly where it was that he was to take refuge, he sat down on a flat rock.

That night the son of a man in the town called old Chang, to whom the Emperor had once shown great kindness, had a dream of good omen. In his dream he saw a boy sitting on a flat rock ten leagues north of the city walls. He was a handsome boy, with all the signs of good lineage. When old Chang's son suddenly woke from his dream, he was covered all over with sweat. As soon as it was light he told his father about the dream. His father said:

'The Crown Prince of the House of Liu has been in flight for some time and I do not know where he is. Without telling anyone, go to the place you saw in your dream and see what you can find out.'

The son did as his father told him. He went to the flat rock, and on it a Crown Prince was sitting in great dignity. He questioned him, saying: 'Where does my lord come from and what is his name and surname, that he should be sitting here?'

The Crown Prince answered, 'I never had a father or mother or clan or branch-clan. It is because my home is so poor that I wander about from one place to another.'

The son then brought him home and as soon as he entered the gate the father at once knew that it was the Crown Prince. He ran down the steps, prostrated himself and performed a dance of homage. When he had heard the prince's story he took him as his adopted son, not letting anyone know. He treated him just as though he were his own son, and he went to school.

After a month a notice was sent round to all districts saying that the Emperor had issued a proclamation:

'The Crown Prince of the House of Liu has fled to another district. Anyone arresting him will be given a fief of ten thousand families.'

The notice was displayed by the Governor of Nan-yang in all wards and lanes; moreover in every ward a cloth drum was hung. If it made a sound when it was struck that would show that the person who struck it was an Emperor and not an ordinary man. In each ward there was a supervisor who saw to it that anyone who came was made to beat the cloth drum. Many did so; but there was never any sound. At last a boy came who passed through the street but did not stop and strike the drum. However, he was allowed to go on. A day later he came down the street, and again did not stop and beat the drum. The third time that this happened, the supervisor called out to him, 'Why did you not stop and beat the drum?'

The boy replied: 'I can't possibly beat it. If I were to beat it, disastrous things would certainly happen.'

'What disastrous things?' the supervisor asked.

He answered, 'If I beat it once, the drums of all the wards would sound of their own accord. If I beat it twice, the rivers would all rise in flood. If I beat it three times, heaven and earth would go dark.'

So saying he beat it three times, and heaven and earth did go dark, so that nothing could be seen.

The Crown Prince then slipped away out of the town. He met a ploughman to whom he explained that he was the Crown Prince of the House of Liu, whose throne had been usurped. He was being pursued, there were placards about him in all districts, and armed horsemen had been sent to arrest him.

The ploughman then buried him under the ridge that his plough had raised, putting seven grains of rice in his mouth. He ate one grain a day, and so just kept alive. He also had in his mouth a bamboo tube that just stuck out above the earth, so that he was able to breathe. His pursuers, having failed to find him, went to the Grand Astrologer, who said, 'The Crown Prince of the House of Liu is dead. He lies beneath three feet of earth. Centipedes are coming out of his mouth and a bamboo is sprouting out of his eye-socket.' In consequence of this the armed horsemen were withdrawn from all districts.

The Crown Prince now came out of the earth and asked the ploughman where he ought next to take refuge, in order to raise an army and recover his inheritance. The ploughman answered: 'Above Mount K'un-lun there is a star, called the Great White Star. Go and see the spirit of this star and get advice from him. Then you will certainly be able to recover your inheritance. But if you trusted to your feet, you might toil all your life and never get there. If you have the power, desire it to the uttermost of your heart, and you will certainly see him.'

The prince uttered his prayer and at once saw the star-spirit. He asked for his advice, raised an army and recovered his inheritance.

Hence comes the saying:

> Mr Chang from Po-shui near Nan-yang
> When he saw the prince, did not get out of bed.

(The last six lines are a mere *résumé*, and the final couplet is, to me at any rate, unintelligible.)

HAN P'ENG

Once there was a good man called Han P'eng. He was an only child; he lost his father when he was quite young, and the care of his old mother fell to him alone. That he might do his duty by her to the full, he decided that he must go away and take service with the King.

Not liking to leave his mother all alone, he married a good wife to keep her company, an accomplished virgin aged seventeen, named Cheng-fu. She was good to the point of being a saint, a flower conspicuous and unique in her beauty, of an appearance which for charm was unmatched by any girl under heaven. Though she was only a woman, she understood classical writings very well, and everything she did was in accordance with the will of Heaven.

When she had been in the house three days and lived with him in harmony, they took a vow each to be faithful to the other: 'You will never take another wife, we will be to each other as water to the fish. I also will never marry anyone else, but serve one husband till death.'

Han P'eng set off and took service in the land of Sung. He meant to be away for three years; but six autumns passed and he did not return. His mother continually fretted at his absence, and his wife, thinking of him all the while, to give vent to her feelings suddenly took a writing brush and character by character wrote a letter. It was in a most elegant style, every phrase a fragment of gold. It was like pearls, like jade. She thought of giving it to a man to take; but she was afraid of men's gossip. She thought of giving it to a bird, but the birds flew too high. She thought of giving it to the wind, but the wind was in empty space.

'Letter,' she said, 'if my feelings have power, go straight to Han P'eng; but if they have not power, fall down amid the grass.'

Her feelings had power, and the letter went straight to Han P'eng. When he got the letter he studied it and read its words. The letter said, 'Far spread the white waters; they flow in eddies. Dazzling the bright moon, shining through the floating clouds. The blue, blue waters winter and summer have their seasons. If one misses the season and does not sow, corn and beans do not thrive. Ten thousand things sprout and change, never countering Nature's times. It is long since we met, but I do not cease to yearn for you. A hundred years we will be true, and in the end good times will come back. Do you not think of your dear ones? Your old mother's heart is sad. I, your wife, am desolate; every night I roost alone, all the while in great sorrow. They say that when a bird loses its mate, its cry is mournful. When evening comes, I lie alone; I am restless all the long night. When one reaches(40) the Great Mountain, high and low there are precipices. On the top are two birds, and at the bottom the holy tortoise. Day and night they sport and play, always going home together. What crime have I done that I alone should be in darkness? The waters of the sea stretch endless, without wind they make their own waves. Those that stand by one are few; those that break one are many. On the southern hill there is a bird; on the northern hill a net is spread. If the bird flies high, what can the net do to it? May you be well and in peace! With me there is nothing wrong.'

When Han P'eng got the letter, his memories were stirred
and his heart was sad. For three days he did not eat, and
never felt hungry. He wanted to go home, but his duties
made this impossible. He put the letter in the folds of his
dress, but not with proper care, and it dropped out when he
was in the palace. The King of Sung found it, and was
enamoured of its style. He summoned all his ministers, the
Grand Astrologer as well, and said to them, 'To anyone who
can bring me Han P'eng's wife, I will give a thousand pounds
in gold and a fief of ten thousand families'.

Liang Po said, 'I will bring her'. The King was delighted
and gave him a carriage with eight wheels, chestnut horses
and more than three thousand followers to attend him.

He set out on his way swift as wind and rain, and in three
days and three nights he had reached Han P'eng's home. The
envoy dismounted, knocked at the gate and shouted. Han
P'eng's mother came out and looked. Startled and afraid she
asked the man who had shouted, 'Whose messenger are you?'

'I am a messenger from the land of Sung and am Han
P'eng's friend and colleague. He is Commissioner for
Appointments and I am Chief Clerk. I have a private letter
from him, which I have come to give to his wife.'

The mother repeated this to her daughter-in-law;

'It seems from what the strangers say', she said, 'that Han
P'eng has entered the King's service and is getting on well.'

'I had bad dreams last night,' said the daughter-in-law,
'very gloomy and distressing. I saw a yellow snake coiled
round the legs of my bed, and three birds flying together.
Two birds attacked one another, and one bird's head was
broken. Its teeth fell out, its feathers showered down and
blood flowed in an endless stream. There was a sound of
horses' hoofs stamping, and there were many ministers in
great splendour.

'I would not show myself to the neighbours, high or low;
much less to strangers from a thousand leagues away. Strangers who come from afar cannot be trusted at all. With artful
and cunning words they have concocted this letter from Han

P'eng. Only if they said that Han P'eng were outside himself, would I go to the gate. Tell them that I am ill and lying in bed, of a sickness that no drug can cure. Say at the same time how sorry I am that they have had the trouble and fatigue of so long a journey.'

When the envoy got this answer he said, 'When a wife hears that a letter has come from her husband, there must be some reason for it if she is not pleased. She is certainly in love with someone else, probably one of the neighbours.'

The mother, being very old, could not make out what it was all about. But when the daughter-in-law was told what the stranger had said she first went blue in the face and then yellow.

'What the stranger has said—that I am in love with some-one else—when I try to grasp his meaning, I cannot make sense of it. If you make me go and welcome these strangers, a mother will lose her wise son for ever, a mother-in-law her daughter-in-law, a daughter-in-law will lose her mother-in-law!'

Then she came down from her golden loom and bade fare-well to bygone things: 'For a thousand autumns, ten thousand years I shall not weave with you again. Water of the well so clear, when again shall I draw you? Pan-stove so deep and broad, when again shall I blow you? Bed and mat of my chamber, when shall I lie upon you? Courtyard so wide, when shall I sweep you? Garden herbs so fresh and green, when shall I pick you?'

Going out and coming in she wept bitterly; all the neigh-bours were harrowed to see it. Then with lowered head she went, her tears falling like rain. She went up to the hall and bowed to the strangers. The envoy helped her into the coach. So soon as she was in the coach, it went swift as wind and rain.

The mother, after she was gone, called on Heaven and invoked Earth, wailing so loud that all the neighbours came round to see what was amiss.

But Cheng-fu, hearing her from afar, said, 'What use is it

to call on Heaven, from what can one escape by invoking the Earth? A team of horses, once it has started, how can it turn back?'

Liang Po hastened on. Day by day she was farther from home, till they reached the land of Sung, nine thousand leagues and more. A light shone on the Palace. The King of Sung marvelled at it. He called together all his ministers, the Grand Astrologer as well. They opened their books and took the omens, to see what this light could portend.

A learned man answered: 'Today is the day *chia-tzu*; tomorrow is the day *i-ch'ou*, when all the ministers must assemble, for the King to take a fair bride.'

He had not finished speaking when Cheng-fu arrived. Her face was like lard, her waist like a roll of silk, she was well versed in literature. Among the Court ladies, the beauties, there was not her like.

When the King of Sung saw her he was mightily pleased. For three days and three nights he made merriment unending.

Then he made Cheng-fu his Queen and, with an escort to wait upon her before and behind, she was brought to the Palace.

When she entered the Palace she wilted and could not be happy. She lay sick and did not rise. The King of Sung said to her: 'You were a commoner's wife, and now you are the mother of a whole kingdom. Why are you not happy? You have the finest gauze to wear and delicious food to eat. Courtiers wait upon you continually, on your left hand and on your right. Why are you not happy? Why are you not glad?'

'I left my father's house', she said, 'and parted from my kinsmen, coming to serve Han P'eng. Life and death each have their place; high and low cannot go together. The rushes have their ground, the brambles their thicket. The panther and the wolf have their mates; the partridge and hare go in pairs. The fishes and turtles have their waters, and would not prefer the high hall. Swallows and sparrows fly in flocks, and would not prefer the company of the phoenix. I am a commoner's wife and cannot be happy as a King's bride.'

'My wife is sorrowful', the King said, 'and is not glad to be Queen. My wife's sad thoughts who can put to right?'

'I can', said Liang Po. 'Han P'eng is not yet a full thirty, but is more than twenty. He is a pretty man, with black hair soft as silk, teeth like shells or girdle-jades, and ears like hanging pearls. That is why she still thinks of him and cannot be happy. All you need do is to spoil his appearance and condemn him to hard labour.'

The King of Sung followed this advice. He knocked out two of Han P'eng's front teeth, put him into old tattered clothes and sent him to build the Ch'ing-ling terrace.

When Cheng-fu heard this, a deep distress cut her to the heart, she was deeply indignant and never ceased to think about it.

'Now that the Ch'ing-ling terrace is finished,' she said to the King later, 'I should very much like to go and have a look at it.'

The King gave her permission and sent her in a carriage with eight wheels, drawn by chestnut horses, with more than three thousand attendants to wait upon her before and behind. At the foot of the terrace she saw Han P'eng cutting hay to feed the horses. 'He is ashamed for me to see him', she thought. 'He is holding up hay in front of his face.' When she saw him do it, her tears fell like rain. 'The King of Sung gives me clothes', she said, 'but I do not wear them. When he gives me food I do not put it to my lips. I think of you always, as a thirsty man thinks of drink. To see your sufferings cuts my heart to the quick. Of the disfigured state you are in I shall certainly inform the King of Sung. How comes it that you are ashamed, that you cover your face with the hay and hide yourself from me?'

Han P'eng said, 'On the southern hill there is a tree; its name is the prickly thorn. On every branch there are two stalks; the leaves are small and their centre flat (with the secondary meaning 'Love has cooled'). In my disfigured state, I cannot be loved. It is said that the waters of the eastern pool have no room for (?) the fish of the western sea. You have left the humble and gone over to the mighty. What possessed you to do it?'

When she heard these words, she bowed her head and went away; her tears fell like rain. She tore three inches of silk from the front of her dress, bit her arm till blood flowed and with it wrote a letter. She tied it to the tip of an arrow and shot it to Han P'eng.

When he got the letter, he died at the mere reading of it.

The King of Sung heard of this, and was much astonished. He asked his ministers: 'Did he die of himself, or was he slain by another?'

Liang Po said, 'When Han P'eng died there was no wound to be seen. But a letter on three inches of silk was tied to his head.'

The King of Sung took it and read it. The letter said:

'The rain pours down from the sky, the fish wander in the pool. The big drum is silent, the little drum does not sound.'

The King of Sung said, 'Who can explain it?'

Liang Po answered, 'I can explain it. The rain that pours down from the sky is her tears. The fish that wander in the pool are her thoughts. The big drum that is silent is her breathing; the little drum that does not sound is her yearning. Her words are an Empire—great is their meaning.'

Cheng-fu said to the King: 'Han P'eng is dead and I will say no more of it. I would only ask one favour from the great King, which is that he should be buried according to the rites. To grant this would bring profit to those that survive him.'

The King of Sung then sent men to the east of the city wall to dig a grave a hundred cubits deep and he was buried with the rites of a Senior Statesman. Cheng-fu asked if she might go and look; she would not presume to stay long. The King of Sung gave her leave. He sent her in a plain carriage, with three thousand attendants and more before and behind.

When they came to the place of the tomb, she got down from the carriage and walked three times round the tomb, uttering a loud and sorrowful lamentation that went far up among the clouds. Standing near the grave she called Han

P'eng by name, but he did not hear her. She turned and said farewell to her attendants: 'May Heaven reward you all for this act of favour. It is said that one horse cannot wear two saddles, one woman cannot serve two husbands.'

She had barely finished speaking when, going back to her room, she steeped her clothes in vinegar till they rotted like an onion. (Then she went back to the tomb[41] and flung herself into it.)

Those to the left clutched at her, those to the right clutched at her; but there was nothing they could take hold of.

The King's servants were scared and amazed; they all beat their breasts, and soon someone was sent to tell the King of Sung. When he heard what had happened, the King was very angry. From above the head of his couch he took his sword and slew four or five ministers. Hastening with flying wheels all his officers gathered together.

Heaven sent down a great rain. The floods poured into the tomb, and the corpse could not be rescued.

Liang Po remonstrated with the King, 'You bring death to tens of thousands', he said, 'but life to none.'

The King sent men to bury Cheng-fu. Her they did not see, but only found two stones, one blue, one white. The King of Sung, when he saw them, buried the blue stone to the east of the road and the white stone to the west of the road.

To the east of the road there sprung up a cassia tree, to the west of the road a kola-nut. The branches of the two trees touched, their leaves intertwined, their roots joined, and underneath them a fountain flowed, that made it impossible to pass.

The King of Sung, when out one day, saw the double tree and asked 'What tree is this?'

Liang Po answered, 'This is Han P'eng's tree'.

'Who can explain it?' said the King.

'I can explain it', said Liang Po. 'The branches that touch are their thoughts. The leaves that intertwine are their love. The roots that join are their life-breath. The fountain that flows beneath is their tears.'

The King of Sung then sent a man to cut down the double tree. When his axe touched it, for three days and three nights blood streamed out in a flood. Two wood-chips fell into the water, turned into two mandarin-ducks that raised their wings and flew high, back to their own home.

Only one wing-feather, very lovely in shape, fell and the King of Sung got it. He stroked his body with it.

'How beautiful is its sheen!' he said. 'But I have not stroked my head.'

So he took it and stroked his head, and his head fell to the ground.

Because he carried off a commoner's wife and wilfully slew the innocent, in less than three years' time the kingdom of Sung was annihilated.

Liang Po and his son were exiled to a far frontier.

Those who do good get blessings; those who do evil come to grief.

THE STORY OF SHUN

When King Yao[42] ruled, every day a thousand kinds of happy portent were sent down by Heaven. Shun had a mother of his own in the hall, who was called Lady Lo-teng. But she fell ill and took to her bed, and for three years never rose from it. She called for her husband Ku-sou and said to him, 'I am leaving an orphan boy and girl in your hands. I hope you will not beat them.'

Ku-sou replied, 'Wife, it is surely possible to get advice about your illness. You must be well looked after and cured.'

But no sooner had he said it, than she died. Shun observed mourning for her for three years, dressing in drab clothes; for ten days he wore no ornaments.

One day Ku-sou sent for Shun and said, 'You lost your mother when you were very young and there is no one to look after the house. What should you think about it if I were to take a second wife?'

Shun folded together the palms of his hands and said to his father, 'Father, if you were to take a second wife, she would be to me just what my own mother was'.

Less than ten days after this Ku-sou married again. He called for Shun and said to him, 'There is fighting under the walls of Liao-yang. I am going there for a while to see if I can't pick up a little profit on the way. I leave the affairs of the family in your charge.'

He spoke of being away for only one year, but three years passed and he did not return. Shun was very unhappy about him. One day he took out (?) his zither,[43] laid it on his knees and while he was playing an old man arrived and stood at the gate. Shun hurried out to the gate. 'Old man, may ten thousand blessings attend your honoured person,' he said. 'Where have you come from?'

The old man said, 'Master, yesterday I came from Liao-yang. I have brought a letter from your father.'

Shun ran into the house, knelt before his stepmother and bowed four times. When she saw Shun kneeling and bowing four times, she fell into a great rage. 'It isn't the Emperor's birthday,' she said, 'nor have you come back from a long journey; yet you kneel down and bow to me four times precisely at noon! What baleful magic rite is this that you are imitating?'

Shun pressed together the palms of his hands and said to his stepmother: 'Father went for a little while to Liao-yang and left me in charge of the affairs of the family. When he went, he said he would only be away for a year. But now three years have passed and he has not come back. I was very unhappy about it. I took out my zither and put it on my knees, and while I was playing it an old man came to the gate, saying he had come yesterday from Liao-yang and had with him a letter from my father. My first two bows were to congratulate you on withstanding the weather and my second two were to share in your joy at getting news.'

When the stepmother heard that her husband was coming back, a plan came into her mind, and she shouted at Shun,

'Well, if your father is really coming back, we have absolutely nothing in the house ready to offer to him. However,
I noticed that in the back garden there is some very nice fruit
—some pink peaches, fresh and tasty. If we were to pick
some of those it would be doing something very useful to the
household.' When Shun heard about picking the peaches he
was delighted, and climbed the tree to pick them. The stepmother also came to the foot of the tree. She loosed her head-
dress and, taking a golden hair-pin out of it, pricked her
foot. Then she shouted up to Shun, 'As you are such an
obedient and filial son why don't you come down from the
tree and attend to my pricked foot?' When Shun heard this
he thought she had really pricked her foot on a thorn, and
hurriedly climbed down from the tree. (There is here a gap
in the text.)

The stepmother took to her bed and refused to get up.
After a day or two her husband arrived. He went straight to
the inner room and found his second wife lying in bed and
refusing to get up. 'I can well understand', he said, 'that when
you were constantly expecting me and I did not come, you
were in low spirits. But now that I have come why do you
lie there in bed and not get up to welcome me? Have you
had a quarrel with some of the neighbours or is the bad
weather affecting you?'

On hearing these words the stepmother burst into torrents
of weeping. 'Ever since you went away to Liao-yang,' she
sobbed, 'leaving me in charge of the affairs of the house,
your child by your first marriage has behaved in a most
unfilial way. Seeing that I was picking peaches in the back
garden he put a lot of frightful thorns into the ground under
the tree. They stabbed both my feet, making wounds the pain
of which goes even to the marrow of my heart. At the time
I thought of going and complaining to the magistrate; and
would have done so, had I not been held back by the bond
that joins man and wife. If you don't believe me, look
at the pus on the soles of my feet. Though like other
men's their heads are black and their faces are white,

this land of Chi does produce people with the hearts of pigs or dogs!'(44)

Ku-sou called Shun to him and said, 'When I went for a time to Liao-yang, I left the affairs of the house in your charge. How is it that someone in the house has been so unfilial? Your stepmother climbed the tree to pick peaches and someone buried sharp thorns, so that she was wounded by them in both feet. Whose villainy is this?' Shun knew quite well what had happened; but he was afraid that if he did not take the guilt upon himself, his stepmother would get into trouble. 'I alone am to blame', he said. 'It was a terrible crime and I invite you to give me a thrashing.' When the father heard this it angered him to hear it, yet he could not be angry; he was glad when he heard it, yet he could not be glad. 'Little Elephant,'(45) he shouted, 'bring three prickly rods; I am going to give your stepbrother a good hiding.' When Little Elephant was told to bring the prickly rods, he rushed into his mother's room and said, 'Father has told me to bring prickly rods, so that he may give my stepbrother a good hiding!' The stepmother turned to Ku-sou and said, 'When children misbehave it is right that they should be thrashed, and no one must be allowed to make excuses for them.' Little Elephant then went to fetch the rods, and Ku-sou chose the stoutest and roughest among them, which weighed two or three pounds and more, hung up Shun by the hair to a tree in the middle of the courtyard, and beat him so that the blood ran down from the top of his head to the soles of his feet, spattering the ground far and wide.

When Ku-sou beat Shun, all the birds of the air were so outraged that they started singing of their own accord, and the merciful crow never stopped shedding tears of blood.

Shun was an obedient and filial child, and Indra(46) in the world above knew all that was happening to him. Changing himself into an old man he came down into the world below and performed a miracle for Shun's benefit, so that he was as though he had never been beaten. So Shun went quietly to the library, where he first recited the *Analects of Confucius*

and the *Book of Filial Piety* and then read the *Book of Songs* and
the *Book of Rites*.

When she saw him do this the stepmother fell into a
great rage. 'Ever since you went to Liao-yang,' she said, 'and
left me in charge of the affairs of the house, your child by
your first wife has been unfilial. He has done nothing but
swill wine in the eastern courtyard, and has never once set
foot in the library in the western courtyard. Night after
night he has gone off roistering with evil companions, never
once coming home. He has sold our fields and orchards and
with the money he got for them has paid some magician to
teach him devilish and disastrous arts, so that when he was
thrashed with a big stick, it had no effect on him. If King Yao
were to hear that we are harbouring a magician, we too
should be involved. If I had any sense I should get a deed of
separation and vanish out of your sight!' 'Wife,' said Ku-sou,
'the life of that wretch is charmed (?) so that it is difficult to
give him a proper thrashing. If you can think of a plan, just
tell me. I leave the thrashing to you.' 'If we can't even
thrash him,' she said, 'there is no more to be said. But even
if we do succeed in thrashing him, I shall be far from getting
my heart's desire.'

After less than two or three days had passed, the stepmother had made a plan. 'I notice', she said, 'that the empty
barn in the back courtyard has been falling to pieces for two
or three years. We'll tell Shun to go on to the roof of the
barn and repair it, and then we will set fire to the barn on
every side, and burn him to death.' 'Although you are a
woman', said Ku-sou, 'you have made a most subtle and
ingenious plan.' Then he called Shun and said to him, 'I
notice that the barn in the back courtyard has been falling to
pieces for two or three years. If you were to repair it, you
would be doing something very useful to the family.' When
Shun heard that he was to repair the barn, he knew at once
that it was a plot laid by his stepmother. He mixed a heap
of plaster, pressed the palms of his hands together and said
to his stepmother, 'I cannot work the plaster just as it is. I

must have two wide-brimmed hats.' She turned to her husband and said, 'This rascal of yours says he needs two wide-brimmed hats. Wait till he is on top of the barn. No matter whether he has two hats or forty hats, he'll be burnt to death all the same.'

No sooner had Shun reached the top of the barn than flames rose from the south-west corner. The first torch was the stepmother's, the next and second was Ku-sou's; the third—would you believe it? was that of little brother Elephant! These three torches were held so that the pigeon-holes caught fire and red flames touched the sky; and so black was the smoke that one could see neither heaven nor earth. Fearing that his life was in danger, Shun used the two hats as wings and, riding the air, flew down from the barn. He was a righteous king,(47) and so moved was the Earth-spirit that he shielded Shun, so that he was not burnt or hurt in any way. He went home to the library, where he first recited the *Analects of Confucius* and the *Book of Filial Piety*, and then read the *Book of Songs* and the *Book of Rites*.

When the stepmother saw him once more do this, she fell into a great rage. 'Ever since you went to Liao-yang', she said, 'and left me in charge of the affairs of the house, your child by your first wife has been unfilial. He has done nothing but swill wine in the eastern courtyard and has never once set foot in the library in the western courtyard. Night after night he has gone off roystering with evil companions, never once coming home. He has sold our fields and orchards and with the money he got for them has paid some magician to teach him devilish and disastrous arts, so that when he was thrashed with a big stick it had no effect on him, and the fire of three torches did not burn him. If King Yao were to hear of it, we too should be involved. If I had any sense I should get a deed of separation and vanish out of your sight.' 'Wife,' said Ku-sou, 'the life of that wretch is charmed, so that it is difficult to correct him. If you can think of a plan, just tell me. I leave the thrashing to you.' 'If we can't even thrash him', she answered, 'there is no more to be said; but even if we do succeed in thrashing him, I shall be far from having my heart's desire.'

Hardly ten days had passed before the stepmother had made another plan. 'I notice that in front of your reception-room there is a dried-up well. It has had no water in it for two or three years. We'll tell Shun to clear it out, and then we'll take a big rock and block up the mouth of the well, so that he'll be bound to die.' 'Although you are a woman', said Ku-sou, 'you have made a most subtle and ingenious plan.' Then he called Shun and said to him, 'In front of my reception-room there is a dried-up well. It has had no water in it for two or three years. If you were to clean it out and get down to the water, you would be doing something very useful to the household.'

When Shun heard that he was to clean out the well, he knew that this was a plot of his stepmother's. But he immediately undressed, knelt down beside the well and bowed, and then went down into the well to clear away the mud. Immediately Indra in the world above secretly sent down five hundred silver coins into the well. Shun put them into his mud-bucket and made his stepmother draw them up. When he had done this several times, he called up to her, 'There is now no more money in the well. Please pull me up, and if you could give me a dish of rice to eat, wouldn't it be a kindness?' When she heard this, she deceived her husband and said, 'This rascal of yours claims that the money is his and we are not to use it. "If you use my money", he says, "when I come out I shall complain to the magistrate and you will all lose your lives." ' Ku-sou at once began to block up the well with large stones. The stepmother's one daughter caught hold of her father and said, 'You have killed my half-brother. How is he to get out of the well-hole?' The father did not listen, but dragged away her hand and rolled the stones into the well. But the god Indra took on the form of a yellow dragon and led Shun through an opening in the side of the well into the well of the neighbours to the east. Shun called out from below, and it so happened that an old woman had come to draw water. 'Who is that down in the well?' she cried. 'It is the unfilial son from the house to the west', answered Shun. When the old woman knew that it was Shun she pulled him up. He bowed to her with tears in his eyes, and the old woman gave him some clothes to wear and a dish of rice to eat. 'You had better not go home', she said. 'Go instead to your own mother's grave, and I warrant she will appear to you.' Nor sooner had she said this than Shun went in search of his mother's grave. She did indeed appear to him, and he wept tears of blood. 'Don't go home', she too said, 'until you are grown up. Only take a plot on Mount Li in the south-west, and plough it for yourself. If you do so, you will rise to greatness.'

After getting this advice from his mother he bade her farewell and went to the mountain, where he found a hundred acres of untilled ground. But he was greatly distressed, for he had neither seed to sow nor oxen to plough with, and could not think where to get them. But Heaven rewards extreme filial piety, and a herd of swine came of their own accord and with their snouts ploughed up the ground and opened the furrows. All the birds brought seed in their beaks and scattered it over his fields, and Heaven sent rain in abundance.

That year elsewhere under heaven the crops did not ripen. Only Shun had a good harvest, getting several hundred tons of corn. He began to think he ought to go home and repay the loving care of his parents. On his way he came to a river and saw a number of deer going together in a herd. He sighed and said, 'How sad that those who have the bodies of human beings cannot be of one mind like these wandering deer!' He also met several merchants, and asked them, 'Are the members of the Yao family at Chi prefecture safe and sound?' 'There are thousands and ten thousands of families with the surname Yao', they replied. 'Who can know to which of them you are related? But we have heard that in one Yao family they sent the boy to clean out a well. His stepmother was jealous of him, and she and her husband stopped up the well and killed him. After that, the father became blind in both eyes and the stepmother became daft. She takes firewood to market. There is a younger brother, and he has also become dumb and idiotic. They are in very bad circumstances and are indeed no more than homeless beggars. That is the only Yao family we know about; but yours may be some other one.' Shun knew at once that this must be his father, stepmother and little brother. He thought so to himself, but he said nothing.

Ten years had passed quickly since he went to Mount Li. He thought he would take rice to his native town, and when he reached the market he saw his stepmother carrying a load of firewood on her back which she had brought to the market to sell and buy rice with the money she got for it. She happened to buy her rice from Shun. He recognized her and when she paid him for the rice she had bought, he pretended to make a mistake, and put the money into her rice-bag. This happened several times. Ku-sou marvelled at it and said to his wife, 'Could it be our Shun?' 'He's buried a hundred cubits deep, at the bottom of the well', she said. 'There is a big rock on top of him, and we filled in the well-hole with earth. How could he possibly be alive?' 'Lead me to the market', said Ku-sou, 'and we will find out.' She led him to the market, and there again was the young man selling rice. 'What saint are you', said Ku-sou, 'that again and again you have forgone your profit?' 'I saw that you were an old man', said Shun, 'and did not like to make profit out of you.' Ku-sou recognized his voice and said, 'Is not this just like my Shun's voice?' 'I am he', said Shun; and he stepped forward and taking his father's head in his arms set up a great lamentation. Then he wiped his father's tears, licking them away with his tongue. Immediately the father regained his sight, and the stepmother recovered her wits. Elephant also was no longer dumb. The people in the market all saw it and were deeply moved.

Shun then took his family back to their former home. Ku-sou, without thought of the damage he was doing to

Shun's record of piety, collected all the neighbours and relations and taking a sword was about to kill the stepmother. But Shun clasped his hands together and said to him, 'If you slay my stepmother, I shall have failed in my duty towards her as a son. Father, please reflect on that.' The neighbours were deeply touched, and said that such a thing had never been heard of anywhere under heaven. After the father had spared his wife's life, they lived united and happy. Shun's name became known in the land. The Emperor Yao heard of him and gave him his two daughters to be his wives. The elder was called E-huang and the younger Nü-ying. Yao then abdicated in favour of Shun. Nü-ying was the mother of Shang Chün; but he was unworthy of his father and Shun therefore abdicated in favour of Yü of the Hsia dynasty.

(The story is then resumed in two poems, each of four lines.)

CHAPTER FOUR

THE STORY OF CATCH-TIGER

WHEN the Hui-ch'ang[48] Emperor came to the throne there was no more religion in the land. The monasteries were destroyed and all the monks and nuns within the Four Seas were obliged to return to lay life and go into hiding. It is told that among them was a monk called Flower of the Law, who lived at Hsing-chou. When he learnt of the ruler's wicked doings he made a parcel of his scriptures and went into hiding in the mountains of Sui-chou, where he built himself a thatched hut, to live in for a while. Every day he prayed and read the scriptures, and every day eight men came to listen to him, without ever telling him their names. One day seven of them arrived first and the eighth, an old man, only turned up later. Flower of the Law was puzzled by this and said to him, 'Aged sir, where do you live and what is your name? You generally come all together; why has one gentleman arrived today so much later than the rest?' 'I will tell you just who we are', the old man said. 'We are the Dragon Kings of the eight great oceans. Hearing that you were in the habit of reading the text of the *Lotus Scripture*, we came to participate in the merit you are acquiring, and you have indeed given to all of us, this watery tribe of kinsmen, a full share of blessing and profit. We kinsmen have nothing to give in return; the best we can do is to help and protect you.

'Do not take it amiss that one of us was late. That was because Yang Chien, the Governor of Sui-chou, is destined within a hundred days to get Heaven's portion.[49] In order that his crown may rest firmly on his head, his skull bone is being changed for him. If you don't believe this, perhaps

74

you will be convinced when I tell you that he has begun to have the most fearful headache, which no one can cure. As we eight brothers have no other way of repaying you for allowing us to hear your recitation, I went to my Palace to fetch a box of dragon-ointment, and that is why I am late.(50) I now hand it over to you. If you go to Sui-chou, obtain an interview with the Governor and rub this ointment on his head, he will recover. After the ointment has had its effect you must give him the following instructions: "Within the next hundred days, you are destined to get Heaven's portion. An envoy will come to summon you to Court, but if you arrive there one day too soon you are finished, and if you arrive one day too late you are lost. For my part, all I ask of you is that, if afterwards you become Emperor, you should make it your business to restore Buddha's Law." For the present, we beg to take our leave.' Whereupon they all suddenly disappeared.

After the Dragon Kings had departed, Flower of the Law went straight to the Governor's office at Sui-chou. The doorkeeper announced, 'There is a monk outside who claims to have a marvellous drug with which he can cure you. I thought it my duty to inform you.' When the Governor heard this he ordered the monk to come and take a seat in his office. 'The thing is', he said, 'that I am suffering from headache. Every sort of remedy has been tried, but I cannot find a cure. I am told that you practise some marvellous system of healing. I promise that, if you succeed in curing me, I will certainly make it worth your while.' When Flower of the Law heard this, he took the little box out of his sleeve and applied the magic dragon-ointment to the Governor's head. It is said that before he had rubbed it on even half his pate, in fact from the very moment it touched his skull, it was as though Buddha had laid his hand upon him. The Governor recovered completely and, prostrating himself twice and again, he said to the monk, 'The Emperor has of course given special orders that no one is to shelter monks. But all the same mightn't it be a good thing if you

were to hide for a while in my official residence?' Flower
of the Law then remembered that he had not yet passed on
the Dragon King's instructions, and not daring to delay he
now said, 'You are destined within a hundred days to get
Heaven's portion. An envoy will come to summon you to
Court, but if you arrive there one day too soon you are
finished, and if you arrive one day too late you are lost. For
my part, all I ask of you is that if afterwards you become
Emperor, you should make it your business to restore
Buddha's Law. I am now going to leave you and return to
the hills.' When the monk had gone, the Governor thought
over what he had told him and could hardly believe that it
would really come true. So lest there should be any mistake
he wrote it on the wall.

Some weeks later, sure enough the Court Astronomer,
when watching the heavens at night, saw signs that Yang
Chien, the Governor of Sui-chou, was going within a
hundred days to get Heaven's portion, and he reported this
to the Emperor. When the Emperor saw the report it was
as though a great mallet had struck him in the chest. He at
once sent a high-ranking courtier to Sui-chou with a
mandate ordering the Governor to come to the capital. On
receiving this order the Governor did not dare delay, but
setting out at once and lingering nowhere soon arrived at
the Ch'ang-lo post-station, some ten leagues or more away
from the capital. Here he halted and reposed himself.
Suddenly he remembered how the monk had told him that
if he arrived at court a day too soon he would be finished,
and if a day too late he would be lost. 'If I see his Majesty
today', he thought, 'he will certainly destroy me.' So he
asked the courtier who had been sent to bring him back, to
go to the capital and arrange that he should have an audience
with the Emperor on the following day. The courtier
undertook to do this and going back to the capital made a
written report to the Emperor. When the Emperor read
the report great joy spread over the dragon-countenance.
But his consort, who was the Governor's daughter, burst

into tears. Seeing this, the Emperor said to her, 'It is only your father the Governor Yang Chien who is in trouble. You are not in any way involved.' The consort bowed and apologized for having wept. When she was back in the women's quarters she thought to herself, 'My father is going to have an audience tomorrow, and the Emperor will certainly destroy him. Of what use to me any longer is the glory of being an Empress? Far better to take poison and die first, rather than live to see my father undone.' So thinking, she bathed in perfumed water, changed her dress, filled a cup with poisoned wine and put it on her mirror-stand. Then she combed anew her cicada locks and repainted her moth eyebrows. While she was busy dressing and combing herself she suddenly saw in the mirror that there was some-one behind her and, looking round, who should it be but the Holy Man[51] who had left his throne and come to her? 'You are combing yourself and dressing just as usual,' he said, 'but one thing is strange. What do you want that wine for?'

When she heard this she knew that Heaven had sent her this opportunity. 'It is for two reasons', she said, 'that I, your concubine, must drink this cup of wine while I am dressing and combing. First, because wine softens the hair, and next because it preserves the complexion. Moreover I hoped that your Majesty would also accept a drink. There is no other reason.' The Emperor was delighted beyond measure with this speech. 'Excellent!' he said. 'For you there will be the additional advantage that you will be preserving your complexion. As for me, whether I have been drinking or not, I am always a proper-looking man.' When she heard this, she hastened to hand him the cup, saying, 'When I drink this by myself I call it my toilet wine. But today, when your Majesty is drinking it too, it must have another name. What shall we call it? Let us call it the Cup of Long Life. May your Majesty live ten thousand, ten thousand times ten thousand years!' Not knowing that it was poisoned wine, he took it and drank it at once. It is said that before he had drunk it, drunk any of it at all, the very moment it reached his mouth, his brain split and he died. When she saw it, she dragged the corpse to the Dragon bed and pushed it underneath and, to hide it for the moment, she took down some wall-mats and concealed the body behind them. Then she left the women's quarters and went to the front part of the Palace. Here she ordered one of the eunuchs to go to her father, Yang Chien, and bid him come at once to the Palace. When Yang Chien received this summons, it was as though a great mallet were pounding his heart. He did not dare disobey, but went at once to receive audience at Court. When he arrived at the gate of the audience-hall, the porter announced him, and his daughter the Empress, hearing that he was there, at once sent word that he was to present himself. He hastened past the screen-wall and without looking up at once prostrated himself and did the dance of homage. When the Empress saw him do this, she said to those about her, 'Support my father the Governor and bring him up to the dais'. Before they could do so, Yang Chien at last lifted his eyes and suddenly saw that it was the Empress, not the Emperor, who was before him. He thought to himself, 'Perhaps, after all, things are not going to go so badly today as I feared'. He went up on to the dais and the Empress said to him, 'It is all right, father. His Majesty the Dragon has gone back to the Great Sea. Today it is you who are the lord of the ten thousand chariots.' He could not believe that this was so. But she said to him, 'If you do not believe it, go and look under the Dragon Couch and you will see his holy relics. Then you will believe me.' 'But I should have no backing', said he. 'How can I carry this through?' 'Father,' she said, 'what particular friends had you at Court?' 'I stood well', he said, 'with the generals of the Bodyguard of the Left and the Bodyguard of the Right.' When the Empress heard this, she was sure the scheme could not miscarry; for these two men had sufficient force at their disposal. So she came forward into the hall and sent someone to fetch Hu and Lang, the Generals of the Bodyguard of the Left and the

Bodyguard of the Right. They came straight to the hall and to their surprise saw Yang Chien standing there, which in itself aroused their suspicion. 'Generals,' said the Empress, 'I know that you and the Governor my father were on good terms. I must tell you that his Majesty the Dragon has gone back to the Great Sea, and I now intend to invest my father as ruler. What do you think of that?' 'As for investing him,' said General Lang, 'that could be done. But how about all the great officers of Court? What is to be done about them?' 'Generals,' said she, 'you must tonight enrol five hundred men of the Imperial Guard, arm them with broad blades and long knives, and hide them in ambush behind lined curtains. When I arrive at Court in the morning, I will say to the ministers, "If you are ready to invest my father the Governor as ruler, there is no more to be said. But if you raise one word of objection, you will all be slain on the spot." In that case, I would appoint a new set of ministers. Would not that be all right?' The two Generals agreed, and enrolled five hundred men of the Imperial Bodyguard, and put them in ambush behind lined curtains. Next morning at the early Court all the ministers, civil and military, were duly in attendance. Addressing them the Empress said, 'His Majesty the Dragon has gone back to the Great Sea. I now intend to invest my father, the Governor of Sui-chou, as lord of Heaven and Earth. How do you feel about that?' and without waiting for an answer she shook out her sleeves and departed. The ministers of the Court, civil and military, feeling themselves to be on the brink of a measureless chasm, were utterly at a loss, when they suddenly saw a white ram(52) twelve feet high, its mouth wide open, showing a set of formidably sharp teeth, running towards the hall. It roared like thunder and looked as though it meant to swallow all the ministers at one gulp. Everyone saw it and at once knew that Yang Chien ought to have Heaven's portion. All of them danced homage to him and shouted 'Ten thousand years'. He then ascended the throne with the title Emperor Wen of the Sui dynasty. The four barbarian lands of the north were in such awe of him that they put themselves under his protection, and the eight savage tribes of the south came and tendered their submission.

(The King of Ch'en decides to revolt against the Sui, and the question is, who is to lead the Sui armies?) There was one man who was not afraid. Who was he? He was the son of the famous General Han Hsiung, who died when the boy was young. He had given himself the name Catch-tiger. Now, not suffering himself to be overlooked, he stepped forward from the ranks of the officers who were present and said, ' "A goblet of water cannot enrich the billows of the great ocean. The highest hill that ants can raise can be no danger to Heaven." Such is the King of Ch'en and, if an army is given to me, within a fixed time I undertake to capture him alive and bring him to your Majesty. How should I dare not to tell you this?' The Emperor saw that Catch-tiger could not be more than twelve years old, and indeed the smell of his nurse's milk had not yet left him. But it was said that he was very brave. 'If I were to make him Commander-in-Chief', the King thought, 'I know that this would offend Ho Jo-pi (the existing high Commander). I might make both of them Commanders-in-Chief with equal power; and indeed such an arrangement is made in the case of the chief ministers at Court. But with commanders in the field it would not work; they would certainly be jealous of one another and quarrel.'

(It ended by Catch-tiger being put in command of the expeditionary force that was to attack Chin-ling, the capital of the King of Ch'en. He advanced unopposed as far as Chung-mou in Honan province, where he encamped. Feeling that he was rather in the dark about the forces that he would have to encounter he ordered a trusted regular army man to go and spy upon the camp of Hsiao Mo-ho, the Ch'en Commander-in-Chief.)

The man disguised himself as a peasant and, carrying a load of dumplings in a withy basket, walked straight into the enemy's encampment and, while selling his dumplings, picked up military information. On returning to Catch-tiger's tent he reported: 'Their cavalry is using black banners with a water-spring design. The infantry is using red banners with the word "Victory" at the centre. The gates of their palisade are left wide open and they let the peasants who come to traffic with them go in and out as they will.'

When Catch-tiger heard this he knew that Hsiao Mo-ho was not a professional fighting general, for from of old there has been a saying, 'If the ruler is lax, his kingdom falls; if the army is lax the general is heading for disaster'.

(Encouraged by this news Catch-tiger advances towards Chin-ling and is met by the enemy General Jen Man-nu. At the commencement of the battle Catch-tiger calls out in a loud voice, 'What is the name of your General and what rank does he hold?')

'My name is Jen Man-nu and my rank is that of Great General of the Defence Forces.' When Catch-tiger heard this he burst into tears, for he remembered that his late father had said to him, 'If it one day should happen that you become a General and are at Chin-ling, you will find there a famous General called Jen Man-nu. He was my school-fellow and used to copy out texts for me. When you see him you must treat him with the respect that a son owes to a father.' 'I little thought', said Catch-tiger to himself, 'that I should meet him here today!' 'The armour that I am wearing', said he, stepping up to Jen Man-nu, 'prevents me from kneeling down before you. I beg you not to take offence!' The General knew at once that this must be Catch-tiger, the son of Han Hsiung, and he thought to himself, 'A father cannot fight against a son'. 'If you will withdraw your troops', he said to Catch-tiger, 'I will ask the King of Ch'en to send an envoy empowered to arrange a treaty of peace between our two countries. Would not that be a fine thing?' When Catch-tiger heard this he was very indignant. 'When I parted with the Emperor Wen of Sui', he said, 'I promised to take the city of Chin-ling. If I return without doing that, I must have three things to bring back with me and offer to the Emperor. Only then will I withdraw my troops.' 'What is the first thing you require?' asked Jen Man-nu. 'First,' said Catch-tiger, 'I must have a full account of the realm of Ch'en, with all its local features, mountains and rivers, and of the number of people who inhabit them. Without that, I cannot withdraw.' 'Later on', said Jen Man-nu, 'I will inform the King of Ch'en of your request. What is your second requirement?' 'Next,' said Catch-tiger, 'I must have the contents of your military treasuries, that I may allot rewards to my armies. Without that, I cannot withdraw.' 'And your third requirement?' said Jen Man-nu. 'As my third requirement', said Catch-tiger, 'I must have the head of Ch'en Shu-pao,(53) to offer up to the Emperor Wen of Sui. Without that, I cannot withdraw.'

When Jen Man-nu heard this he knew that his 'son' did not mean to treat him as a father, and he was very angry. Catch-tiger, seeing this, drew his sword and threatened him. 'The sword in my hand', he said, 'was given to me by the Emperor Wen of Sui by special decree in his Palace. The blade is cold as frost and when the battle begins it will take no account of kith or kin.'

(In the description of the battles that follow there is a great deal about magical battle-formations. Here I am quite out of my depth, and I will go on to the arrival of Catch-tiger at Chin-ling.)

When the King of Ch'en saw that the armies of Sui had arrived he fled and tried to hide in a dry well. But the gods were not on his side and changed the well into flat ground. An officer saw him, took him prisoner and brought him to Catch-tiger where he sat on his horse. 'Cursed rebel', cried Catch-tiger, 'who sought to turn against your ruler and plunge the land into disorder! Now that you are my captive,

what have you to say for yourself?' The King shut his mouth
and did not say a word. He was now put into a cage and
carted towards the capital, where Catch-tiger intended to
hand him over to the Emperor Wen of Sui. They travelled
fast, not stopping anywhere, until they came to the borders
of Hsin-an. Here an officer of the front line brought information that the Ch'en General Chou Lo-hou, with an army of
over 200,000 men, was intending to snatch the King of
Ch'en out of Catch-tiger's hands. When he heard this,
Catch-tiger was very angry and raged against the King,
saying, 'He who rebels against his rightful lord is not helped
by Heaven. I shall first cut off your head and display it in
the middle of my camp and then go and do battle with
Chou Lo-hou.' 'Mayn't I write a letter to him', said the
King of Ch'en, 'telling him to surrender to you? Wouldn't
that be a good thing?' When Catch-tiger heard this, he told
him to write the letter. The King of Ch'en said in his letter:
'When I was in Chin-ling my territory contained fifty great
districts and three hundred smaller districts. I had in my
grasp ten thousand leagues of river and hill, and under my
command was an army of a million men. I intended to
master everywhere under heaven and make myself Emperor.
How could I know that, when Catch-tiger came with his
armies, at the first blow all my power would crumble away?
Now I am a prisoner, and even though you still have a strong
army, what can you do against the House of Sui? If you
doubt what I say, remember that Heaven does not help
those who rebel against their rightful lords. From the King
of Ch'en to Chou Lo-hou, to be opened only by him.'

When he had finished the letter, he sent it to Chou
Lo-hou's palisade, by the hand of a junior officer. When
Chou Lo-hou read it, his eyes filled with tears. He thought
to himself, 'My lord being a prisoner, even if I were to
return victorious, to whom would the credit of the deed
revert? No, a sensible man is capable of changing his plans
according to the circumstances. I had better surrender.' So
he sent 200,000 cuirasses, had himself bound with straw

ropes and went straight to where Catch-tiger was sitting on his horse. 'I am the leader of a defeated army', he said, 'and it is for you to decide whether I live or die. I beg to be allowed to surrender.' 'Glad to make your acquaintance,(54) General', said Catch-tiger. 'If you had come as an enemy, I should have taken your life. But as you have come to surrender, we are now both members of one household. . . .'

Some time later the Khan(55) of the Ta-hsia, who were northern barbarians, sent a Turkish chieftain as envoy to Ch'ang-an, to declare war on the Emperor Wen of Sui. When the Emperor heard this, he gathered all his officers, civil and military, in the hall of audience and said to them, 'The Khan has declared war on me. What do you think of that?' He had hardly finished speaking when the barbarian envoy, knowing nothing of Court etiquette, stepped forward from the ranks and said, 'Bows and arrows are what we barbarians care for most and our shooting matches are all held in front of the Khan's Palace. We will hold such a match now, and if anyone can dislodge my arrow we will send you tribute every year and for ever call ourselves your subjects. So set up a shooting-target in front of this Palace.' When he heard this, the Emperor set up a target in front of the Palace and painted a deer(56) on it. Then he ordered that the shooting-match should begin. The barbarian, when he saw it, was delighted beyond measure, bowed a salute to the Emperor, and shot at once. The arrow left the bow-string with a sound like the splitting of a bamboo; not east, not west, it went straight into the deer's navel. When the Emperor saw this, he said to his ministers, 'Who can dislodge it?' 'I want to dislodge that arrow', said Ho Jo-pi, the General of the Left. 'Your wish is granted', said the Emperor. Ho Jo-pi then rested the bow on his arm, took an arrow from beside his waist, fitted the bow-string into the arrow-notch, and shot. The arrow when it left the string flew not west, not east, and entered the same hole as that made in the target before. When the Emperor saw this, great joy spread over the dragon-countenance, and all the ministers of the Court did the dance of homage crying, 'Long life to your Majesty!'

But Catch-tiger saw that the previous arrow had not been dislodged. He was not at all awestruck and did not do the dance of homage, but stood apart. 'What is on your mind?' asked the Emperor. 'I want to dislodge that arrow', said Catch-tiger. 'Your wish is granted', said the Emperor when he heard this. Catch-tiger then bowed a salute to the Emperor, rested his bow on his arm, took an arrow from beside his waist, fitted the bow-string into the arrow notch, and shot. The arrow left the string with a sound like the roaring of thunder. Not east, not west, it struck the notch of the barbarian's arrow and carried it bodily, from butt to tip, right through the target and some ten steps beyond, where it plunged three feet into the ground. When the barbarian saw this he was uncommonly surprised and alarmed. He hastened forward and bowed low to Catch-tiger. Seeing him do so, Catch-tiger rated him soundly: 'You cursed little beast', he said. 'You thought to make trouble in the Middle plain. Now, in front of the Palace, what have you to say for yourself?' When the barbarian leader heard this, he was uncommonly surprised and alarmed, and immediately took his leave, intending to go home at once. Seeing this the Emperor Wen of Sui ordered Catch-tiger to go with him and arrange peace terms at the barbarian Court. Hearing this command, Catch-tiger did the dance of homage, thanked the Emperor for this favour, said farewell to the Holy Man (i.e. the Emperor) and set out with the barbarian envoy.

Not many weeks passed before they came to the frontier of the barbarian land. The Khan brought the celestial envoy (i.e. Catch-tiger) to sit with him in his tent. He then summoned into his presence thirty-six eagle-shooting princes and said to them: 'On the occasion of this celestial envoy's visit we will not have any singing or other music. Bows and arrows are what we barbarians care for most, and we will shoot down eagles and wild geese by way of entertainment for the celestial envoy.' The princes assented and all sprang into the saddle. Suddenly they saw an eagle coming from the north. When the princes saw it, they shot at once; but when the arrows left their bow-strings, not east, not west, they passed through the eagle's wings. When the Khan saw this, he suddenly became very angry and said to those about him, 'Take those princes and scoop the hearts out of their bellies, for they have brought disgrace upon the ancestors of my barbarian house!' Catch-tiger, seeing this, contrived to rescue them. 'Let the princes off this time', he said. 'Just give me a bow and arrows, and I will shoot down an eagle and offer it to your Majesty.' When the Khan heard this, he gave Catch-tiger a bow and arrows. Catch-tiger took the bow and arrows and was meditating, when two eagles suddenly appeared, fighting for a morsel of food as they flew. When he saw them he could scarcely contain himself for joy. Having saluted the barbarian King he walked his horse ten paces forward, while he was preparing to shoot. When he had gone twenty paces, he rested his bow on his arm. At thirty paces he took an arrow from his waist-side, at forty paces he fitted the bow-string to the arrow-notch and drew his bow to the full. At fifty paces he turned in his saddle and shot behind him. The arrow left the bow-string with a sound like the splitting of a bamboo. Not east nor west, it passed straight through the first eagle's neck and then pierced the second eagle's heart. Both eagles fell to earth in front of his horse. When the barbarian King saw it, he burst into applause. But Catch-tiger at once shouted to him, 'I do know something about bows and arrows. But King Wen of Sui has a hundred and twenty commanders who are all great experts at shooting wild geese.' When the barbarian King heard this, he hastened to dismount and did a dance of homage, directed towards the Sui Court in the south, shouting, 'Long life to his Majesty!' When his dance of homage was over, he chose a hundred fine horses and a thousand splendid camels, together with narwhal ivory, wild sheep, elks and musk, for the Sui envoy to take

with him on his journey. Catch-tiger then said farewell and
set out. In a few weeks he was back at Ch'ang-an, and went
straight to the Palace gates. The gate-keeper announced him
and the Emperor at once granted him audience. . . . The
Emperor was overjoyed to see him and made him a present
of brocades and fine silks, vessels of gold and silver, and a
pair of beautiful girls; after which he went back to his
private mansion to rest. . . .

Less than two weeks later he suddenly felt uneasy in spirit
and mind and his eyelids twitched and his ears burned. He
thought he would go and sit for a while in his reception hall;
but he had scarcely settled down there when suddenly
cracks in the shape of a cross appeared in the ground, and
out of them leapt a man clad in chain-mail armour all of
gold and on his head a phoenix-wing helmet. Holding his
weapons top to bottom he shouted a salutation. When
Catch-tiger saw him he cried, 'What man are you?' The
apparition replied, 'I am the General of the Five Ways.'(57)
'Why have you come?' 'Last night at the third watch a
written order came down from the Court of Heaven, saying
that you have been appointed Chief Clerk in the World of
the Dead.' When Catch-tiger heard this, 'Delighted to make
your acquaintance, Great Spirit of the Five Ways', he said.
'But I must ask you for three days' leave. Will that be all
right?' 'At present', said the Spirit, 'there is no one at all
to take charge of the Courts of the Dead. I cannot give you a
single hour, a single minute.' When Catch-tiger heard this,
he suddenly became very angry. 'Under whose orders are
you?' he asked. 'Those of the King of the Dead himself',
the Spirit replied. 'If you don't let me take leave of my
sovereign', said Catch-tiger, 'it will mean a hundred blows
under your left ribs with an iron cudgel.' When the General
of the Five Ways heard this, he was so terrified that sweat
poured down all over his back. 'Great sovereign,' he said,
'why say three days? You shall have a month's leave, or more
if you like.' 'You'd better go back at once to the Court of
the Dead and keep an eye on the ghosts', said Catch-tiger.

'On the third day from now I will be at your disposition.'
The General of the Five Ways assented, and disappeared.
When he saw that the General was gone, he drew up a
memorial and sent it to the Emperor, relating in it all that
had just happened. When the Emperor saw the memorial,
he was uncommonly surprised, and at once summoned
Catch-tiger to the Palace. 'It was through no merits of my
own', he said, 'that I arrived at my present lofty position,
which far exceeds anything to which I am properly entitled.
I can't imagine what will become of my realms if you leave
me and become Chief Clerk of the Courts of the Dead.' 'I
will tell your Majesty', said Catch-tiger. 'If ever you find
yourself in any great difficulty, just let me know, and I will
bring ghostly armies to help you.'

Having been told this, the Emperor summoned all the
great ministers to a revel that was to last for three days, in
honour of Catch-tiger's departure. On the third day, just
when the singing and revelry were at their height, there
suddenly appeared a man dressed in purple and there
suddenly appeared a man dressed in scarlet, riding on a
black cloud. They alighted and standing in front of the
Palace gave a loud cry of greeting. When Catch-tiger saw
them, 'Who are you, standing in front of the palace?' he
asked. 'Answer immediately!' 'We come,' they said, 'the
one of us from the Court of Heaven, the other from the
Tribunal of the Underworld. We have come, great sovereign,
to fetch you; that is all.' When Catch-tiger heard this, 'If
you will retire to one side for a moment', he said, 'I will
see to it that you are given wine and something to eat.' The
two men assented and retired each to one side. . . . Having
taken leave of the Emperor and all the ministers of the
court, Catch-tiger came to his own house and gave final
instructions to his wife and sons, and his whole household,
freemen and slaves, and said farewell to them. He then ran
to his bed, lay down (and died). Then, taking only the
brocade bed-spread to cover him he rubbed down his
horse, saddled it and rode on it up into the clouds, waving

farewell to his Majesty the Emperor Wen of Sui as he passed by the Palace. When the Emperor saw him, his eyes filled with tears. He took a cup, made a libation of wine and pronounced the formula of offering, saying. . . .

The illustrated text ends thus; I have not left anything out.

(The last two lines are a comment by the scribe. The prayer of offering may have been omitted because such addresses to the dead follow a fixed pattern, familiar to everyone.)

CONFUCIUS AND THE BOY HSIANG T'O

INTRODUCTION

The Prose Story

There exists in a popular modern Chinese children's book, the *Tung Yüan Tsa Tzu*, a dialogue between Confucius and a boy called Hsiang T'o. The boy answers with complete success conundrums put to him by Confucius, while Confucius fails to answer satisfactorily questions put to him by the boy. The story is alluded to from the second century B.C. onwards. At Tun-huang it was evidently very popular, for eleven MSS of it were found there, five of which are now at Paris and six at the British Museum. As well as these eleven versions in Chinese there are two Tun-huang versions in Tibetan, and in later times the story spread to Mongolia, Japan and Siam. The popularity of the piece is easy to account for. Stories in which less consequential persons score off Confucius are common in early Taoist writing and even percolated into Confucian texts; there are several of them in the *Analects* of Confucius, the basis of all Confucian education. In one case (the Taoist collection *Lieh Tzu*) two little boys draw Confucius into an argument and deride his pretensions to learning.

The story of Hsiang T'o, treated as a story for the young,

points the moral that even children can, by diligence in their studies and refusal to be drawn into idle pursuits, become wiser than the wisest adult. Indeed, this aspect of the story is already stressed in the earliest mention[58] of Hsiang T'o: 'Lu Wang (who at ninety became the adviser of King Wen of Chou) gave an impetus to the aged; whereas Hsiang T'o gave self-confidence to children.'

The Song

In all the five MSS that are complete at the end, the prose story (rhymed prose in part) is followed by a ballad or song in fifty-six lines which also deals with the story of Hsiang T'o, but which (though it may have been intended to be sung along with the prose version) is a separate composition. The prose story is almost entirely in literary language, the song is in colloquial. It begins (perhaps on the principle of 'Some talk of Alexander. . . .') by mentioning a number of other worthies. One is reminded (though the parallel is not complete) of the stock opening of song-sequences in the thirteenth and fourteenth centuries: 'Today you are not going to hear about so and so, and so and so (mentioning favourite heroes and heroines), but about a new theme.'[59]

The subject of this song is the murder by Confucius of his youthful rival. One is surprised at finding such an atrocity attributed to the apostle of Benevolence; but the boy Hsiang T'o was not the only rival whom Confucius was supposed to have liquidated. It is said that at one time his pupils began to stray away to the classes of a teacher called Shao-cheng Mao. Confucius discovered that this rival[60] was publicly advocating the dismantling of a certain fortress, while at the same time secretly supplying the Governor of the fortress with arguments in favour of its not being dismantled. Confucius who was then, according to the legend, Acting Chief Minister, executed Shao-cheng Mao on a charge of political duplicity.

The natural inference (though this was not explicitly drawn till modern times) was that Confucius merely used the dismantling episode as a pretext for getting rid of a rival. In any case both in this and the Hsiang T'o story Confucius kills a rival wiseacre.

Another violent act commonly attributed to him was the slaying of some dwarf jesters[61] whose presence at a peace conference he thought unseemly or even dangerous, because they might well be kidnappers in disguise. The idea of Confucius as a man of violence is therefore by no means foreign to Confucian legend.

Anyone wanting to know more about the Hsiang T'o story in its various versions should read Michel Soymié's article in the *Journal Asiatique*, 1954. This is an exemplary piece of research.

CONFUCIUS AND THE BOY HSIANG T'O

In days long ago the Master travelled to the east. When he reached the Ching hills he met on his way three small boys. Two of them were playing, but one was not. This surprised him and he asked, 'Why don't you play?' The small boy who was not playing answered, 'In big games children kill one another; in small games they wound one another. Play does no one any good. One's coat gets torn, the lining is in holes, one child chases the other, throwing stones. Far better to go home and pound grain. . . . Having thought this well out, I decided not to play. Why should you be surprised?'

Hsiang T'o with some others heaped up earth on the road and made a 'city wall', and then sat down inside it. The Master said, 'You are preventing my carriage from getting by'. The boy said, 'I have heard that wise men of old had a saying, "The Sage knows all the constellations in heaven above and all the conformations of earth below. He knows all the feelings of man, who lies between." From of old till now one has heard of carriages getting out of the way of city walls; but who has ever heard of a city wall getting out of the way of a carriage?'

Confucius could think of no reply, and turned his carriage

aside, so as to avoid the 'wall'. He sent someone to ask, 'Whose little boy are you? What is your surname and name?' The small boy replied, 'My surname is Hsiang; my name is T'o'. The Master said, 'Although you are so young, you seem to know a great deal'. The small boy answered, 'I have heard that three days after it is born a fish goes swimming in the rivers and seas. The hare, three days after it is born, goes chasing round three acres of land. A foal, three days after it is born, can keep pace with the mare. A child three days[62] after its birth knows its father and mother. These things are all natural and inborn. What difference does it make whether I am little or big?'

(Confucius then asks the boy a series of questions, such as 'What cow has no calf? What horse has no foal? What sword has no ring?' To these conundrums the boy successfully replies, 'A clay cow has no calf, a wooden horse has no foal, a chopping-knife has no ring.' The clay cow, it should be explained, was used in expulsion rites and the wooden horse was an instrument of torture. Old Chinese swords had rings at the top; the word for knife and sword, *tao*, is the same.)

The Master said, 'Good! Very good indeed! I should like to take you with me on my travels round the world. Is that possible, or not?' The small boy answered, 'I cannot travel. I have a revered father, whom I must wait upon. I have a kind mother, whom I must look after. I have an older brother whom I must obey and a younger brother whom I must instruct. So I cannot go with you.' The Master said, 'In my carriage I have a backgammon board. How would it be if we were to have a game?' The small boy replied, 'I do not play games of chance. If the Emperor loves gambling, rain and wind come at the wrong times. If the barons love gambling the affairs of their States fall into disorder. If clerks love gambling, they get behindhand with their documents. If farmers love gambling, they fail to plough and sow at the right time. If students love gambling, they forget to read the

Book of Songs and the *Book of History*. If little boys love gambling, they end by being birched. It is a profitless business and there is no use in my learning how to do it!'

The Master said, 'I should like to take you with me to level the world.[63] Is that possible or not?' The little boy replied, 'The world can't be levelled. There are bound to be high hills as well as rivers and seas; nobles as well as slaves. Consequently it cannot be levelled.' The Master said, 'But I'll level out the high hills for you, fill in the rivers and seas, abolish the nobles, do away with slavery. Then surely the world would be dead flat?' The little boy replied. 'If you levelled the high hills, the beasts would have nowhere to go; if you filled in the rivers and seas, the fish would have no home. If you abolished the nobles, the people would do right or wrong as they chose. If you abolished slavery, who would there be to work for gentlemen?'

The Master said, 'Very good! Very good indeed. . . .'

(Then follows another series of rather feeble conundrums including, 'When does the wife remain seated, while the mother-in-law does things for her?' Answer: 'When she first comes under the flowers', i.e. on the night of the wedding.)

The small boy in his turn asked the Master: 'How is it that ducks are so good at swimming and cranes have so mellifluous a note? How is it that the pine-tree is green in winter and summer alike?' The Master replied, 'Ducks swim well because their feet are square. Cranes sing well because their necks are long. The pine-tree is green winter and summer alike because it is tough inside.' The small boy replied, 'That is not so. The frog can sing, but its neck is not at all long. The tortoise can swim, but its feet are far from square. The bamboo is green winter and summer alike, but it is not tough inside'.

(The boy then answers questions about cosmology—the height of the sky, the thickness of the earth, etc.—and

Confucius winds up by saying, 'Good, very good indeed. Now I know that the young are indeed to be feared', thus quoting a saying attributed to him in the *Analects*.[64])

THE POEM

When the Master debated with Hsiang T'o, he was defeated by him again and again. The Master determined to kill Hsiang T'o, and I have made a poem, as follows:

Sung Ching hung himself by the hair and pricked his legs;[65]
K'uang Heng made a hole in the wall to steal the lamplight[66] at night.
Tzu-lu excelled in acts of courage;
Tzu-chang[67] was an avid reader of the *Songs* and *Book*.
Hsiang T'o at the age of seven was already a clever talker
And in his replies to Confucius he got the upper hand.
Then Hsiang T'o went away to the hills to pursue his studies;
Folding his hands in front of the hall he addressed his father and mother,
'Beneath a hundred-foot tree I am going to continue my studies;
And what's to prevent my being notified of a glorious future career?'
His father and mother, being very old, were somewhat confused in the head;
The Master left in their charge two cartloads of hay,
But years passed and the Master never returned to claim it,
And in the end the father and mother gave up hope of his coming
And took a hundred bundles of the hay and burnt them up as fuel;
What was left one day they fed to their cattle and sheep.
But in the end the Master came and laid claim to his hay;
The father and mother at this request looked exceedingly blank.

They at once offered to settle the matter by giving him the
price of the hay,
Even offering for each bundle three bars of gold.
'For gold money, silver money I have not any need;
Old lady, what I want to know is where is Hsiang T'o?'
'My boy went away many years ago;
Under a hundred-foot tree he is studying learned books.'
The Master when at that time he heard what the mother
said
Felt in his heart a burst of joy such as he had seldom known.
The Master at once got into his carriage and went off to the
hills.
He mounted the hills, he crossed ranges, searching in every
direction.
He carefully measured every tree, but none was a hundred
feet;
Dolichos and creepers entwined his feet, spreading every-
where.
The Master told his followers to take spade and pick;
Digging a pit deep into the ground they found a stone hall,
Inside a gate with single flaps a stone lion stood,
Outside a gate with double flaps, a stone Vajrapāni. (68)
When he reached the middle gate he pricked his ears and
listened;
Two rows of students were reading from a book, ranged like
wild geese.
The Master at once drew his sword and struck out wildly,
But on those people in the two rows (?) he could inflict no
wounds.
For they all turned into stone men and did not speak a word;
He cut into them with an iron knife, and blood began to flow.
Thereupon those two people(69) each sought for victory;
Expect it or not, the first to fall was the boy Hsiang T'o.
But Hsiang T'o, while still there was in him some remnant
of life,
Turned his head and looking afar spoke thus to his mother:
'I am sending to you my red blood; I have put it into a jar

To be brought home, where you must keep it (?) seven days
 or more.'
The old mother could not bear the sight of her son's blood;
She took it in her hand and dribbled it out at the side of the
 rubbish heap.
After one day, two days a bamboo root sprouted;
In three days, four days it grew thick and green.
The bamboo grew till it was a hundred feet high;
At every joint were mounted warriors,[70] looking like
 spirit-kings.
They had about them bows and swords—all the implements
 of war.
Confucius at that time was very much afraid
And ordered (?) a temple to Hsiang T'o to be built in every
 town.

CHAPTER FIVE

THE STORY OF HUI-YÜAN

W E are taught that the King of Religion is most mighty and the teachings of the Buddha are very lofty. In this King's law there is no bias; in the works of Buddha there is absolute justice. The King left behind him the nine kinds of teaching, the Buddha expounded the True Tenets. These are all comprised in the twelve divisions of the honoured Canon and are the bridges to Salvation built by Śākyamuni. But after the Nirvāna of the Tathāgata,(71) no saints any longer appeared.

Once in the Second Phase(72) of the religion there was a monk-tutor called Chan-t'an. He had a pupil called Hui-yüan. It is said that this Hui-yüan lived at Yen-men, where he had a brother, but no other kinsmen. Hui-yüan was the older of the two, and he became a monk. The younger, who was called Hui-ch'ih, stayed at home and looked after their mother, while Hui-yüan continually recited the True Law at Chan-t'an's school, and constantly scanned the True Scriptures. Knowing the delight that was to be found in the practice of the Three Concentrations and discerning that the end of the dynasty(73) was at hand, he one day pressed together the palms of his hands and said to his teacher, 'I have now been humbly serving you for a great many years, but I feel that in the cultivation of learning I am still hopelessly defective, which is no doubt due to my own stupidity. I think of seeking a famous mountain, investigating streams, crossing waters, searching for the Way, visiting monks, living as a hermit at the side of some precipitous gorge, that I may be free to pursue my natural bent.' The Master said, 'When you go, what mountain do you think of going to?' 'East and west are all one to me; I cannot say if it will be to the north or the south', said Hui-yüan. 'I only know that I want to go away; I do not know where I shall go to.' 'When you go', said the Master, 'go to the east (? west) of the River and plan your pilgrimage. Then when you come to the Lu Shan, stop there; for that is the place where you are to carry out your spiritual exercises.' When Hui-yüan heard this, he could hardly control his delight. Having received such definite instructions from his Master, how could he dare disobey? So he stepped forward, pressed together the palms of his hands, bowed low, twice took a formal farewell of his teacher, and then set out on his long journey. He went by by-ways, bringing with him a copy of the *Nirvāna Sūtra*,(74) to study while on his way to the Lu Shan.

Spring was beginning, the air was full of the scent of flowers, the green willows were gently swinging their tails in the breeze. He gazed on cloudy peaks jutting up far away, he watched the winter wild geese hurrying home. He felt confidence in his power to apply himself to study and was determined quickly to penetrate the True Principles. After travelling for several days he reached Kiukiang, wandered about the streets, rested for a day or two and then set out once more. He had gone about fifty leagues to the west when right in front of him he came upon a mountain. 'What mountain is this?' he asked, and a villager said 'This is the Lu Shan'. 'When I parted from him', said Hui-yüan to himself, 'my Master in his final instructions directed me to stop when I came to the Lu Shan, saying that this was where I was to pursue my religious exercises.' He saw that it was no common mountain. What kind of fairyland was it? I will tell you. A myriad sharp crags soared into the sky, piled thousandfold one upon another, the high peaks were precipitous and bare, the lofty ridges were cleft and rugged. Monkeys twittered in the dark valleys, tigers roared in the deep ravines. On withered pines hung immemorial creepers, peach-blossom displayed its perennial glow.

Hui-yüan was eager to taste the joys of this mountain, and

though the sun was sinking in the west he went far up it, looking for a place to settle in. He chose a spot on the northern side of the top of the Incense-Burner Peak, and here for temporary shelter built himself a thatched hut. Then taking the fire-stone that he carried at his waist he struck it, lit—treasure beyond all value—an incense-stick, and sitting cross-legged recited several chapters of the *Nirvāna Sūtra*. In so clear and resonant a voice did he recite this scripture that it could be heard far and near. The tones of the Law resounded, the sound of his chanting carried far afield. Moved by it, great rocks shook, the grass bent low, birds magical and of good omen all drew near and sighed their praise. Moreover the Spirit of the Mountain in his shrine witnessed these portents and being much astonished said to his followers, 'Who is on duty today?' The Spirit of the Solid Tree ran to the hall of the shrine and cried, 'At your service'. He was like a leopard or thunder-god, with one head and three faces, big eyes like hanging mirrors, and in his hand an iron club the same length as his body. 'It is I who am on duty', he said. 'Oh, it is you, is it?' said the Spirit of the Mountain. 'Well, when I arrived at my shrine just now I noticed that the rocks of the mountain were shaking and that the birds and beasts had been startled by something. I wish you would inspect this mountain for me and find out what is the meaning of those portents. Probably some saint or sage from other parts has arrived here, or some strange species of sprite or divinity is taking refuge in this mountain. If he brings peace and joy to this mountain, let him be; but if not, you must at once drive him away.' The Tree Spirit accepted the command and went everywhere, up hill and down dale, searching streams and crossing waters. He even searched one by one under every tree in the mountain woods, but could find no one. However, when he reached the northern side of the Incense-Burner Peak he saw that a monk had built himself a meditation-hut and was sitting in it cross-legged, reciting the scriptures. Hiding his spirit form and appearing in the guise of a very aged man, the Tree Spirit came up to the hut and said in a loud voice: 'I have not the pleasure. . . .' 'Ten thousand blessings on you!' said Hui-yüan. The 'old man' came closer and said, 'I, your disciple, do not know where you come from, how you got here or what it is you want. I humbly beg you to take pity on me and give me a little information.' 'I came from Yen-men', said Hui-yüan, 'and have settled here to perform religious exercises.' 'What marvellous sounds were those that I heard just now proceeding from your mouth?' asked the old man. 'What you heard just now', said Hui-yüan, 'was me reciting the scriptures. All living things, when they hear those sounds, want to escape from sorrow and obtain Release.' 'Excellent, excellent!' said the old man over and over again. 'Now that you are here,' he said presently, 'is there anything further that you need?' 'It would be very nice', said Hui-yüan, 'if I could have a monastery to live in. I should not then suffer so much from the wind and frost.' 'Well, if that is all you want', said the old man, 'it's a very small matter. I live in the village to the west. When I get back there, I will have a word with the village elders, and then come and see about your monastery.'

The old man went off; but when he was about a hundred steps away from the hut, he suddenly vanished. He had in fact changed back from the guise of an old man to being once more a Tree Spirit. When he reached the hall of the Spirit of the Mountain he bowed low and said, 'I searched everywhere, up hill and down dale, for goblins or fox-spirits, but found nothing. However, when I got to the north side of the Incense-Burner Peak, I saw a monk, who has put up a meditation-hut, sitting cross-legged and reciting the scriptures. He said he had come from Yen-men and had taken refuge for a time in this mountain in order to devote himself to the pursuit of religious studies.' 'Extraordinary!' said the Spirit of the Mountain, when he heard this. 'I have been the guardian of this mountain for countless aeons and have never once known a monk to take refuge here. His presence will certainly bring us perpetual blessings and drive away all calamities.' 'Has he got all he needs?' the Spirit of the Mountain added. 'I asked him that just now,' the Tree Spirit replied. 'He said the only thing he wanted was a monastery to live in.' 'Well, if that is all he wants', said the Spirit of the Mountain, 'it's a very small matter. You need not go far afield. Just get together the ghosts and spirits of this mountain, and tell them to build a monastery for this monk.'

Having received this order, the Tree Spirit went on to the western slope and gave three long cries. In an instant all the ghosts and spirits of the mountain arrived, darkening the sky like a cloud. For a day and a night they forged magic implements. There was flash after flash of lightning, peal after peal of thunder, a mighty uproar that went on till dawn and, when daylight came, lo and behold the ghosts and spirits had built a monastery, and no ordinary monastery at that! It was piled up many storeys high, like the palaces of the God Indra's heaven; its jewelled halls and terraces matched those of the Western Paradise. Around it lay groves of flowering trees in bloom throughout the whole year. Rivulets flowed past it never ceasing, spring and winter alike. Rare flowers and tender grasses grew beside these halls of Enlightenment, birds magical and of good omen flew up to the roof of this sanctuary.

When Hui-yüan came out of his hut and suddenly saw that a monastery had been built, he uttered a cry of surprise. After reflecting for a while he thought, 'It is not I who have brought this about; it can only be due to the mighty power of the *Great Nirvāna Sūtra*', and contemplating this miracle he made a stanza:

The tall bamboos, rustling in the breeze, turn every
    season into spring;
Waters flowing on every side wash all dust away.
Along the walls the spindle rears bough on bough of green,
Over the earth the mosses spread their freshness, patch
    by patch.
In these far wilds there is no commerce with the din of
    great towns;

These clear spaces are not neighboured by the common
  life of men.
The Spirit of the Mountain in this place has built me a
  monastery,
And I must invite monks to come and turn the Wheel of
  the Law.

Hui-yüan then entered the monastery and went round from
cell to cell and courtyard to courtyard. Nothing seemed to
be lacking, except that he could not find any drinking-water.
'This is a fine monastery', he thought, 'and everything is in
order. The one defect is that there is no drinking-water, and
that makes it impossible to live in. Afterwards, when a community of monks arrives, what will they do about water?'
But when he was on his way to the Buddha Hall he noticed
a large rock which looked as though it might have a spring
under it. He scrabbled with his monk's staff, and sure enough
there was a spring. It bubbled up out of the earth, and is still
called today the Monk's-staff Spring. There is also a monastery called the Monastery Built by Magic, and below it there
is a pool of running water called the White Lotus Pond.

When he had been settled at the monastery for several
months, a crowd of people came from every side to hear him
preach. On this occasion he delivered a comprehensive discourse on the doctrines contained in the *Great Nirvāna Sūtra*,
and in the course of a year his hearers had become many as
the clouds, and donations poured in like rain. He was told
by many of these hearers that an old man had been coming
regularly to the assemblies for a whole year without ever
giving his name or style. He was always in his seat when the
sermon began and went away directly it was over. Hui-yüan
was puzzled as to who he might be and at last asked some of
those who sat in the same row to bring the old man to him.
The old man, when he was sent for, came at once. 'Where
do you live?' asked Hui-yüan. 'You have been listening to the
Law for a long time, but we do not know your name or
surname. I should like the facts.' 'It is true', said the old man,

'that I have listened for a whole year; but I still do not at all understand the doctrines contained in this *Nirvāna Sūtra*, and until I do, I am reluctant to tell you my name and surname.' Having said this, he ran out of the monastery gate and when they followed to see which way he went, they could see no trace of him.

Who was he? I will tell you; it was the dragon of the thousand-foot deep pool of the Lu Shan who had all this while been coming to hear Hui-yüan preach.

After the old man had gone, Hui-yüan kept on thinking about him with great remorse. 'This old man,' he said to himself, 'who has been listening to my preaching first and last for a whole year, still does not understand the doctrines contained in the *Nirvāna Sūtra*; how much the less can the ordinary rank and file of my listeners understand what they hear? I must certainly make a commentary on the *Nirvāna Sūtra*.' He then addressed the Buddhas of the Ten Quarters, saying, 'At present all living creatures go astray because their hearts have not been opened to the Mahāyāna. I, your disciple, now intend to make a commentary on the *Nirvāna Sūtra*, that all living creatures may have their hearts opened to Enlightenment and when they have clear knowledge of Buddha's Law may reject the false and return to the true, abandoning for ever the workings of doubt.' Then in front of the Buddha Hall he took a holy writing-brush made of vetch-down and addressed the Buddhas of the Ten Quarters, the Tathāgatas, local spirits and divinities, informing them of his intention. 'If all you saints and worthies do not approve,' he said, 'then make this brush immediately fall down.' Having burnt incense and reverently made this address he threw his brush into the air. It remained fixed and immovable, so that he knew that his project was pleasing to the Buddhas and Tathāgatas. He then asked that the brush might come down, and it did so. How do we know that this is true? There is still to this day a peak at the Lu Shan called Throw-brush. He then made his commentary, which took him three years in all before it was finished. But in case there were mistakes in the writing and the meaning was not intelligible he took all the eight hundred scrolls of his commentary to a place outside the eastern gate of the monastery and put them on top of a bonfire made of incense-sticks, and once more addressed all the Buddhas of the Ten Quarters, the Bodhisattvas and saints and worthies: 'Because all living creatures are confused and do not understand and are not enlightened concerning the Mahāyāna, your disciple in order to remove their doubts has composed a commentary. If his explanations concord with the scripture, signify this by fire failing to burn this commentary and water failing to submerge it.' The crimson flames stretched up to the sky and black smoke curled; but the commentary remained completely unharmed. He was now pretty well convinced that the commentary was pleasing to Buddha. But he was still not quite satisfied, so he took it to the edge of the White Lotus Flower Pool and threw it towards the water. But it remained suspended in the air ten feet above the surface of the pool and dropped no farther. Then he was sure that Buddha was pleased with it. He took it into the monastery and put it in the library. Soon great multitudes came to listen and he used it to expound the meaning of the *Great Nirvāna Sūtra*. People from every direction poured in like rain, determined to hear the Law. First and last he addressed these great crowds for several years.

There suddenly arose at this time in the neighbourhood of Shou-chou(75) a robber band led by a man called Po Chuang. It was said of this man that from his earliest years he had piqued himself on his valour and had always been engaged in deeds of violence and robbery, regardless of all risks to his own safety and by nature disposed towards slaughter. One day he heard that a monastery had been built by magic and that it was immensely wealthy owing to the vast quantities of silk and other goods that benefactors donated to it. He assembled his five hundred followers and brought them, travelling double stages by starlight, to within the borders of Kiukiang, where they encamped. He then addressed them as follows: 'Say nothing to anyone; for this must not get out beforehand. Tomorrow at the hour of the monks' repast we are going to pillage that monastery.' They all gave their promise.

There is a proverb that says: 'Profess a good intent, and Heaven will prosper it; profess an evil intent, and Heaven will frustrate it.' The moment that Po Chuang said what he meant to do, the local deity of the place took note and, displaying his magic powers, came to the monastery and told the monks what was going to happen. The word soon went round from cell to cell and courtyard to courtyard, for speaking out of the sky the deity said, 'Tomorrow at the time of your repast a band of robbers is going to pillage the monastery. I strongly recommend you to go into hiding.' When the monks heard this they were in a terrible fright and at once made themselves scarce, scampering some this way, some that. The only one who did not rush off was Hui-yüan's chief disciple Yün-ch'ing. Because of the rules of behaviour towards a teacher and because of his strong attachment to him he did not dare attempt to evade the robbers, but went straight to the Master's meditation-hut and said, 'Just now a divinity came and announced that a band of robbers is about to pillage the monastery. I respectfully desire that your Reverence may go off into hiding.' 'You may not have known this', said Hui-yüan. 'But I have known for a long time that this was going to happen. However, in the Nirvāna doctrine fear has no place, and where there is fear there is no Nirvāna. You and the other monks had better hide swift as fire, each shifting for himself. I intend to stay here.' When Yün-ch'ing saw that, though he begged him twice and again to get away, the Master could not be persuaded, with tears streaming down his face he left the monastery and all alone set out to follow the other monks in their flight. Hui-yüan, when he saw that the monks were all gone, sat alone in his meditation-hut not in the least afraid. Before long Po Chuang and his followers reached the monastery. He drew up his troops in battle formation across the hill-crest, and also spread them out down the length of the valley. Such was their violence that the hills crumbled and rocks split. East and west they charged wildly, north and south they scurried, and at last all pressed into the monastery, shouting, 'Catch them alive!'

Po Chuang arrived in the monastery expecting to find a great store of valuable goods; but though he searched in courtyard after courtyard, he found the whole place utterly empty and deserted. 'Extraordinary!' he exclaimed. 'Yesterday we held our consultation in absolute secrecy. Who can have given the monks warning and caused them to make off, taking everything with them?' He then told his assistants to search in every nook and cranny inside the monastery and outside, and if they found any teacher or monk bring him along at once. They acknowledged his order and again searched in every possible place, but could find no one. At last outside the eastern gate they saw a monk sitting quietly in a meditation-hut. They thought this should be reported at once and, turning on their heels, went straight back into the monastery and coming into Po Chuang's presence they announced, 'In accordance with your orders, General, we made a thorough search for monks, both inside the monastery and outside, and could find none anywhere. At last outside the gates we saw a monk and dared not fail at once to report this.' 'Where was he?' asked Po Chuang. 'He was sitting outside the eastern gate in a meditation-hut', they said.

Po Chuang at once shouted to his followers in a loud voice, bidding them bring the monk to him. 'If you have any money or silks or clothing in your monastery', he said, 'they must be produced immediately.' Stepping forward Hui-yüan said, 'This monastery has always been very badly off; there is not a thing in it. There have of course been some small offerings, but only trifling contributions to the day by day expenses of the refectory, nothing in the way of valuable stuffs. You may be sure, General, that I would not dare deceive you.' Po Chuang now took a closer look at him and began to take a great fancy to him; for Hui-yüan had the marks of a Bodhisattva. A silver light shone from his body, he was seven feet tall, his hair was as though smeared with lacquer, and his lips as though stained with cinnabar. 'This monk', said Po Chuang to those about him, 'would be very useful to me as a servant.' Then, turning to Hui-yüan, 'I should like to take you into my service. Would you be willing?' 'I am willing to be your slave, General,' said Hui-yüan, 'and have only one small condition to make, which I think I ought to make clear. Is it my bodily service that you require or my professional service?' 'What is the difference?' asked Po Chuang. 'My profession', answered Hui-yüan, 'is to recite the scriptures. If you only want me to fetch and carry for you, that would merely be bodily service. If that is what you want, I must make it a condition that my duties do not prevent me from reciting the scriptures.' 'So long as you do your work properly, nobody is going to prevent you from reciting your scriptures,' said Po Chuang. Hui-yüan assented to this arrangement and followed behind the General's horse as he rode away. When they were a hundred steps or so from the monastery, he said, 'Let me go back to the monastery and get out of my monastic dress. I will come back here at once and follow your flags.' 'Don't be long about it', said Po Chuang, 'or I shall be very cross. If you keep me waiting too long I shall tell my followers to seize you and cut you into three pieces, here in front of me. Don't say I did not warn you!' Hui-yüan assented and went back to the monastery. He was standing in front of the hall when his chief disciple Yün-ch'ing, who had taken refuge on the top of a high peak, looked down and saw him. He immediately came running down, and when he reached his Master said, 'Just now when the mad brigands were careering about I was very much afraid. I have now come to share your joy in the fact that the robber armies have withdrawn.' 'In the Nirvāna doctrine there is no fear,' said Hui-yüan, 'and where there is fear, there is no Nirvāna. From now onwards you must strive hard to improve yourself and administer this place properly. We shall never meet again in this life.' 'What *can* make you say that', exclaimed

Yün-ch'ing. 'Outside the monastery, over there,' said Hui-yüan, 'I have just sworn to be that brigand General's slave. I have only come back here for a moment. You must try to do your best.' When Yün-ch'ing heard this, he smote himself with such violence that fresh blood flowed from all his seven apertures. At last he revived and rising from the ground recited this stanza:

> All of us were like the birds of the air;
> You, our Teacher, were like a great tree.
> Now that the great tree is taken away
> Where shall his followers find a perching-place?
> In changed guise where will he now dwell
> Bequeathing us only a Nirvāna couplet?
> Oh may the lamp of Highest Wisdom avail
> To light us on our path, lest we should go astray!

Having recited those verses, he burst out again into lamentation. 'I must go now or I shall get into trouble with the General', said Hui-yüan. He hastened out of the monastery, caught up with the banners and followed on behind them. Days came and months went; he followed them for several years.

After Hui-yüan left, Yün-ch'ing reassembled the monks, took the commentary on the *Nirvāna Sūtra* and gave lectures founded upon it. Tears streamed from the eyes of his hearers, for it was as though they were listening to the Master. At last Yün-ch'ing, having had no news of Hui-yüan for several years, took the commentary and gave it to a teacher called Tao-an, who took it to the Fu-kuang Monastery at Nanking and began lecturing upon it. Not knowing what sort of man this Tao-an really was listeners were moved to flock to him like clouds, and donations poured in like rain.

Now it happened that at this time the Emperor Wen of the Chin dynasty ruled at Nanking. When Tao-an was going to lecture showers of heavenly flowers dropped out of the

sky . . . and five-coloured clouds appeared. The concourse
of people that gathered to hear him was so immense that
they trod the seats to bits and he could not begin his lecture.
He therefore sent in a petition to the Emperor saying:
'Your servant received orders from your Majesty to preach
upon the *Nirvāna Sūtra* in the Fu-kuang Monastery. Those
who came to listen were so many that disturbances took
place among the audience and it was impossible to hold the
session. I humbly beg your Majesty to issue special instructions.' The Emperor accordingly ordered that everyone
wishing to hear Tao-an's discourse must pay a length of silk,
which would entitle him to admission on one day only. It
happened that peace prevailed in the land, prices were very
low, and twenty to thirty thousand people came every day
with their length of silk. The monastery courtyard was not
very spacious and it was impossible to accommodate so
large a number. Tao-an sent in a second petition saying that,
despite the charge of a length of silk, more people than ever
were seeking admission and it was impossible to control them.
The petitioner humbly begged for further instructions. The
Emperor then commanded that in future the charge was to be
a hundred copper cash a day. This charge brought the attendance down to not more than three to five thousand auditors
a day, who came to listen to Tao-an's preaching at Nanking.

Meanwhile, where was Hui-yüan? He was still with
Po Chuang who was pillaging every place, big or little, that
he came to. By day he wandered beside waters and through
the wilds; by night he lay in mountain woods. His head
shaved to the level of his eyebrows and wearing a short
serge jacket he waited all the time on his master. This went
on year after year. He thought often about the Gateway into
the Void,(76) but had no chance to re-enter it; and all the
while Po Chuang was committing crime after crime,
consorting only with abandoned ruffians, loving slaughter,
hating to let live and dealing only in pillage.

One day when they were in the mountains, Po Chuang
encamped on the eastern ridge and Hui-yüan bivouacked on

the western slope. The autumn wind suddenly rose, the falling leaves whirled, the hills were quiet, the trees wide apart, frost was wet on the grass. The light wind in the woods blew the bamboos as though they were silk thread. A moon shone in the clear sky, pink mists like a brocade trailed along the side of the stream. Hui-yüan was heavy at heart. Presently he dozed off, and in his dream saw the Buddhas of the Ten Quarters appear among the clouds, with a numberless host of saints and worthies. They called to him, 'Bodhisattva, arise! Do not hanker for the sleep of the witless. Take your stand upon the Nirvāna! Why are you not preaching the *Nirvāna Sūtra* to all living creatures?'

Hui-yüan in his dream prostrated himself time and again. Taking pity on a common mortal, Akshobhya, the Buddha of the East, now revealed to him his future. Calling him into his presence, Akshobhya said, 'There is no need for you to despair. In a former existence you contracted a debt which you have not discharged. You acted as surety for someone and you must settle with the creditor in your present incarnation. This creditor is not hard to find; he is the present Chief Minister. You have only to get into touch with him and sell yourself to him. You will get five hundred copper cash which, in fulfilment of your guarantee in a previous existence, you will hand over to Po Chuang. You will then be able to return to the Lu Shan, where we shall meet again.'

Hui-yüan woke up feeling much moved. He sat up and began to recite several chapters of the *Nirvāna Sūtra*. The sound woke Po Chuang, who was sleeping on the eastern ridge, and he said to his companions, 'What is that noise coming from the western side?' 'General,' they replied, 'that is the low slave, whom you captured and brought along with you, reciting the scriptures.' When he heard this, Po Chuang was very angry. He sent for Hui-yüan and scolded him at the top of his voice: 'It would be bad enough if you went to a monastery and recited like that; but that you should do so when you are supposed to be in attendance on me is intolerable.' 'General,' said Hui-yüan, 'at the time when you captured me, you said there was nothing to prevent my reciting the scriptures.' 'On what occasion did I say that?' asked Po Chuang. Hui-yüan did not reply at once, and one of Po Chuang's followers said, 'General, as a matter of fact you did say he might recite his scriptures'. 'It's quite uncalled for, this reciting of scriptures', said Po Chuang. 'I, like the rest of you, have done a lot of killing, and I don't like the sound of scripture being read.' 'If I may not read scripture out loud', said Hui-yüan, 'I suppose there would not be any objection to my reading silently?' 'No, that won't do either', said Po Chuang. 'One reason why I took you on, after you fell into my hands, was that I wanted compensation for not finding money or anything else at the monastery; another was, that I was short of servants. But now I am no longer short of servants; in fact, I have a very large number of them, and I'm quite ready to let you go back to your monastery and pursue your devotions there to your heart's content.' 'Sir,' said Hui-yüan, 'I undertook to be your slave for life, and if I withdraw my service half-way through, how can that be called being a slave for life? If you still need me, then there is no more to be said. If you don't, sell me to someone else and buy wine and meat with the proceeds. Wouldn't that be possible?' Po Chuang gave a great guffaw. 'You are quite wrong', he said. 'If the position had been that I obtained you by purchase, I could produce the deed of purchase and should be able to sell you. But as matters stand, I got you by capture and consequently I cannot sell you.' 'If you won't sell me', said Hui-yüan, 'there is no more to be said. But if you really want to sell me, you have only to pass me off as having been born in your house, as the child of a slave, and in that case you can sell me without producing a deed of purchase.' 'Even if I did that,' said Po Chuang, 'where do you suggest that I should sell you?' 'The best way to sell me', said Hui-yüan, 'would be to take me to Nanking.' When Po Chuang heard this he became very much alarmed, and also very angry. 'These low-class creatures', he cried, 'never for

a moment quit their scoundrelly tricks! What you mean to
do is to go the round of the various government offices at
the capital, give an account of my career and get me
arrested as a brigand.' 'If such an idea ever entered my head,'
said Hui-yüan, 'or I am scheming any plot against you, may
I in every future existence drop straight into hell and stay
there. There is no need at all for you to worry about
anything of that sort.'

Po Chuang believed him. He dismissed the bulk of his
followers and, only keeping with him three or five, he
disguised himself as a merchant and taking three or five
beasts of burden he loaded them with market goods and
went to the capital to sell Hui-yüan in the livestock row of
the market. On arriving at the market Hui-yüan displayed a
placard announcing that he was for sale. The myriads of
people in the market-place burst into cries of astonishment.
For Hui-yüan was seven feet tall, a silver light shone from
his body, his forehead was broad and his eyebrows high, his
face was like the full moon, his hair was as though smeared
with lacquer, his lips as though stained with cinnabar. His
stride was that of a King, his hands fell to below his knees.
When he strode this way and that in the market-place, all
beholders gasped with astonishment and admiration. They
gathered together in groups, saying to one another: 'I have
seen in the course of my life thousands and tens of thousands
of low-class people, but never such a one as this.' And while
they were marvelling they were continually joined by more
and more people who came to look at him.

Hui-yüan naturally felt cast-down at having to dispose of
himself in this way. But he knew that the debt he had
contracted in a former existence was not yet paid, and he
was eager to sell himself in order to discharge his obligation
to Po Chuang. In a little while the god Indra, appreciating
his plight, came down from heaven disguised as a member
of the Chief Minister Ts'ui's staff. He went straight to the
livestock row and shouted to the livestock broker, 'This
chattel is not to be sold to anyone else. The Chief Minister

Ts'ui needs him in his mansion, and no offers for him are to be made by anyone else.' When the broker heard this he fully believed that the Chief Minister had given this order, and at once took Hui-yüan to his mansion. Po Chuang followed them; but Hui-yüan said to him, 'You need not come; for good or ill, I will make myself responsible for the rest of the proceedings. If the minister is pleased with me, I will hand over to you whatever price he pays.' 'Well,' said Po Chuang, 'when you meet the minister be sure to answer all his questions properly and make no mistakes.' Hui-yüan promised, and followed the broker to the minister's gate. The gate-keeper asked the broker, 'Who is this that you have brought?' 'I have come at the bidding of one of his Excellency's personal followers', said the broker. 'Owing to what he told me I did not dare sell this chattel in any other quarter, but have specially brought him for his Excellency's use.' 'Stay here for a moment', said the gate-keeper, 'while I go in and announce you.' 'There is a slave-broker at the gate', the gate-keeper announced when he reached the Minister's office. 'He has brought a low fellow to see you, and I thought I had better let you know.' 'Bring them in', said the Minister. The broker dragged Hui-yüan in and they were taken to the Minister's office, where Hui-yüan prostrated himself before his Excellency and then stood to one side. The Minister exclaimed in surprise, 'Last night in a dream I saw a divinity who came into my house, and I wonder whether the arrival of this slave may not be what was foretold by my dream?' 'Was he born in the house of his present owner', said the Minister to the broker, 'or was he obtained by purchase?' 'The fellow was house-born', said the broker. 'In that case, of course,' said the Minister, 'there would not be any deed of purchase. By the way, how much is being asked for him?' Before the broker could reply Hui-yüan stepped forward and said, 'If you are willing to sell me cheap, charge his Excellency five hundred cash.' 'What arts and accomplishments have you', asked the Minister, 'that I should spend five hundred cash upon you?

Just give me a short account of what you can do, and I will decide if you are worth the money.' 'I can say just how rich anyone's family was three hundred years ago', said Hui-yüan, 'and just how poor it will be two hundred years hence. I can fold and iron (?) clothes, concoct the drugs needed at all four seasons, carry messages. There is no question I cannot answer. I have a rough knowledge of the various styles used by the different schools of calligraphy. In all this, "single horse and lonely spear",(77) I am ready to be tested against anyone you like to name. About hoeing grain and reaping corn I understand quite a bit. In business transactions of every kind I know my way about. As for fetching and carrying in domestic service, I am swift as the wind, and indeed far from stupid or slow. If you don't believe me, I will myself write out for you a contract for the sale of my person, that there may not be any doubt that what I have told you is true.'

The Minister ordered his attendants to furnish Hui-yüan with paper and writing-brush. When they were brought he asked for an incense-burner. He was immediately supplied with one and, having bowed to the Minister, there and then in the office he wrote out a contract for his own sale, indeed a most singular document. It ran as follows: 'In such and such a month of such and such a year I sold myself to be the Chief Minister's slave, undertaking to serve him faithfully so long as he is alive. If I fail in this and desert him half-way may I in every future existence drop into hell when I die and when my punishment there is done be reborn as an animal and chafed by the saddle, the stirrups dangling at my sides and a bit in my mouth, pay the penalty of my transgression. If on the other hand I serve my master so long as he lives, may I in every future existence complete the Ten Stages and be born as an auditor of Buddha's preaching.'

When the contract was written, he handed it to the Minister who, on seeing it, burst into cries of admiration: 'It must be a Bodhisattva, a Mahāsattva (Great Being) who has come to my house.' He then gave orders for the five hundred cash to be given to the broker and passed on at once to Po Chuang, who when he got the money did not dare stay any longer at the capital, but made off at once for the borders of Shou-chou.

The Minister, having bought this slave, told his servants in the western courtyard to prepare quarters for him in a room there. Knowing that he had to work off his debt, Hui-yüan felt no grudge against anyone, but gladly bustled about on errands here, there and everywhere, held his master's whip or ran by his stirrup-side.

It happened that once, when Hui-yüan was sitting alone in his room very late at night, he had several times meant to snuff out the lamp. But seeing how still and clear was the Milky Way and that the moon was shining brightly, he sat up for a long while. When at last he dozed where he sat, he once more saw in his dream the Buddhas of the Ten Quarters all appearing in the sky, along with countless saints and worthies, assembled there in a vast throng. They called to him, 'Bodhisattva, arise! Do not lie sunk in witless slumber, but take your stand on the Nirvāna. Why are you not reciting the scriptures to all living creatures?'

He woke with a start and, sitting up, began to recite the *Nirvāna Sūtra*, going on till daylight came. The Minister in his office, hearing the sound of a scripture being recited, slipped away all by himself to the gate of the western courtyard to listen. Presently he had his wife sent for and, when she arrived at the western gate, both of them listened to the recitation of the scripture till daybreak. Early next day when the Minister returned from his morning audience at Court and was sitting in his office, he sent for the servants attached to the western courtyard. Thirty of them came and he asked them, 'Which of you was reciting the scriptures last night in the western courtyard?' 'It was none other than the slave you have just bought', said the chief of the group of servants. When the Minister heard this, he sent for Hui-yüan and asked him whether it was true that it was he who had been reciting scriptures last night. Hui-yüan confessed that it was. 'And what is the title of the scripture you were reciting?' asked the Minister. 'The *Great Nirvāna Sūtra*', said Hui-yüan. 'How many chapters are you able to recite?' 'A whole section, in twelve chapters', he replied. 'Last night I recited them from beginning to end.' 'That can't be true', said the Minister. 'I would not dare deceive your Excellency', said Hui-yüan. The Minister then made him sit down and recite the *Nirvāna Sūtra* again. Whereupon he started again, from the title onwards, and recited it right through without any omission or mistake. The Minister constantly broke out into cries of applause, and afterwards sent for all his household, young and old, freemen and slaves alike, three hundred persons in all, and when they were assembled in his office instructed them that from now onwards the new slave must not be looked down upon by anybody. He also gave him the additional name Shan-ch'ing.(78)

It was the Minister's practice every day after the morning audience to go to the Fu-kuang Monastery and listen to Tao-an's exposition of the scriptures, paying his hundred cash like everyone else. He would often take Hui-yüan with him, but as Hui-yüan came in the capacity of the Minister's servant he was not allowed to go in and listen, but only to keep an eye on the Minister's horse outside the monastery gate. Soon the audience began to arrive in vast throngs, passing on into the monastery. The tolling of the monastery bell stopped, and Tao-an gave out the title of the scripture. The sound of his chanting echoed far afield and even reached Hui-yüan outside the gate, making him very sad. 'How, I wonder,' he said to himself, 'did Tao-an get such eloquence in preaching? If only I could one day mount the high dais again, give witness to the fruit of the Ten Stages and save all living creatures from calamity, that the shaped and the unshaped, the embodied and the unembodied(79) might all be absorbed into Nirvāna!' Soon the preaching ended and the audience, men and women, all dispersed. The Minister went back to his house and after a rest sat in his office. His wife, with her hands hidden in her sleeves, came to him and said, 'You have for several years been listening to his

Reverence Tao-an preaching about the *Nirvāna Sūtra* at the Fu-kuang Monastery. What doctrines has he told you about? They say that the *Nirvāna Sūtra* has countless inner meanings. You must surely remember how he explains some of the passages. Why do you keep silent about what you hear and never tell me? You have not so much as repeated to me one stanza or half-stanza.' 'Have you ever read the *Lotus Scripture?*' asked the Minister. 'Indeed I have', she said. 'In that scripture it is written,' said the Minister, ' "Only those words are listened to which are spoken by request".' 'I do wish', said his wife, 'that you would give a short talk about it to all the members of the household, freemen and slaves, so that they might have at any rate the beginning of an understanding.' 'I might try to tell you something about the inner meanings of the *Nirvāna Sūtra*', said the Minister. His wife then told servants to sweep and sprinkle the audience room and arrange benches. She sent for the three hundred members of the household, young and old, freemen and slaves, and begged the minister to give a talk about the meaning of the *Nirvāna Sūtra*. Everyone then listened in complete silence while the Minister that night, as his first talk, spoke about the assault of the Eight Woes.

(I shall not translate the minister's talk, or the other sermons which follow. It is, of course, in order to work them in that the writer tells his lively and exciting story and they do in fact constitute for him the whole point of his tale. But they could only be made intelligible with the aid of a vast amount of commentary. My book is after all a literary anthology, not a treatise on Buddhism. There do exist large numbers of such treatises in most European languages, and a reader who wants to know can easily find out what, for example, the Eight Woes (sorrows, pains, uneasinesses) are. I will only say here that the author takes them in this order: Birth, Old Age, Illness, Death, Woes arising from the Five Constituents (form, feeling, perception, impulses, consciousness), Seeking but not getting, Anger, and Parting

from what we love. These are not all such plain sailing as
they sound. 'Parting from what we love' (*priya-viprayoga* in
Sanskrit), for example, is understood quite differently in the
Nirvāna Sūtra, coming out in the Chinese translation as
something like 'the destruction and dissolution of pleasure-
objects', and elsewhere it is given an even more technical
and specialized meaning. But the Minister, though he was
nominally expounding the *Nirvāna Sūtra*, seems to have in
mind more popular, unscholastic interpretations, such as
those of the *Sūtra of the Five Kings*, a work which though
purporting to be translated from Sanskrit was obviously
composed in China; for it is moulded on an episode in the
Analects of Confucius.[80] This book takes *priya-viprayoga* in
the human and natural sense of 'parting with those one
loves'. Here is the Minister's paragraph on it):

'Suppose a family brings up a son. To the father and
mother he is precious as pearls or jade. When he reaches
manhood and is beginning to "distinguish east from west"
he leaves his native place. His father and mother think of
him perpetually day and night, always expecting his return.
Day after day they stand at the door, weeping and lamenting.
Their constant longing for him at last makes them ill; but
he is not there to look after them and give them medicine.
Winter comes and all the rest of the family is there; but
suddenly the father and mother think of the boy who is not
there, and the breath is stifled in their breasts. That is what
is called "Being parted from those one loves".'

(The three hundred members of the household were
delighted with their master's discourse, but Hui-yüan was
observed by the Minister to be weeping bitterly.)

'What is the matter?' the Minister asked. 'I take the
trouble to expound the scripture for you, and you burst
into tears. If you have a grievance against someone, the
sensible thing would be to tell me all about it immediately.

If you don't, you'll be in for a thrashing!' Hui-yüan came
forward and addressed the Minister: 'I have no grievance
against anyone else. It is only because, when he preaches,
Tao-an makes distinctions; that is why I am sad.' 'Since
Tao-an has been preaching at the capital', said the Minister,
'the Emperor, the nobles and all the ministers have come
every day to hear him. You haven't heard him, so how can
you know that he "makes distinctions"?' 'Well, for example
last night,' said Hui-yüan, 'when I went with you to the monastery, I was left outside the gate, where I could not hear the
scripture. That is why I say that when he preaches he makes
distinctions. Though I am in a humble station of life, I do
understand a little about Buddha's religion. I may not be robed
as a monk, but the religion is the same for everybody. That is
why I say that Tao-an, when he preaches, makes distinctions.
He does not know that he ought to transmit the religion to
the three classes, to those born in the four different ways, and
to the ten kinds of listener.'

(The Minister asks what these categories mean, and is
told, for example, that the three classes are those who lie
ill in bed, prisoners shackled and confined, and those who
are not their own masters. A long sermon follows, on the
four ways of being born (from the womb, from an egg, etc.)
and the sort of conduct that leads to each form of birth.
Then follows the exposition of the 'ten kinds'. As an
example may be taken the third kind, those who 'go to a
monastery to listen to the preaching, see that the preacher
is sleek and white, take a fancy to him and being completely
captivated let their thoughts stray away from the preaching.
When their thoughts stray, folly arises. . . .' and so on in a
long chain, till they fall into Hell.
The Minister is deeply impressed and asks for another
discourse. Hui-yüan explains the doctrine of the Twelve
Causes and Effects, much as it will be found in any ele-
mentary book on Buddhism. Hui-yüan then asks if he may
not be taken into the monastery and conduct a debate with

Tao-an. 'All that Tao-an says', complains Hui-yüan, 'is like trying to build a palace in the air. It can lead to nothing, just as a palace built in the air is bound to come down with a crash. Though I am in a humble position, the religion of Buddha is the same for all. There is a difference of garb, but not of substance. I should very much like to go with your Excellency into the monastery and challenge Tao-an's views.' 'If you have a mind to do that', said the Minister, 'I for my part will not do anything to prevent it.' Next morning the Minister sent for Hui-yüan and said, 'This Tao-an is one of the most celebrated monks in the land. You had better consider carefully before embarking on a debate with him.' 'A proverb says,' replied Hui-yüan, ' "A brave woodman does not keep away from the hills for fear of meeting wolves or tigers. A brave fisherman does not shun a stream for fear of being attacked by dragons." To debate with Tao-an would be for me like drink to one who is athirst, like fire to one who is acold. I assure your Excellency that you need not worry on my account.' So as soon as it was time for the preaching to begin, they set off. When they arrived the minister paid two hundred cash and took Hui-yüan into the monastery.

The proceedings began as usual with an introductory invocation, doing homage first of all to Buddha and the Saints and Worthies of the religion, and then praising the virtues of the reigning Emperor and praying for the temporal good fortune and spiritual welfare of the Emperor, the Crown Prince, the Princesses and Imperial Consorts, the Court Ministers and provincial officials, and lastly of the 'good men and good women' in the audience. There are numerous such introductory invocations among the Tun-huang manuscripts, existing either as separate texts or occurring at the beginning of popular sermons.

Tao-an is just about to explain the title of the scripture, when Hui-yüan comes forward and begins to heckle him. The disputation that follows could only be made intelligible by a vast amount of commentary and I skip on to the passage where Hui-yüan challenges Tao-an to confess how he got hold of the commentary he has been using.)

'I won't ask anything else. I will just ask this one question: how did you get hold of the commentary on the *Nirvāna Sūtra*?' 'It came from the Lu Shan,' said Tao-an, 'from the great Master Hui-yüan's place.' 'Would you know Hui-yüan, if you were to see him?' 'No,' said Tao-an, 'I confess I should not know him.' 'In that case', said Hui-yüan, 'you cannot have got the commentary direct from the Master himself.' 'I got it from his chief disciple, Yün-ch'ing', said Tao-an. 'I don't know who you imagine I am', said Hui-yüan. 'Perhaps it may surprise you to learn that you need look for Hui-yüan nowhere else; for I am he.' When Tao-an heard this he felt completely bewildered and was not at all sure that it was true. 'I have heard', he said, 'that the Great Master Hui-yüan had a birthmark on his arm in the form of a ring. If you are he, show me this mark.' To convince him, Hui-yüan bared his left arm and there sure enough was the ring. A great light shone from it, and was seen by all the hearers.

Tao-an arose, came down from the high dais and smote himself till the fresh blood poured from every one of his seven apertures. Then step after step he came forward and to expiate his offence was about to take an awl and gouge out his eyes, in token of his blindness in not having recognized Hui-yüan. Weeping and wailing he prostrated himself and begged the Master to accept his repentance.

'Don't take on so about it', said Hui-yüan. 'There is no need for all this lamentation. You are only a common mortal, and how could you be expected to recognize in me the expounder of the true sense of Nirvāna? As soon as may be I will occupy the seat you have vacated. But I must first make my apologies to the Chief Minister. After that I will come back and preach the True Law to you.'

(Hui-yüan then goes to the Minister, apologizes for creating a disturbance and admits that he deserves a sound thrashing. The Minister, on his side, is appalled to think of all the rude things he has said to Hui-yüan during the six years of his bondage, and implores his forgiveness. Hui-yüan explains the circumstances in a previous existence which led to his becoming the Minister's slave. But we have heard all this and need not have it over again. The Minister reports to the Emperor the extraordinary happenings of the day; Hui-yüan is sent for to the Palace and acts as chaplain for another six years, finally converting the Emperor and administering to him the Five Vows of Abstinence, that is, installing him as a lay convert. A curious passage follows: 'Ever since he had been in the Palace Hui-yüan had noticed that in all the different apartments the Palace people were in the habit of using paper with writing on it for unclean purposes in the privy. He scolded them all and made a stanza.'

The text of the first four lines of the stanza is corrupt and partly unintelligible. But it goes on: 'Examination essays, too, are all written with the same characters as the scriptures of the Buddhist Canon. Yet some people show them no respect and use them for filthy purposes in the privy. To atone for their sins, numerous as the sands of the Ganges, many incarnations would not be time enough. For five hundred aeons they will be degraded, never ceasing to be reborn as insects inhabiting the privy.'

The passage has importance to readers of Tun-huang literature; for it was probably owing to this taboo against throwing away any kind of written matter, secular or religious, that so great a mass of texts was preserved in the walled-up library.)

The time came when Hui-yüan insisted on being released from his chaplaincy and allowed to go back to the Lu Shan. When he left the capital, clouds gathered under his feet and supported him . . . like the outspread arms of a strong man. In a twinkling he was at the Lu Shan, but he did not go back to his old monastery. He made himself a temporary thatched hut some ten leagues away, on a high ridge. Here he sat cross-legged, again seeking his old scrolls and once more filling the air with the sound of scripture. Several months went by, till suddenly he noticed a high plateau, to which he climbed. Cranes sang on lofty peaks, down in the gulleys dragons boomed. On every hill and dale the flowers were in bloom. Over level spaces streams ran that never dried, the gardens were spread with flowers that never withered. For it was a place where a Buddha had once pursued his spiritual ends. Here Hui-yüan sat upright and entered into concentration, purified his thoughts, cleansed his heart and meditated about Buddha's way. He dwelt on the thought that this fleeting life cannot be for long, that nothing in the common world can endure. Then out of his own self-nature and master-mind he made a Boat of the Law, that he might commit himself to the Heavens of the Upper Sphere. To make this boat he did not use the common substances of the world. All he needed was the passionless Mahāyāna to make the rigging, Bodhi and Prajñā to make the rails; he used the Secret Thunder-bolt deity[81] to make. . . .'

(Here the manuscript abruptly ends. But probably only a few lines, describing Hui-yüan's death or transference to some higher sphere, are lost. The legends embodied in this work evidently had a wide circulation. P'u-tu in his *Lu Shan Lien-tsung Pao-chien* (A.D. 1305; *Taishō Tripitaka*, XLVII, 321) denounces a book called *Lu Shan Ch'eng-tao Chi* for giving apocryphal information about Hui-yüan: the teacher of Hui-yüan is wrongly called Chan-t'an, it is falsely asserted that he was captured by a robber called Po Chuang and then sold himself as a slave to the Minister Ts'ui; also that he had a birthmark on his arm, when in reality it was Tao-an who had this birthmark, and so on. These false stories, says P'u-tu, are known to everyone and are so universally accepted that it is now by no means easy to discredit them.)

CHAPTER SIX

THE WIZARD YEH CHING-NENG

... CHING-NENG lived at the Hui-yeh Taoist cloister in the Kuei-chi mountains, where he studied with a Taoist monk. He applied himself with the greatest diligence to his tasks, and at the age of twenty he too became a monk and wore the ailanthus-bark hat and yellow cape. There was always a scroll in his hand, and his diligence so much moved the Spirits that one day a certain Spirit appeared to him, he having no idea where it came from. 'The god Indra in the Ta-lo Heaven', said the Spirit,[82] 'has been so much impressed by the concentration with which, despite your tender years, you have been devoting yourself to Taoism, that he has told me to bring you this scroll of magic spells, which he wishes you to study with great application and on no account show it to anyone else. When you have mastered it, there will be nothing you cannot accomplish. You will be able to rise into the sky at will and come and go just as you please. If you want to move the Five Mountains you will be able to do so in a twinkling. You will be able to check the waters of the great ocean and make them flow backward, penetrate all mysteries and probe into the subtlest atoms, control the universe and all created things that are in it. There will be none to compare with you. For anyone not bent upon exploring the mysteries of the Way these spells would be perilous to his wits, for they contain the names of all divinities in heaven and below heaven and if you were an ordinary man I would not reveal to you the lore of heaven. Now I must leave you; we shall one day meet again in the Ta-lo Heaven.' In a twinkling the Spirit disappeared. Henceforward Yeh Ching-neng applied his mind to the Way with unflagging devotion. As soon as he opened the scroll of spells, their use was immediately clear to him. The names of all demons and spirits were listed, along with those of every monster and hobgoblin in the world. Apart from being able to ward off evil influences of a lesser kind, if at any time he wanted to uproot a mountain and put it in another place, he had only to use one of his spells. . . . So Yeh Ching-neng, living in the Kuei-chi hills, could enlist in his service men, demons, spirits and hobgoblins, setting them to work for him how and when he pleased. For ripe mastery of the Way and consummate skill in the use of spells there was not in the whole universe anyone that surpassed him.

In addition to all this he was a fine-looking man, very conversable, pleasant and easy-going, and always remaining quite unruffled even in the most awkward predicaments. If at any time he wished to travel, he had only to concentrate his mind on the idea for a moment and in one day he could go thirty to fifty thousand leagues. If he chose not to eat, he could go thirty to fifty days without food; and when he ate, he could consume sixty to seventy or more rations at one meal. He could become invisible, or again make himself into a hundred people.

There was at that time an Emperor of T'ang the like of whom there had not been since the days of the Three Sovereigns and Five Emperors at the Beginning of Things. This was our Emperor Hsüan Tsung, so wise and illumined that at his Court all his ministers were able to speak the truth to him, without a word of flattery. This Emperor in the Kai-yüan period of his reign (713–42) greatly fostered Taoism. He gave orders that throughout the Empire images of Lao Tzu were to be made and shrines built to contain them. He paid great honour to the Taoist religion. Hearing this, Yeh Ching-neng set out from the Kuei-chi hills to Ch'ang-an, the capital, to hand in his name. When he had travelled for several days, Indra, the monarch of the Ta-lo Heaven, by his magic produced a river more than five leagues broad, without any bridge or boat or place where one could cross; doing this in order to test Yeh Ching-neng's powers. But Yeh immediately wrote out a spell and threw it into the water. The river dried up, and he was able to proceed on his way. Several days later he reached a place about five leagues east of Hua-yin, in the district of Hua-chou. Now it happened that this year in the fourth month there took place the gathering of officials at the capital, at which new posts were allotted to them, and they were now proceeding to various places to take up their appointments. Among them was a certain Mr Chang who had been appointed Prefect of Wu-hsi. On his way, having with him his wife and children, he passed the temple of the God of Mount Hua and taking his wife and a supply of meats and wine he galloped off to make an offering to the God, and so obtain blessings. Now it happened at that time that the God had two wives, but lacked the third, to whom he is entitled. So he sent a messenger to the inn at which the Prefect had put up, and at the third watch of the night the messenger carried off the Prefect's wife to act as third wife to the God. Precisely at the third stroke of the third watch she suddenly died. The Prefect did not know that the God of Mount Hua had taken her away to be his wife, and cried out to Heaven with bitter lamentations, quite beside himself with grief.

Now it happened that Yeh Ching-neng had also put up at this inn, and he had a room close to that of the Prefect. When he suddenly heard a great noise of lamentation, he went to the Prefect and asked what had happened. 'My wife has just suddenly died', said the Prefect. 'She has certainly been taken away by the God to be his bride', said Yeh Ching-neng. 'Do you want her to be brought back to life?' 'If you can do that for me', said the Prefect, 'my life is in your hands; you have only to demand it, and I shall not dare refuse.' 'Had she been ill at all?' asked Yeh Ching-neng. 'Not in the least', said the Prefect. 'She suddenly died immediately after we got here.' And he swore again that if the Master could save her he would be eternally indebted to him. Yeh Ching-neng then took a brush and wrote a black spell which he blew up into the air. Here it changed into a divinity clothed in black who swift as a cloud hastened to the God's temple. When the gate-keeper saw him he went and announced to the God, 'A messenger has come from the Great Unity'.(83) The God at once invited the messenger into his temple. 'The Great Unity', said the messenger, 'told me to ask you why you have wrongfully taken a living man's wife to be your bride, cruelly separating a loving married couple?' 'She was assigned to me as third wife by the Tribunal of Heaven', said the God. 'Tell the Great Unity to mind his own business.' And he dismissed the messenger, telling him to inform the Great Unity of what he had said. The messenger promised to do so and at once went back to Yeh Ching-neng and repeated to him what the God had said. Yeh made a very angry face and, taking a brush, wrote another spell, this time in red. He blew it into the air, where it turned into a messenger dressed in red, who in a trice reached the image-hall. The God hastened down the hall to receive him. 'You should not have taken a living man's wife to be your bride', said the messenger. 'The Great Unity is very angry. Where is she now?' 'I would never have ventured to take a living man's wife to be my bride', said the God, 'simply at my own pleasure. She was assigned to me by the Tribunal of Heaven. I should be most obliged if you would make this clear to the Great Unity.' 'First of all you risk your life for the sake of a woman, and then you try to lay the blame on the Tribunal of Heaven', said the messenger. 'You had better take care!'

'Great messenger,' said the God, 'I am sure you will know how to state my case for me, and if you do so, I will never forget your kindness.' The messenger went straight back to the inn and saw Yeh Ching-neng, to whom he repeated what the God had said: 'He makes out that the Court of Heaven definitely allotted her to him as third wife and that he would never have dared to take her simply at his own discretion.' When he heard this Yeh Ching-neng looked very angry. He scolded the messenger, saying, 'You don't know your business at all', and he made him stand to one side. He then took realgar and two feet of white silk, drew a magic diagram on the silk and blew it up into the air, where it changed into a huge General, wearing golden armour and sporting a helmet. He was ten feet tall and several arm-hugs round the waist. He drew his sword and shouted with a voice like thunder, his eyes flashing like lightning. In a trice he was standing in front of the temple. Just at this moment the Prefect's wife appeared, to perform the ceremony of 'bowing to the Hall'.[84] The General screamed angrily, 'Fie upon you, God of this temple, how dare you take a living man's wife to be your bride? The Great Unity is furious about it and sent me to cut off your head and bring it to him.' He gave the God no chance to justify himself, but sword in hand strode up the hall, evidently intending to cut off the God's head. When the God saw him coming, he was terribly frightened and could think of nothing better to do than take to his heels. His relations, who had assembled for the 'bowing to the Hall' ceremony, now came forward and, throwing themselves on their knees, implored the General to content himself with merely taking the Prefect's wife back to him. 'We, his relations,' they said, 'will persuade the God that it is a mistake to retain this lady if, by doing so, he incurs the anger of the Great Unity.' Acting on their advice the God now prostrated himself before the General and implored him to take the Prefect's wife away. The General took her back to the inn and in less than no time she came to life. She said to her husband, 'While I was performing the 'bowing to the Hall' ceremony in the God's presence, a General suddenly appeared, wearing golden armour and with a tall helmet on his head. He drew his sword and advanced up the hall, meaning to behead the God. The God was so frightened of him that he released me.' Hearing this, the Prefect was delighted beyond measure and both he and his wife politely thanked Yeh Ching-neng. The Prefect said, 'My gratitude to you for rescuing my wife and restoring her to life is high as the hills. I wish I knew what I could do for you in return.' He then took twenty lengths of silk out of a hamper and offered them to Yeh, saying, 'All that I have with me is this silk. Unfortunately "The indigent cannot be bountiful". I and my wife ought to be your slaves for ever if we were properly to repay what you have done for us. Meanwhile I do hope you will accept this small present.' 'The Taoist religion', said Yeh Ching-neng, 'is not concerned with the acquisition of property nor with the satisfaction of desire. The Taoist does not covet glory or high place, but only seeks to relieve the distress of men in this world. Such is our religion. Seeing that you were so deeply attached to your wife, I saved her life. You will need this silk to pay for your travel expenses during your further journey to your place of office. Do not give me the trouble of refusing twice and again. When I get to Ch'ang-an, I shall be amply provided for.' The Prefect and his wife therefore bowed to Yeh and took their leave.

That evening Yeh Ching-neng took up his staff and went on his way; in a few days he had reached Ch'ang-an. Here he stayed at the Hsüan-tu Taoist Monastery and for a month never left the courtyard, distracting himself only by playing the zither and making long-drawn-out mouth-noises.[85] The monastery servants who sometimes came and peeped at him could see no sign of any cooking having been done, nor indeed of his having eaten or drunk anything. A few disciples visited him and questioned him about his arts. To these, readily answering all their questions, he explained the use of his spells and how they were able to cure illnesses caused by hobgoblins and other evil spirits. 'What comes out of one mouth enters ten thousand ears', and it was not long before all the common people of both the eastern and the western markets at Ch'ang-an knew that at the Hsüan-tu Monastery there was a Taoist from far away who could cure illnesses caused by hobgoblins and understood the uses of magic spells. It happened at the time that a common man of the Tse-hsien Ward, called K'ang T'ai-ch'ing, had a daughter aged sixteen or seventeen who was possessed by a fox-spirit. Sometimes she laughed, sometimes she moaned, now she ran, now she sat; sometimes she charged wildly down the street cursing everyone she met in the most dreadful language. A neighbour said to K'ang T'ai-ch'ing, 'At the Hsüan-tu monastery there is a monk from far away who knows how to cure illness caused by fox-spirits'. When K'ang T'ai-ch'ing heard this, he and his wife went to the monastery, bowed down before Yeh Ching-neng and described the case to him. 'If by any chance your Reverence can cure her,' they said, 'we shall be grateful till our dying day.' 'It is certainly an illness caused by a fox-spirit', said Yeh Ching-neng. 'If you want her to be cured all you have to do is to get a piece of serge-matting and four big nails, and she can be cured at once.' K'ang T'ai-ch'ing went straight home, got hold of a piece of matting and the nails and went back again to the monastery, bringing his daughter with him. Directly Yeh Ching-neng saw her he was more certain than ever that it was an illness caused by a fox-spirit. He took a sword in his left hand and, grasping the girl in his right, he cut her into three pieces, the blood flowing all over the ground. Everyone in the courtyard was horrified, and K'ang T'ai-ch'ing and his wife called upon Heaven and cried to Earth. 'Run at once to the local magistrate's office', they shouted to those who were standing around, 'and say that a monk in the Hsüan-tu Monastery has committed a murder.'

Yeh Ching-neng showed no sign of alarm. He covered the dead girl's remains with the matting and then nailed the matting at the four corners, fastening it down firmly to the floor. The blood still kept on oozing out from under the matting, and the spectators, who were by now very numerous, all said to one another, 'To think that such a thing as this can happen in the middle of a great Imperial city!' and there was a tremendous uproar and to-do. But Yeh Ching-neng, quite unconcerned, sat in his cell playing the zither and making mouth-noises.

In a short while the Chief of Police and a number of constables arrived in the courtyard. 'Where is the monk who has committed a murder?' they asked. 'I'm the man you want', answered Yeh Ching-neng from inside his cell. 'I am curing an illness caused by a fox-spirit. These ignorant people do not understand this and have told you that there has been a murder.' The official turned to K'ang T'ai-ch'ing. 'It's the person under the matting', said K'ang. The official saw blood oozing from under the matting and said to Yeh Ching-neng, 'How dare you deny that there has been a murder, when I can see the evidence of it right in front of me, with my own eyes?' 'How would it be', said Yeh Ching-neng, 'if you were to raise the matting and make sure, rather than skimp the law in this hasty way?' The Chief of Police then told his assistants to raise the matting and report on what was under it. Having done so they announced, 'K'ang T'ai-ch'ing's daughter and the fox-spirit responsible for her illness are both there. The girl is quite unharmed; the fox is cut into three parts.' The Chief of Police was astounded; K'ang T'ai-ch'ing and his wife crawled to the Master's feet and did him reverence. The girl's hobgoblin-illness was completely cured.

The Chief of Police made a full report of what had happened and sent it to the Mayor, who came to the monastery, called upon Yeh Ching-neng and enquired about his name and surname, treating him with the utmost deference. The Mayor said that Yeh evidently possessed supernatural powers, and submitted an account of the affair to the Emperor. This Emperor of the K'ai-yüan period loved Taoism and did not respect the religion of Śākyamuni; so he sent a eunuch to the Hsüan-tu Monastery, commanding Yeh Ching-neng to present himself at the Palace. When he got there and the Emperor saw him, Yeh Ching-neng proceeded to expound the Taoist religion to him and the pure, subtle and abstract character of his discourse made a deep impression upon his Majesty. The Emperor was anxious to hear about the art of living for ever. 'My spells', said Yeh, 'are the best (?) in heaven or earth for curing illnesses caused by hobgoblins, elves and other evil spirits. But if you want to compose the Elixir of Life, there is nothing to stop you; so that if your Majesty is set upon living for ever, that can easily be managed.' The Emperor was delighted to hear this and said to Yeh Ching-neng, 'I will be your disciple and you shall be my Master'. He gave orders that the people of the monastery should select a courtyard and settle Yeh in it. Every day they were to send someone to see if he had all that he required. The Emperor constantly drove in person to visit him in his courtyard, and discoursed with him on Taoist topics. The ministers of the Court also all wanted to go with him, and every one, commoners and gentlemen alike, all revered the Taoist religion.

Suddenly one day the Emperor wanted to go and look for the drug of immortality. He summoned Yeh Ching-neng to visit him at the Palace, and Yeh said to him, 'You and I will go a great way off, to gather herbs of immortality'. He left his ordinary body in the monastery and created a second body to go with the Emperor and gather herbs. When they got to the Ch'ien-t'ang river he saw that its waters were very deep and vast; indeed it was so broad that the other shore seemed endlessly far away. In the river was an evil sea-serpent, so that no boat dared to go across. Yeh Ching-neng wrote out a spell and threw it into the river. The river began to dry up, and after three days the evil sea-serpent was left high and dry on a sand-bank. When Yeh Ching-neng saw this he at once went and cut it into three parts. He was then able to go across to the other shore and get the herb of immortality, which he presented to the Emperor, who was delighted. But the eunuch Kao Li-shih did not believe that it was really a herb of immortality and said to the Emperor, 'I fear this herb is not the true herb and I propose that this wizard should be put to the test.' 'How will you test him?' asked the Emperor. 'What I shall do', said Kao Li-shih, 'is to dig a tunnel between the gate-screen and the gate and make five hundred drummers beat their drums in the tunnel. Your Majesty will send for Yeh Ching-neng and say to him, "There are strange sounds in the Palace; it is haunted by baleful powers. Could you not exorcize them for me?"' The Emperor accepted Kao Li-shih's proposal. Kao Li-shih had a tunnel dug and when it was completed he put five hundred drummers into it and made them beat their drums. The Emperor then sent for Yeh Ching-neng, to whom he accorded an interview in the upper hall. When he arrived, the Emperor told him that the Palace was haunted by a sound of drumming which was evidently caused by baleful powers. Having been told that he was to exorcize the supernatural drumming Yeh Ching-neng asked for a cup of water and standing face to face with the Emperor took some of it in his mouth and spat it out again, at the same time making a magic pass. The moment the water left his mouth the room was suddenly darkened by a cloud that turned into a great snake, which at once entered the tunnel. Its eyes were like hanging mirrors, its mouth was like a blood-bowl,[86] it belched thick and poisonous vapours. The five hundred drummers caught their breath as though suddenly overtaken by a polar blast, and the drum-sticks dropped from their hands. When Yeh Ching-neng heard that the sound of drumming had stopped, he said, 'I can now inform your Majesty that the drumming was not supernatural'. 'Well, then, what was it?' asked the Emperor. 'Your Majesty', said he, 'sent men to beat drums, in order to test the validity of my spells.' Hearing this, the Emperor was ashamed to face Yeh Ching-neng and sent him back to the monastery.

Not long afterwards, however, the Emperor invited Yeh Ching-neng to a drinking-party at the Palace. There was to be music and the ritual dances of ancient Kings. It was the first month of autumn and a chill was coming into the wind. At this Palace festivity the ladies of the Court took their part. The wine went round several times and there was much singing and flute-playing; but the Emperor was in low spirits. He said to Yeh Ching-neng, 'I am not enjoying this party as much as I usually do. Can't you invent some drinking-game to make things more lively?' In obedience to his Majesty's command Yeh Ching-neng at once got up and advanced towards the western corner of the hall where there was a painted pottery jar made by the aborigines of Chien-nan (Szechwan), of a size to hold more than a gallon. He concentrated his mind and made a magic pass, seeking silently for the best means to cheer things up and revive the Emperor's spirits. Then taking a brush out of the folds of his dress he painted on the jar a picture of a Taoist holding a wine-cup in his hand and drinking. On to the jar he stuck a magic spell-sheet, and the jar at once changed into a little Taoist three feet high, wearing the ailanthus hat and yellow cope, standing there in the western corner of the hall. 'I saw that you were not enjoying yourself', Yeh Ching-neng said to the Emperor, 'so I have invited a drinker who will certainly make the party more enjoyable.' 'What sort of drinker is he', asked the Emperor, 'that you should think he would take my fancy?' 'Though he is a Taoist', said Yeh Ching-neng, 'he is an adept at drinking-games. He can also, at a drinking-party, discourse on all subjects ancient and modern. There is nothing that he does not know; indeed he has innumerable accomplishments and understands everything in the world.' The Emperor called the Taoist to him and the Taoist at once obeyed, advancing from the western corner of the hall and crying 'Your servant, your servant' at every step. When the Emperor Hsüan Tsung saw him, the dragon-countenance beamed with joy, and all the Court ladies laughed merrily. The Taoist displayed a faultless knowledge of Court etiquette, and the Emperor accorded him the honour of coming up on to the dais and sitting by him, that they might converse. 'What is his drinking capacity?' the Emperor asked. 'He can hold an immense quantity,' said Yeh Ching-neng, 'indeed he is really an adept drinker. You can add thirty to fifty parts each time the cup goes round and you will find it impossible to make him drunk.'

The Taoist went on accepting round after round and never once refused. The Emperor was exceedingly pleased with him and all the guests entered into the fun. The Court ladies now urged him to drink from a three-pint flagon, and each time it reached him he never failed to finish it. From the Hour of the Snake (9 a.m.) to that of the Monkey (3 p.m.) he drank steadily, consuming more than a gallon. The great wine-jar was now almost empty, but in a tankard there were still five pints. As though wishing to display the Taoist's full powers Yeh Ching-neng now said, 'Your Majesty's guests will no doubt soon be dispersing. I hope your Majesty will accept my proposal that the Taoist should be asked to finish up the remaining wine.' 'As you like', said the Emperor, and the wine was handed to the Taoist. This time however he absolutely refused to drink it, saying, 'I am afraid if I drink any more I may get out of control and do something contrary to Court etiquette'. 'We know that your Reverence is a drinker of great capacity', said Yeh Ching-neng. 'What is your real reason for refusing?' 'The truth is', said the Taoist, 'this wine is of such poor quality that I cannot drink it.' Seeing him persistently refuse Yeh Ching-neng, putting on an expression of furious rage, said to the Emperor, 'Pray do me the favour of condemning this Taoist to decapitation'. 'What has he done', said the Emperor, 'that he should suddenly be decapitated?' 'It is because he has insulted us extremely', said Yeh Ching-neng. 'As you like', said the Emperor, and he told Kao Li-shih to cut off the Taoist's head. When the head fell, he cast it aside and it turned out to be the lid of a wine-jar, the body being the wine-jar itself, with a picture of a Taoist painted on it and a spell pasted to it. The jar was full of wine to the brim, which was why the Taoist could hold no more. When he saw this the Emperor gave a great shout of laughter, the Court ladies all congratulated him on the performance, and all the people of the Palace were astonished and amused beyond measure. Kao Li-shih could not take his eyes off the astounding sight and repeatedly gasped in admiration and astonishment. The Emperor and the great ministers of Court declared that Yeh Ching-neng had no rival in ancient times or today; his magic arts, they said, were inexhaustible, his talismans and spells full of wisdom and deep mystery. In all the world there could rarely have been such an exponent of transformations and manifestations. Indeed he was, they said, the equal of Lao Tzu himself. . . .

In the fourteenth year (A.D. 726) the Emperor declared an amnesty throughout the land and allowed the people to light lanterns and make offerings. All the officials were allowed to go to see the lanterns, and there was uncommon rejoicing. Another edict permitted the common people of the wards and markets to light lanterns, and the curfew was abolished.(87) After looking at the lanterns the Emperor returned to the Palace and said to Yeh Ching-neng, 'Have all the cities great and small made lantern displays like this?' 'At Ch'eng-tu (the capital of Szechwan, in the south-west) the lanterns and offerings are particularly magnificent, perhaps better even than those here in the capital.' 'How far away is Szechwan from here?' asked the Emperor. 'Three thousand leagues', said Yeh Ching-neng. 'In that case', said the Emperor, 'how do you know what is going on there?' 'I went to have a look', said Yeh Ching-neng. 'I have just come back. If you do not believe what I have told you about the lanterns there, it would be difficult for you to go there on your own; but if you went with me, you could be there in a trice.' 'Suppose you were to take me,' said the Emperor, 'what attendants could come to wait upon me, how many other people could come with us?' 'You could bring a hundred or more', said Yeh Ching-neng. 'What colour should they wear?' asked the Emperor. 'Those in personal attendance on you', said Yeh Ching-neng, 'should all be dressed in white.' 'In that case', said the Emperor, 'tell Kao Li-shih and the rest to pack for the journey swift as fire and be ready to come with you to Szechwan, to look at the lanterns.' Kao Li-shih and the rest, on receiving this order, immediately made ready. Yeh

Ching-neng made magic and took the Emperor, along with all his retinue, to Szechwan to look at the lanterns. They travelled swift as flying clouds or lightning flashes. When they got there they strolled through the streets, wandering about everywhere. Lanterns were set out in all the wards and markets and there were offerings in profusion. The music was at its height, and the Emperor was delighted. Yeh Ching-neng then took him to the Prince of Shu's Palace and he and his escort had a look at it. Finally Yeh told the musicians in the retinue to play a few tunes. 'Heavenly Master,' said the Emperor to Yeh, 'it is very late. I think I ought to be getting back to Ch'ang-an.' 'Your Majesty', said Yeh Ching-neng, 'has really seen very little of this city. But if you want to go back to the capital, we'll go at once. I think', he added, 'that as your Majesty has visited this commandery you ought to let the authorities of the commandery know that you have been here and seen the lanterns and also played music in the Palace.' 'How can I let them know that I have been here and seen the lanterns?' asked the Emperor. 'You must leave some article of clothing in the Palace of the Prince of Shu', said Yeh Ching-neng. 'People will have heard the music, and the Commandant is certain presently to have this Palace searched. If he finds, say, a shirt of yours there, he will be sure to send a messenger to bring it to your Majesty at the capital. Your Majesty will then say to the messenger, "I went in person to your city, saw the lanterns and made music. I left my shirt on purpose, lest there should be any mistake about it". Then the men of Shu and all the people of the world will know that your Majesty saw the lanterns. Would not that be a good plan?'

The Emperor therefore left a piece of clothing, in fact a small shirt, in the Prince of Shu's Palace. As soon as Yeh Ching-neng saw that the Emperor had left a garment, he made magic, and in a trice he had brought the Emperor back to Ch'ang-an. 'This is the Palace', he said to the Emperor. . . . Suddenly there came from within the Palace the sound of four drum-beats, clearly announcing the hour.

'Heavenly Master,' said the Emperor, 'you had better return for the moment to your monastery, and come and see me at dawn tomorrow. . . .'

During the night the Commandant at the capital of Szechwan, his officers, and all the common people had heard the sound of music coming from the Palace of the Prince of Shu. The staff of the commandery were so much puzzled by this that when dawn came they made a further search, suspecting that the Palace was haunted by strange manifestations or hobgoblins of some kind. But despite all their investigations they found nothing at all except a small shirt. They continued the search for several days, but found nothing to indicate how it got there. The Commandant felt that the matter ought to be reported to the Emperor and drew up a memorial, describing the strange things that had happened. He entrusted the memorial to a member of his staff, the Censor Ti Ch'ang, to deliver to his Majesty, and in no great while he arrived at Ch'ang-an. When the Emperor saw the memorial he spread it out on his jade desk and recited it from beginning to end. When he saw that the shirt was mentioned, there was great joy on the dragon-countenance, for he now knew that there could be no mistake. He asked for a further account of the circumstances, and the envoy reported, 'At the second watch on the night of the fifteenth day of the first month a large retinue, with carriages and horses, all clad in white, numbering more than a hundred persons, arrived at the Palace of the Prince of Shu and made music. When the piece was over they went away, but left a shirt behind. Investigations were made, but failed to reveal who the visitors were. This seemed so strange a portent that the Commandant thought it proper to send me with a report on the occurrence.' 'On the night of the fifteenth day of the first month', said the Emperor to the envoy Ti Ch'ang, 'I and Yeh Ching-neng, together with my escort, rested in the Palace of the Prince of Shu, where I ordered my musicians to perform. When the tune was over and we were about to return to the capital, I was afraid that the people of the commandery of Shu would not know that I had visited the place, so I left behind a shirt. Pray tell the Commandant, when you get back, that I shall be issuing a special edict in which I shall confer on him suitable rewards.'

Ti Ch'ang bowed, took his leave of the Emperor, and set out on his way, rejoicing that the rain and dew of Imperial favour were about to fall upon his chief, bringing glory to his whole clan. Before many days had passed he was back at Shu, where he reported all that the Emperor had said. All the people of Chien-nan, both officials and peasants, said that the Emperor was in spiritual communication with the whole universe, and could wander at will to any place under heaven. From that time onwards no officials either within the confines of Shu or in any city or region dared to flout the Emperor's laws. . . .

On the night of the fifteenth day of the eighth month the Emperor, Yeh Ching-neng and a retinue of attendants all climbed to a high place to enjoy the spectacle of the full autumn moon. 'Can one find out anything about what goes on in the moon?' asked the Emperor. 'It would be no use my merely telling you about it', said Yeh Ching-neng. 'I should like to take your Majesty with me on a visit to the moon. Would you allow me to do this?' 'How should we get there?' asked the Emperor. 'If you were to try to get there on your own', said Yeh Ching-neng, 'you would not be able to. But if I take you, there will be no difficulty.' The Emperor's dragon-countenance beamed with delight. 'Should I be able to take followers with me?' he asked. 'It won't be the same as going to Chien-nan to see the lanterns', said Yeh Ching-neng, 'for that is only a place in the common world. The Palace of the moon is in the upper realms and is quite a different matter. But as your Majesty has some degree of Taoist sanctity, it will be possible for you to go there for a short while.' 'What colour ought we to be dressed in', asked the Emperor. 'You had better wear white damask quilted clothes', said Yeh Ching-neng. 'Why clothes of that sort?' asked the Emperor. 'Because', said Yeh Ching-neng, 'all the halls and towers are of crystal, and that makes the air very cold.'

As soon as the Emperor had made his preparations, they started off. Yeh Ching-neng made a magic pass and in a trice they had reached the Palace of the moon. The towers and halls, terraces and pavilions that they saw before them were quite unlike those in the realm of men. The panels of the gates and doors belonged to a completely different world. After looking for a while at the towers and halls the Emperor reached a pair of double gates. He went in, and saw more towers and apartments and finally came to the Great Hall, which was made, every bit of it, entirely of crystal, beryl and agate—an unfathomable wonder. All the windows were of crystal and the towers and terraces too, all of solid crystal. He also saw several beautiful women clad in dresses of strung (?) pearls and carrying in their hands crystal trays on which were vessels all compounded of crystal and the seven kinds of jewel. The Emperor saw them, but maintained an attitude of strict decorum.

Yeh Ching-neng brought him straight on to see the *sāla* tree that grows in the moon. The Emperor saw that it was of immense height, its branches stretching straight up to the topmost spheres of heaven. The colour of its leaves was like that of silver and its flowers were the colour of clouds. The Emperor walked about slowly under the tree and then stood still for a moment. But the air was bitterly cold and its snowy chill pierced him to the bone. 'I find it very cold here', he said. 'I think I had better go back to my Palace.' 'I hoped', said Yeh Ching-neng, 'that you would let me take you round and see the sights. You would find fairy flowers quite unlike any flowers in the world below. Your Majesty is wrong to be in such a hurry. Surely it would be better to enjoy your visit to the moon in a leisurely way, and then go home.' The Emperor was leaning against the tree, and felt more freezingly cold than ever. 'This cold', he said, 'is more than I can stand. Let us go back at once. A little more of this, and I shall be incapable of moving.' Yeh Ching-neng could not help smiling. However, he made a magic pass, and in a twinkling they were back at Ch'ang-an. . . .

Several days later Yeh Ching-neng saw a Palace lady of great beauty, who enjoyed the Emperor's special favour. Going back to his monastery he wrote a spell which created a magic menial, who every night at the third watch came to the Palace and fetched this lady to sleep with Yeh in the monastery. Just when day broke he brought her back to the Palace. This went on for days and months, and when half a year had passed the lady felt dazed as though by wine and scarcely knew what was happening. She hastened to report to the Emperor, 'I am with child and am awaiting the labour of child-birth. I thought I had better inform your Majesty.' The Emperor at once became convinced that this had happened because Yeh Ching-neng by his magic had made someone bring her to him. He told the lady not to speak of it to anyone, and then sent for the eunuch Kao Li-shih, to ask his advice about how to slay Yeh Ching-neng in the Great Hall of the Palace. Yeh in the monastery was at once aware of what was afoot.

'He can shift mountains and overturn oceans', said the Emperor. 'He can transform Heaven and Earth, control the universe, soar freely into the void and by his transformations avoid every peril. I don't think it's going to be easy for me to kill him. Can you think of any plan for killing him?' 'He can only soar about among the clouds', said Kao Li-shih, 'because of the power of his spells. He has no means of knowing about any scheme that we devise for killing him in the Palace. What your Majesty must do is to send for him here and permit him to sit with you on the dais. At the back of the hall you will secretly install five hundred swords-men. Your Majesty will keep on plying him with a flood of questions about the Way, and while he is busy answering them you will display your dragon might; that to say, I shall give a signal to the five hundred men, who will at once rush

on to the dais, close upon him and put him to death.' 'That's
a very good plan', said the Emperor. Kao Li-shih, having
received this authorization, took five hundred men of the
Guard, armed with swords that gleamed like snow and frost,
and set them in ambush at the back of the hall. No one else
knew that they were there. Then the Emperor summoned
Yeh Ching-neng. He knew all about there being an ambush
at the back of the hall, but made nothing of it and came
straight to the Palace. The Emperor made him sit by him
and talk about Taoism. After a while the Emperor said,
'Have you any further doctrine to expound to me?' Yeh
Ching-neng knew that if the Emperor started asking about
all the different doctrines and arts of the religion, they
would prove too numerous to deal with. 'If your Majesty
intends to ask about them all', he said, 'we can't possibly
ever get to the end of it. I have told you all that on the
present occasion is possible to tell.' When the Emperor
heard this, he put on a terrible expression of rage, preparing
to display his dragon might. Kao Li-shih signalled to the
five hundred men, who rushed in a body on to the dais,
intending to hew down Yeh Ching-neng. But when he saw
them mount the dais with drawn swords he was not in the
least afraid. He rose slowly and standing before the Emperor
said, 'I am not at all scared'. The five hundred men, all
raising their swords at the same moment, closed upon him.
But he concentrated his mind, made a pass and by a trans-
formation of his body entered into one of the pillars of the
hall, so that no one could see what had become of him.
The Emperor, amazed, walked round and round the pillar
examining it. Then he called out again and again, 'Heavenly
Master, Heavenly Master, it was not my idea. It was the
eunuch Kao Li-shih who arranged this plot against you. I beg
your Holiness to realize that I for my part meant you no
harm.' 'My one desire', said Yeh Ching-neng from within
the pillar, 'was to serve your Majesty all your days. Little
did I think that your Majesty would turn against me in mid-
course.'

The Emperor then told Kao Li-shih to take a sword, pare away the pillar and see what was inside it. When about half had been pared away it became clear that there was no trace of Yeh Ching-neng in the pillar. Yet a voice seeming to come from the pillar said, 'Your servant is now going off to the Ta-lo Heaven'. Both the Emperor and Kao Li-shih then saw a streak of purple vapour soar up into the sky and disappear. It was now too late for the Emperor to repent of what he had done. The officers and ministers at Court all said that he had been too hasty in accepting Kao Li-shih's advice, in consequence of which the Heavenly Master was now no longer in the world of men, but had returned to the upper realms. They did not in fact regard Yeh himself as at all to blame.

After this the Emperor pined continually and did not either eat well or sleep quietly. After some ten days a Court messenger who had been sent to Shu and was on his way back to the capital, at a point about a hundred leagues from Shu, suddenly saw Yeh Ching-neng strolling along in a calm and leisurely way. When he saw the envoy he called out to him in a loud voice to stop. When he heard that he was being called to, the envoy dismounted and having done obeisance asked Yeh whether the Emperor's holy person had enjoyed good health when he left him, and also asked what the Heavenly Master was doing here. 'I am on my way back to the Ta-lo Heaven', said Yeh Ching-neng. 'I left Ch'ang-an in a hurry and was not able to say goodbye properly to the Emperor. Please, when you see his Majesty, tell him from me that being on a journey I cannot compose a proper memorandum; I hope he will understand. If he would care ever to see me again, he must wait till the rivers run dry and there is no more water in the sea, till the mountains have moved and the earth has vanished.' A moment later he had disappeared.

The envoy went on to the capital and had audience with the Emperor. After giving an account of his mission to Shu he added, 'When I was returning from Chien-nan and was

about a hundred leagues away from Shu, I met Yeh Ching-neng
strolling along in a leisurely way. He called me to him and
gave me the following message for your Majesty: "The other
day I left in a hurry and could not say goodbye to your
Majesty properly; moreover, being on a journey I cannot
compose a proper memorandum. If your Majesty would
care ever to see me again you must wait till the mountains
move and the earth vanishes, till there is no more water in
the sea and all the rivers run dry." That is the message he
gave me and I thought I ought to inform your Majesty of it.'
When the Emperor heard this message he looked out from
his hall towards the river of Shu, his eyes full of tears, and
he made a lament saying. . . .

(There follow some forty lines of verse, resuming the
story of Yeh's achievements.

Yeh Ching-neng is in the above stories, as often, confused
with his great-nephew Yeh Fa-shan. The latter was a Taoist
master much favoured by the Court in the early part of the
eighth century. He was known as a stout opponent of
Buddhism, but also of the pretensions of rival Taoists who
undertook to prolong the Emperor's life by alchemy. Most
of the stories told above occur, in a less complete form and
with considerable variations, in the printed collections of
marvel-stories. Some of them give the Taoist magician a
quite different name.)

CHAPTER SEVEN

MENG CHIANG-NÜ

INTRODUCTION

THIS is one of the best-known Chinese legends. It has existed in various forms for over two thousand years and has been the subject of innumerable ballads and plays. In the present version the story is placed in the time (third century B.C.) of the First Emperor, who built the Long Wall ('Great Wall'). Meng Chiang-nü's husband, who was employed in the building of the wall, succumbs to the hardships of the task, and is buried in the wall. His wife comes to bring him winter clothes, and is told that he has been buried in the wall. She prays that the wall may crumble, and the intensity of her love is such that it falls down, she finds her husband's bones and brings them back for burial. In later versions of the story we are told how she came to meet her husband; on his way to the wall he came across her when she was bathing, and as he had seen her naked he was bound to marry her. This, of course, is connected, though in a tenuous way, with the Swan Maiden story (see below, p. 149). The text is incomplete at the beginning.

'. . . weary and destitute (?) Farewell! If you were to send me winter clothes, I do not know what return I could make.'

At the time of his taking leave from his wife he did not
    speak for long,
For he hoped as it were between morning and evening to
    come back to his home.

Who could think that he would suddenly meet disaster
by pestle and hammer,
His soul be dissolved, his life finished—that he should
perish at the frontier wall?
After he had taken leave and reached the Long Wall
The officials in charge of the work there treated him with
bitter harshness.
When he died his body was at once built into the wall,
His wandering soul strayed afar amid the thorns and
brambles:
'Weary and destitute (?) on this long journey you came
on purpose to see me
Bravely meeting wind and frost, wasting your energy.
A thousand times farewell! Go quickly home;
A poor soldier[88] under the earth will not ever forget
you.'
When his wife heard this, she burst into great sobbing;
'Little did I know that you my lord had perished at the
Long Wall!
You tell me now that the bones of your body are built
into the Long Wall,
But how am I to know in what part of this Long Wall to
look?'
Chiang-nü smote herself and wailed to mighty Heaven,
Making plaint that so good a husband had perished all too
soon.
A wedded wife's intense devotion can move rivers and
hills;
Her great wailing had such power that the Long Wall
fell.

An old poem says:

Over the ridges sad clouds rise,
In the empty wastes sorrowful is the voice of wailing.
If you say that men have not the power to move,[89]
How was it that the Long Wall toppled?

Those stone ramparts, ranging over a thousand cubits,
At one stroke melted into the streams and hills.
Could it be that the Wall had crashed and fallen
Only because a wedded wife had come?
This frontier land—strange beyond reason—
With cold heart could not endure to hear.

When she had finished wailing, her heart and soul were still lost in sorrow, grieving that her husband had suddenly been destroyed. She sighed out her faithful heart, anguish ever added to anguish. There were skulls without number; many dead men lay there. Among all the bones that were strewn this way and that, how was she to tell which were his?

She bit her finger till it bled, and dripped the blood on to the Long Wall to show her singleness of heart, that she might be able to pick out her husband's bones.

Chiang-nü said sobbing, 'I am at my wit's end;(90)
His lovely substance is scattered about among the yellow
    sands.
I say to all these ridges and hummocks "Vouchsafe me a
    clear sign;
Among all these piles of skulls, tell me which is his".
Alas, alas, it is very hard to choose;
To see them causes sad thoughts to rise.'
One by one she takes them in her hand and looks hard
    at them;
Then she bites her finger and draws blood and puts them
    to the test:
'If it is my husband, the blood will sink deep into the
    bones;
But if it is not Chi Liang, the blood will remain apart.
If only I can recognize them, I will take them home with
    me;
Let them not on any account leave me still in doubt.'
Stifled by her great sobbing, her voice then ceased,

From her two eyes there still flowed tears that were hard
    to stop.
'If Mighty Heaven does not consent to give me what I ask
Then certainly I too will die at the Long Wall.'

(The text here becomes fragmentary; but it is clear that
the test works. Meng Chiang-nü recovers all her husband's
bones.)

But there were as well many skulls that had no one to
carry them away. Chiang-nü was sorry for them and asked
them: 'All you skulls, in what prefecture is your home?
When taking my husband's bones back, I could bring a
message for you. If you have souls, I could guide them on
their way.'

The skulls having thus been questioned by Meng Chiang-nü
Knew now that they could send a message to their
    homes.
The souls of the dead then replied to Chi Liang's wife:
'All of us were sons born into good families;
But the ruler of Ch'in sent us to work on the building of
    the Long Wall;
The hardships we endured were more than we could bear
    and we all died at our tasks:
Our corpses were scattered over the wastelands, no one
    knew what had become of us,
Spring and winter for ever we lie amid the yellow
    sands.
Bring word to our wives that pine desolate in their
    bowers
Telling them to chant the Summons to the Soul and keep
    up the sacrifices.
Make sure to record in your heart what we tell you
    now,
And if you see our fathers and mothers do us the kindness
    to tell them. . . .'

(Here the manuscript again becomes fragmentary. It ends with the sacrificial address, *ch'i wen*, which accompanies Meng Chiang-nü's offerings to the souls of the dead; but this, too, is fragmentary.)

T'IEN K'UN-LUN

(A SWAN MAIDEN STORY)

Once upon a time there was a man called T'ien K'un-lun.(91) He was very poor, and was not able to marry a wife. In the land he owned there was a pond which was deep, clear and beautiful. Once when the crops were ripe he went to his field and saw that there were three beautiful girls washing themselves and bathing in the pond. Wanting to have a look at them he watched them from a hundred paces away. They at once changed into three white cranes, two of which flew to a tree that stood by the pond and perched on top of it. But the third stayed in the pond, washing herself.

T'ien K'un-lun pressed low down between the cornstalks and crept forward to look at her. These beautiful girls were Heavenly Maidens (*t'ien-nü*). The two older ones clasped their heavenly robes and rode off into the sky. But the youngest, who was in the pond, did not dare come out. She made no secret of this, saying to K'un-lun: 'We three sisters, who are Heavenly Maidens, came out to amuse ourselves for a while in this pond. But you, the owner of the pond, saw us. My two elder sisters were able to rescue their heavenly robes in time and escape. But I, the youngest, lingered all alone in the pond and you, the owner of the pond, took away my heavenly robe and I cannot come naked out of the pond. Please do me the kindness to give it back to me, that I may cover my nakedness and come out of the pond. If you do so, I will marry you.' But K'un-lun debated the matter in his mind and decided that if he gave her the heavenly robe, there was a danger she might fly away. So he

149

answered: 'Madam, it is no use your asking for your heavenly robe, for you will never get it. But how would it be if I were to take off my shirt, so that for the time being you could cover yourself with that?'

At first the Heavenly Maiden refused to come out on these terms, and K'un-lun at last declared that it was getting dark and he must go. She tried to detain him, still asking for her robe; but when she found she could not get it, her tone changed and she said to K'un-lun, 'Very well then! Give me your shirt to cover me while I come out of the pond, and I will marry you.' K'un-lun was delighted. He rolled up the heavenly robe and hid it away. Then he took off his shirt and gave it to the Heavenly Maiden, to cover her when she came out of the pond. She said to K'un-lun, 'Do not be afraid I shall go away. Let me put on my heavenly robe again, and I will go along with you.' But K'un-lun would rather have died than give it to her, and without more ado he took her home with him to show her to his mother. The mother was delighted and ordered mats to be set out. All the friends and relatives of the family were invited and on the appointed day the girl was hailed as New Bride. Although she was a Heavenly Maiden, they had intercourse after the manner of people in this world, and lived together. Days went and months came, and presently she bore him a son, a fine child, whom they named T'ien Chang.

Soon afterwards K'un-lun was marked down for service in the west, and was away a long time. The Heavenly Maiden said to herself, 'Since my husband went away I have been bringing up this child for three years'. Then she said to her mother-in-law, 'I am a Heavenly Maiden. At the time I came, when I was small and young, my father made for me a heavenly robe,(92) and with it I rode through the sky and came here. If I were to see that robe now, I wonder what size it would be. Let me have a look at it; I would dearly love to see it!'

Now on the day that K'un-lun went away, he had given strict orders to his mother, saying, 'This is the Heavenly

Maiden's robe. Keep it hidden away and do not let her see it. For if she sees it, she will certainly ride away with it through the sky, and will never be seen again.' Whereupon the mother had said to K'un-lun, 'Where would be the safest place to hide it?' So K'un-lun made a plan with his mother, deciding that nowhere would it be more secure than in the mother's bedroom. The thing to do was to make a hole under one of the bed-legs, stuff the robe into it and herself always lie on top. Then the Heavenly Maiden would certainly not get at it. So they hid it away like this, and K'un-lun went off to the west.

After he went away, she thought constantly about the heavenly robe, fretting about it all the time and never knowing a moment's happiness. She said to her mother-in-law, 'Do let me just have a look at the heavenly robe!' She kept on worrying her about this, and at last her mother-in-law decided to fall in with her wish. So she told her daughter-in-law to go outside the gate for a little while and then quietly come back. She went out at once and the mother-in-law took out the heavenly robe from under the bed-leg, and when the Heavenly Maiden came back, showed it to her. When she saw it, her heart was cut to the quick, her tears fell like floods of rain, and she longed to ride off through the air. But having thought out no plan to do this, she had to give it back to her mother-in-law, who again hid it away.

Less than ten days later she said once more to her mother-in-law, 'Let me have another look at my heavenly robe'. The mother-in-law said, 'I was afraid you might put it on, and fly away from us'. The daughter-in-law said, 'I was once a Heavenly Maiden. But now I am married to your son and we have had a child. How can you think I would leave you? Such a thing is impossible.' The mother-in-law gave in, but was still afraid that she might fly away, and set someone to keep strict watch at the main gate.

But the Heavenly Maiden, as soon as she had put on the robe, flew straight up into the sky through the roof-vent. The old woman beat her breast (?) and in great distress hurried out of the door to see what happened to her. She arrived in time to see her soaring away into the sky. The mother-in-law, when she knew that she had lost her daughter-in-law, let out such a cry as pierced the bright sky; her tears fell like rain, she became utterly desperate and in the bitter sorrow of her heart all day she would not eat.

The Heavenly Maiden had passed more than five years in the world of men, and now she had spent her first two days in heaven above. When she escaped and reached her home both her sisters cursed her for a shameless baggage. 'By marrying that common creature of the world of men', they said, 'you have made your father and mother so sad that they do nothing but weep.' 'However,' the two elder sisters said to the younger sister, 'it is no good your continually lamenting as you are doing now. Tomorrow we three sisters will go together and play at the pool. Then you will certainly see your child.'

The child T'ien Chang had just reached his fifth year. At home he was constantly sobbing and calling out for his parents, and out in the fields he continually wailed in sadness. At that time there was a certain Master Tung Chung(93) who was always seeking for persons of superior conduct. He knew that this was the child of a Heavenly Maiden and knew that the Heavenly Maiden was about to come down to the lower world. So he said to the child, 'Just at midday go to the side of the pond and look. Three women will come all dressed in white silk robes. Two of them will raise their heads and look at you; but one will lower her head and pretend not to see you, and that one will be your mother.'

T'ien Chang did as Tung Chung told him, and just at midday he saw beside the pond three Heavenly Maidens, all dressed in white silk robes, cutting salad-herbs at the edge of the pond. T'ien Chang went nearer and looked at them. Seeing him from afar they knew that it was the child who had come, and the two elder sisters said to the younger, 'Your child has come'. Then he wailed and called out to his mother. But she, although she hung her head in shame and did not look at him, could not stop her sorrow from coming out of her heart, and she wept bitterly. Then the three sisters took their heavenly robes and carried the child away with them into the sky. When God (literally 'the heavenly elder', *t'ien-kung*) saw them, he knew it was his daughter's son and he felt very tenderly towards him, and taught him magic arts and accomplishments. When he had been up in heaven for four or five days, he (no longer) looked like a child of the world below. When he had studied for more than fifteen years, God said to him, 'Take these eight volumes of my writings and they will make you glorious, rich and honoured all your life. But if you go to Court, you must be careful not to tell anyone about them.' The young man then went down into the world below. Everything that there was to hear he got to know of, and he understood the whole universe. The Emperor heard about him and summoned him to be Chief Minister. But he committed an offence in the Back Palace,(94) and was banished to a place in the western wilds.

Afterwards, when all the officials were out hunting in the fields they shot a crane, and gave it to the kitchen-man to cook. When he slit its throat, he found in it a child three inches and two part-inches tall, wearing cuirass and helmet, and pouring out a flood of abuse. The kitchen-man reported the matter to the Emperor, who at once summoned all his ministers, officials and counsellors, and asked them about it. But they all said they did not know.

On another occasion one of the princes, when out hunting, found a front tooth three inches and two part-inches long. He brought it home and pounded it; but it did not break. All the officials were again asked; but they all said they did not know. The Emperor then issued a proclamation which was distributed everywhere under heaven, saying that anyone who could explain these two things would be given a thousand catties of gold, a fief of ten thousand households and any rank he liked to name. But no one came forward.

Then all the ministers and officials consulted together and agreed that only T'ien Chang(95) could recognize these things; no one else could explain them. The Emperor then sent an envoy galloping full tilt on relay-horses to bring back T'ien Chang. When he arrived, the Emperor said, 'I have always heard that you are a man of great intelligence and wide knowledge, and that in fact you know everything. Here is a question. Have there been any giants anywhere under heaven?' T'ien Chang answered, 'There have'. 'What giant has there been?' asked the Emperor. 'Once upon a time', said T'ien Chang, 'there was Ku Yen of Ch'in, who was the son of the Emperor. During a battle with the people of Lu, one of his front teeth was knocked out, and no one knows what became of it. If someone finds it, the truth of what I say can be tested.' The Emperor then knew that it was this that had passed into his possession.

He then questioned him a second time: 'Have there been any pygmies under heaven?' he asked. 'There have', said T'ien Chang. 'What one has there been?' asked the Emperor. 'Once upon a time', said T'ien Chang, 'there was Li Tzu-ao. He was three inches and two part-inches tall and wore a cuirass and helmet. Once when he was out in the fields he was swallowed by a crane(96) and is still playing about in its throat. If a huntsman gets that crane and brings Li to you for verification, you will know who he is.' 'Excellent', said the Emperor. And he asked another question. 'Is there anywhere under heaven a really big noise?' 'There is', said T'ien Chang. 'And what is it?' 'Thunder shakes things seven hundred leagues away, and its rumbling can be heard one hundred and seventy leagues away. Those are both big noises.' 'And is there any very small sound under heaven?' T'ien Chang answered, 'There is'. 'Which is it?' 'Three men walking shoulder to shoulder. One man whispers something and the other two hear nothing. That is surely a small sound.' The Emperor asked again, 'Is there anywhere under heaven a large bird?' T'ien Chang answered, 'There is'. 'What is it?' 'The great rukh which in one flight can reach

Hsi Wang Mu.⁽97⁾ It can wing its way nineteen thousand leagues before it needs a meal. This is surely a large bird!' The Emperor asked again, 'Is there a small bird under heaven?' He said, 'There is'. 'Which is it?' 'There is no smaller bird than the *chiao-liao*. It brings up a family of seven children on the antennae of a fly and still finds its territory far too thinly populated. Meanwhile the fly does not know that there are birds on its head. Surely this is a small bird?'

The Emperor then made T'ien Chang High Chamberlain, and because of what had happened both the Emperor and everyone under heaven knew that T'ien Chang was the son of a Heavenly Maiden.

(It may be worth mentioning here that a quasi-Swan Maiden story is told in the *Hsüan-chung Chi*, *c.* A.D. 300?, in order to explain why the goat-sucker bird carries off children: 'Once upon a time a man of Yü-chang, capital of Kiangsi, saw seven girls in the fields. He did not know that they were really birds. He crept towards them, meaning to take their feather robes and hide them. When he advanced upon the birds they rushed to their robes, put them on and flew away—all except one bird, who was too late. The man took her as his wife and had three girls by her. Afterwards the mother made the girls question their father. She learnt that her robe was under a pile of rice-stalks. She took it, put it on and flew away. Afterwards she came with feather robes to fetch her three daughters. When the three little girls got the robes they too flew away.)

THE BALLAD OF TUNG YUNG

When one carefully considers the life of man as lived in this
    world,
There is no objection, for a little while, to making a lively
    din.

But now I must ask you many hearers to listen earnestly and
　　quietly,
While I tell you how your first duty is to cherish and obey
　　your parents.
Good deeds and wicked deeds are all listed and recorded,
There is a Boy who records evil deeds, and another who
　　records good.
Among ancient worthies whose piety was rewarded, we are
　　told of Tung Yung,
Who was getting on for fifteen when both his parents died.
He sighed to himself that by ill luck he had not any brothers,
Down from his eyes the tears flowed in several thousand
　　rows.
On account of causes in many incarnations he also had no
　　sisters,
Nor had he at hand acquaintances or friends nor kinsmen of
　　the same branch.
In his home there was utter destitution, he had neither
　　money nor goods.
And thus was obliged to sell himself that his parents might
　　be put in their coffins.
Soon there appeared the slave-dealer who had come to take
　　him away,
And now he was able to make arrangements for fulfilling his
　　pious plan.
His purchaser handed over eighty strings of cash,
Tung Yung only required a hundred thousand odd.(98)
In possession now of the money he needed he went back to
　　his home
And choosing by the calendar a lucky day he put his parents
　　in their coffins.
His parents that were his flesh and blood were still in the
　　main room;
He now had the coffins moved and taken outside.
Seeing thus his flesh and blood, his voice was choked by sobs,
At last he was able to burst out into loud lamentations.
On this occasion various kinsmen came to attend the funeral,

And making to the east they came straight to where the
tomb had been dug.
When every rite of internment was over and the grave
filled in
Tung Yung howled and wept for his father and his mother.
As soon as the third day came and the grave had been
filled in
He said farewell to both parents before fulfilling his pledge.
'Father and mother, here is your son kneeling[99] to say
farewell.
I pray that soon and in good health I shall manage to return
home.'
Then he parted from the neighbours to the east and the
people who lived to the west,
And setting out had already covered several leagues or more
When on the road he met a girl who began to question him,
'Tell me, young gentleman, in which direction do you live?
What is your surname and what your name? Tell me only
what is true.
Begin at the beginning, hold nothing back, but tell the whole
tale.'
'Lady, since you have already asked me such a number of
questions
If I answer them all one by one do not break away.
The home where my family has always lived is under the
Lang Hills;
Would you know my surname and the name I go by—I am
master Tung Yung.
All of a sudden my kind mother's health gave way
And after an illness of a few days she died before her time,
My kind father had already been ill, he was the first to die;
It was only after he died that my mother passed away.
When it came to the time for burying them, I had not any
money,
So I sold myself to get money to bury my father and mother.'
'Surely you must have orchards or fields that you might
have disposed of,

Rather than sell yourself and quit the ranks of free man?

Or why not borrow (?) the sum you need on security of your orchards and fields

Rather than give up all you have and become this man's slave?'

'Lady, possessions of that kind are indeed[100] good things,

For I, Tung Yung, by means of them may repay my parents for their love.'

'Young sir, by doing this you are behaving in a filial fashion,

And the sight of this conduct of yours has moved the Halls of Heaven.

One of their number has been sent down into the world below

To dwell for a while amid dirt and evil far away from home.

The god Indra in his high Palace has himself sent instructions:

"I am sending you straight away to help him in buying his freedom."

If you will accept me just as I am and be mine for a thousand years

I will go with you on your journey and serve the master who has bought you.'

Tung Yung knelt before his master[101] and did humble obeyance.

'When I was young I lost my parents and was very unhappy indeed. . . .'

'Yes, but according to the arrangements we made I bought one person.

Who is this young woman standing beside the gate?'

Tung Yung answered him by telling the whole truth:

'The woman who is with me lives at the village of Yin-shan. . . .'

'Yes—but I should like to know in what arts she is skilled.'

'At the bright loom she has marvellous skill in weaving pictured patterns.'

At once her master fetched thread and handed it over to her;

She said that in all she would only need one single room.

The master of the house went into the figures and did the whole sum;

To pay back what was owed meant a thousand lengths or
    more.
So soon as the thread, every bit of it, had been properly
    smoothed out,
At the bright loom with marvellous skill she wove pictured
    patterns.
The first thing she began to weave was a bundle of brocade,
So even her shuttle that earth was moved to a fragrance of
    glad flowers (?).
All day long and every day she never once weaved;
It was only at night that she turned her loom and called
    upon the goddess Śrī.[102]
On the brocade golden symbols were all ranged in pairs;
Two by two the mandarin-ducks confronted pairs of phoenix.
When she had finished weaving the brocade, she cut it down
    from the loom,
She folded it, she put it into a box.
The master of the house going to see what was lying in the box
And having examined the pictured patterns that this girl had
    made
Said to himself, 'This girl is not a common mortal;
I feel sure that she was brought up living in the Halls of
    Heaven.
She has now woven gauzes and satins to the full number agreed;
I shall send both of those two people back to their native
    village.
Farewell, you two people! May you go in peace,
Not feeling any grudge against your former master!'
So the two people bade farewell and set out on their way;
They had only ten leagues to go to get to Yung's farm.
When on their way back they reached the place where they
    first met:
'So now, goodbye! I must go back to Heaven, where I
    belong!'
The lady at once riding on a cloud made straight for the sky,
But before this, she entrusted to him their little baby boy.
She only said: 'Take great care of this small child.'

Tung Yung at parting wept a thousand rows of tears.
Tung Chung⁽¹⁰³⁾ grew up and soon was aged seven;
He ran out into the street and played at the side of the road.
But other boys strolling by spoke very rudely to him,
They all said that Tung Chung had not any mother.
He ran home and when he was there reported this to his
    father.
'Tell me, father, how comes it that you have not any wife?'
'At one time I sold myself, in order to bury my parents;
A Heavenly Maiden, moved by this, helped me to purchase
    freedom.
Even now every time I think about your mother
From both my eyes the tears flow in several thousand rows.'
Tung Yung told the child to go and look for his mother.
He started off and went straight to see Sun Pin.⁽¹⁰⁴⁾
The Master when he saw him coming at once consulted the
    diagrams:
'I feel certain that this young person is looking for his mother.
At the Anuttara lake-side she has come to wash and bathe,
But first, before she goes in, she is hiding under the trees.
She is not alone, three girls have all gone together;
Now they are all making a dash straight for the water side.
One takes off her heavenly garments and goes at once into
    the water,
Holding her purple coat and skirt rolled up in her arms.
It is this one, among the three, who is Tung Chung's mother;
But this time she is ashamed to see her little son come.'
'Little son, you are young and small and could not know
    where to come;
Sun Pin certainly told you, through his skilful divination.
I, your mother, indeed mean to take you and bring you up;
But, son, it is not right that you should stay where you are
    now,
Take this golden vase and give it to Sun Pin.'⁽¹⁰⁴⁾
He did so, and suddenly flames from heaven rose in the
    wizard's face,
The wizard turned on his heels and fled as fast as he could run.

It certainly seemed at that time that everything would be burnt;
Though search showed that there still remained the Sixty
  Cyclical Signs.[105]
Because of this we do not know the doings of Heaven above;
It is all because Tung Chung went to look for his mother.

This legend, as you will have noticed, has a great resemblance to the Swan Maiden story. It has enjoyed immense
popularity in China and been the subject of endless plays
and ballads. The story figures in most of the collections of
'Paragons of Filial Piety'. It is also closely connected with
the story of the Herd Boy and Weaving Maiden, lovers who
were turned into stars on opposite sides of the Milky Way
and only allowed to meet once a year.

As a footnote to the 'bondage' theme of this ballad I
append the following contract,[106] found at Tun-huang, and
now at Peking:

Contract entered into on the first day of the first month
of the year *chia-hsü* (914?). Lu Pei-po-t'i, a peasant of the
village of Tzu-hui, being short of man-power in his own
family, agrees to hire from Teng No-erh-po of Lung-lo
village his son Yen-shou, to work for him from the first
month till the end of the ninth month. It was settled that
the payment for the hiring should be one load (of corn)
every month, one suit of spring clothes, one shirt, one
apron and one pair of leather shoes. From the time of the
hiring onwards he must work with might and main and
must not take a single day off. In the busy season he is to be
fined two pecks (of corn) for every day on which no work
is done; in the slack season, one peck. If the hireling drops
on to the path and loses or damages such baskets, sickles,
hammers, shovels, bags and other gear as he is using in his
work, he himself is to be held responsible; the master is not
involved. But for damage to such things if they have been
brought back safely to the house the hireling is not to be
held responsible. If the hireling steals someone else's melons,

fruit, greens, sheep, cattle and so on, should he be arrested, he has to meet the charge in his own person. If the hireling falls ill, compensation has to be paid to the owner according to the number of days the illness lasts. If the hireling is attacked by brigands and carried off, it is to count as though he were dead (?). The two parties to the agreement having met face to face and discussed these terms in due form, it must not be broken off unilaterally. Either party so breaking it off is to be fined ten loads of new wheat, to be paid to the party that still abides by the contract. To meet the possibility of bad faith this deed has been drawn up as evidence.

The following extract from a set form of prayer to be used by the bridegroom as part of the wedding ceremony shows the very varied uses to which slaves were put. He prays for:

Gold and silver to fill my store-house year by year;
Corn and rice to crowd my sheds at every harvest.
Chinese slaves to take charge of treasury and barn,
Foreign slaves to take care of my cattle and sheep.
Strong-legged slaves to run by saddle and stirrup when I ride,
Powerful slaves to till the fields with might and main,
Handsome slaves to play the harp and hand the wine;
Slim-waisted slaves to sing me songs, and dance;
Dwarfs to hold the candle by my dining-couch.

It is interesting that the use of slaves for agricultural work is mentioned, for it has sometimes been said that slaves were not used in China for this purpose.

THE DOCTOR

Once in old times the Duke of Ch'i had a dream at night in which he saw demons of sickness take the form of two insects. He fell sick and sent to another State for the doctor

Ch'in Huan to come to Ch'i. His dream had been this: he saw two demons of sickness in the form of two insects come out of his nose and then transform themselves into two boys both dressed in blue. They stood by his bed, talking together. One said, 'Ch'in Huan is a very skilful doctor. He has just entered the borders of Ch'i and will certainly slay us two people, unless we find some way of escaping from him.' But the other boy was against this and said, 'Heaven sent us to take the Duke of Ch'i; we can't run away. You must install yourself just above the midriff and I will install myself just below it. These are secret cavities where neither the needle nor the moxa can reach, nor can any drug find its way there. Even if Ch'in Huan does come he won't be able to get at us.'

Then, in the duke's dream, the two boys turned once more into two insects and flying into his mouth made their way down into his entrails. On waking, the duke knew that he would die.

Before ten days were out Ch'in Huan arrived. He felt the duke's pulse and said after a while, 'This illness cannot be cured. And why? Because the demons of sickness are installed above the midriff and below the midriff. These points are secret cavities, where neither the needle nor the moxa can reach, nor any drug get there. You will certainly die; there is nothing to be done about it.' The duke said, 'That is all just as in my dream'.

Ch'in Huan did not attempt any treatment; but the duke rewarded him handsomely and sent him on his way with every mark of courtesy. Three days after Ch'in Huan's departure, the duke died.

CHAPTER EIGHT

THE WORLD OF THE DEAD

THE following five pieces all deal with the World of the Dead. Popular Chinese ideas about what happens to the dead were in Tun-huang times a mixture of Buddhism and Taoism. The Buddhist World of the Dead was reigned over by King Yama who enquires or gets his subordinates to enquire into the record of the dead person and gives judgment accordingly. The number of people who had behaved sufficiently well to be sent to the Halls of Heaven was very small. There was a proverb that said, 'In the Halls of Heaven things are very quiet'. The great majority of the dead were 'sinners' who were sent to one section or another of Hell to be tortured.

The Taoist Hell was under or on Mount T'ai in Shantung, near the eastern coast, and its authorities are often conceived of as working in with King Yama and his judicial Court. Finally the ancient Chinese idea of Heaven (T'ien) as arbiter of human destinies comes into play, and both Yama and Mount T'ai are shown as subject to the higher dictates of Heaven.

Most of what the living know about the dead comes, naturally, from people who have, for one reason or another, returned to life after spending some time in the World of the Dead. They may have been sent for by mistake, they may have influence with the authorities of the underworld or they may be employed by King Yama or Mount T'ai on secret missions in the World of the Living. Or they may have been sent for to do some special job for King Yama, such as painting his portrait or curing his ague, after which they were returned to their families on earth.

The mixture of Taoism and Buddhism in popular beliefs

about Hell is well illustrated by a short text[(107)] called 'Manual of the Procedure for making offerings to King Yama'. Here the General of the Five Ways (who occurs above, in the Story of Catch-tiger), the Court of Heaven and the Court of the Underworld all figure. A special offering to Yama and the General of the Five Ways, we are told, will make possible 'the rescue of sinners from Hell, the erasure of their names from the Registers of the Dead and the restoration of their names to the Registers of the Living'. But 'offerings of money, silk and so on must not be made'.

It might be assumed that proceedings at the Court of the Dead are naïvely modelled on those of the living world, without any intention of parody or 'take off'. I am inclined to think that this is seldom so and that a 'dig' at mundane institutions is usually intended.

T'AI TSUNG IN HELL

'I (i.e. the Emperor T'ai Tsung) remember that from the third to the fifth year of Wu-te (A.D. 620–2) I went on several military expeditions, took part in every engagement and killed a large number of people. I have not yet paid the penalty for those sins of former days, and how can I now return on the road to life?' Very despondent, the Emperor staggered on like a drunk man. However, led by his escort, he managed to follow on till they came to the gates of the Court, and going in halted at the screen-wall. Here his escort announced, 'We wish to leave in your hands the living wraith of a certain person called Li, known in the world as His Majesty T'ai Tsung, Emperor of T'ang'. The Court servants said, 'By all means', and brought the Emperor into the Audience Hall to make his obeisances. His Majesty, however, did not perform the rite of prostration. A certain high-ranking official up in the hall shouted out, 'Why does not the Emperor of T'ang perform the dance of homage?' If he had not been shouted at like this, the Emperor might not have been altogether unwilling to make the obeisance. But nettled by being shouted at he retorted in a loud voice, 'Who was it that ordered me to perform the dance of homage? When I was in Ch'ang-an, people did homage to me; I am quite unused to doing homage to others. Is the person up in the hall who ordered me to do homage by any chance a subject of mine? I am the Emperor of Great T'ang. King Yama is only sector-leader of a parcel of demons; how can I be expected to dance homage to him?'

King Yama, hearing himself spoken of in this insulting way, hung his head, ashamed to look Hell in the face, humiliated in the presence of all his officials. Scowling angrily he ordered those about him. . . .

(There are now gaps in the text; but it appears that King Yama orders the case to be enquired into by the Assessor Ts'ui Tzu-yü, so famous in Chinese legend.)

When the Emperor reached the gate of the courtyard, the escort said to him, 'I must trouble your Majesty to wait here for a little, while I go in and announce to the Assessor that you are here. I'll be back in a minute.' The escort went to the Assessor's office and, bowing low, announced that in accordance with the Great King's orders he had brought the living wraith of the Emperor T'ai Tsung to be put on trial by the Assessor. 'He is outside the door', said the escort. 'I did not venture to bring him in.' When Ts'ui Tzu-yü heard this, he hurriedly rose to his feet and muttering, 'This is most unfortunate!' he added, 'I am a subject of the Emperor's and as such I ought to have gone a long way to welcome him; instead of which I have kept a lord of men waiting outside the gate! This is an act of gross impoliteness on the part of a minor official like myself. Moreover, in the living world I am clerk in the town of Fu-yang. My household consists of more than five hundred persons and all of us have a horse to ride and meat to eat, a state of affairs we owe entirely to his Majesty's bounty. But now owing to my having this post in the Underworld I am neglecting my governmental duties at Fu-yang. If on looking into his Majesty's record I find that his span of life is at an end, there is no more to say. But if it turns out that he still has some years to live, and goes back to reign at Ch'ang-an, those five hundred and more members of my household will have to change over to a fish diet, and that will all be the result of my rudeness on this occasion to his Majesty in my capacity of Assessor in the World Below.' Ts'ui Tzu-yü continued to be very worried about this.

Meanwhile the Emperor, seeing that his escort was a long time before coming out to fetch him, thought to himself, 'Perhaps he is telling the Assessor about various wicked deeds of mine'. So the Emperor, too, could not help being very worried. Now however Ts'ui Tzu-yü hastened to ask for his official dress and tablet and, going to his office, tried to compose himself. After a while he came running out to where the Emperor was waiting, himself announcing his name and rank. When he reached the Emperor he did the dance of homage before him, crying, 'May your Majesty live ten thousand years!' and, crawling towards him with his face on the ground, awaited the Emperor's commands. 'It seems then that you who are doing homage to me are Ts'ui Tzu-yü, the clerk of Fu-yang. Is that so?—I give you leave to interview me without standing on ceremony, in an ordinary posture.'

The Emperor now remembered the letter that he was carrying in his bosom, and he said to Ts'ui Tzu-yü, 'I believe that you knew Li Ch'ien-feng at Court. Is not that so?' 'Yes,' said Ts'ui Tzu-yü, 'from the time we began to be at Court together we were like Kuan and Pao.'(108) 'That is to say, very close friends indeed', observed the Emperor. 'He gave me a letter for you. I've got it here.' When Ts'ui Tzu-yü heard there was a letter for him, he did not seem best pleased. The Emperor then took the letter and gave it to Ts'ui Tzu-yü, who knelt to receive it and did a dance of homage to thank the Emperor. But instead of reading it, he put it in the folds of his dress. 'Why don't you read the letter?' the Emperor asked. 'I am low in rank', replied Ts'ui Tzu-yü. 'It would be a breach of Court etiquette if I were to read it in your Majesty's presence.' 'But I gave you leave not to stand on ceremony', said the Emperor. 'I have no objection to your reading it.' Having received this command and bowed, Ts'ui Tzu-yü in the Emperor's presence opened the letter and read it. What he read so much agitated him that he abandoned all the etiquette belonging to a subject in the presence of his ruler, and looking afar towards Ch'ang-an he said, 'Li Ch'ien-feng! It is true that we served together at Court. But does that give you the right to demand things of this sort from me?'

When the Emperor heard him say this, he felt as though the ground had been withdrawn from under his feet, and very humbly, with soft words, he asked Ts'ui Tzu-yü, 'Is there any chance of your being able to do what the letter suggests? Please, tell me at once, so as to put my mind at rest.' 'There's nothing impossible about it,' said Ts'ui Tzu-yü, 'but under the circumstances it might be rather difficult.' When the Emperor heard that it might be 'rather difficult', his spirits fell. 'You have had me brought here under arrest', he said, 'and I am entirely at your disposition. But the Crown Prince is very young and important points of policy have to be settled. I don't expect to be allowed to return to life for very long. But if you could allow me three or even five days at Ch'ang-an, it would give me time to leave instructions about State affairs and about the Crown Prince, and it would still not be too late for me to come and report here.' When he spoke of the Crown Prince the Emperor wept floods of tears. When Ts'ui Tzu-yü saw how upset he was, he said, 'Your Majesty may put your mind at rest. Come with me, and we will discuss terms.'

The Emperor, as desired by Ts'ui Tzu-yü, then followed him, and once inside the screen-wall he saw that on the east side there were more than twenty offices. In No. 6 office there were two men wailing. 'What are they so unhappy about?' asked the Emperor. 'Who else should they be', replied Ts'ui Tzu-yü, 'but the two princes Chien-ch'eng and Yüan-chi?'[109] 'If you had not brought me here', said the Emperor, 'I should never have had a chance to see my brothers!' 'Since they've been here', replied Ts'ui Tzu-yü, 'the two princes have been constantly sending in statements about you, demanding that you should be brought here for trial. They feel they have been deeply wronged and their complaints are worded in the most bitter terms. It was to meet these charges that you were sent for. If you keep away from the princes, I may be able to find some way of arranging matters for you fairly well; but if you insist on going into that office and meeting them, you will be face to face with your accusers, and even I will not be able to save you. In that case you will certainly not be able to get back to Ch'ang-an. Your Majesty had better not even go and look at them; it would be far safer not to.' When the Emperor heard this, he did not dare insist, but hurried on to the Assessor's office and took a seat there. Ts'ui Tzu-yü did not go in, but stood on the steps, calling for the heads of the six offices to come and pay their respects. After they had bowed and enquired after the Emperor's health, they bowed again and retired. 'Who were those people?' asked the Emperor. 'Why did they bow to me in front of your office?' 'They are the heads of the six offices', said Ts'ui Tzu-yü. 'And who are the heads of the six offices?' he asked. 'In the World of the Living', said Ts'ui Tzu-yü, 'there are people called "the heads of the six offices" and in the World of the Dead they have the same name.' 'Why don't you come up into your office', said the Emperor, 'and keep me company?' 'I am too low in rank', said Ts'ui Tzu-yü. 'It would not be fitting for me to sit with you in the same office.' 'When you were in Ch'ang-an', said the Emperor, 'you held a low rank. But here in the Court of the Dead it is quite otherwise, and there is no reason you should not come up.' Ts'ui Tzu-yü bowed and, coming up into the office, took a seat.

(The text here becomes fragmentary, but it is evident that the Two Boys,[110] who record good and evil deeds, are sent for.)

Ts'ui Tzu-yü asked the boy who records good deeds, 'What good deeds did his Majesty do when he was in Ch'ang-an?' The boy pressed together the palms of his hands and said, 'It does not appear that at Ch'ang-an he did any good deeds. He certainly did not have any *sūtras* copied or any images painted. . . .

(Two incomplete lines follow, and the text then breaks off. The second portion, after an incomplete line, goes on with words spoken by Ts'ui to the Emperor.)

'The three rolls of writing here on my desk contain the facts about your Majesty's life-span and fortunes. If you want me to go through them for you and make changes, I must have your authority for doing so.' 'Do as you propose', said the Emperor. 'Make any changes for me that you think desirable.' Ts'ui Tzu-yü returned to his seat and began to examine the documents.

He . . . and then added the minute 'Ten years as Emperor; to go back again to the World of the Living.' But when he had given the Emperor this extra span, he thought to himself, 'My rank in the Living World is so low that if the Emperor had not been brought for trial here, I should never have set eyes on him. I ought to avail myself of this opportunity to get from him a post in the Government.' So he . . . his tablet and said, 'I have made the necessary changes in your Majesty's papers.' 'To what effect?' said the Emperor. 'Do tell me at once.' But Ts'ui Tzu-yü again thought to himself, 'I had better not tell him at once that I have put in "To be Emperor for ten years", for if he doesn't in return give me what I've set my heart on, I shall have no remedy. I had better pitch it lower than that, and tell him "three years" or "five years".' So he said to the Emperor,

'Your humble servant is deeply indebted to your Majesty for coming here in person, and as a small return he has altered the record of your destiny to five further years and a return to the World of Life.' 'If I do succeed in reaching the city of Ch'ang-an', said the Emperor, 'all the things sent as tribute to my Palace shall be yours.' Ts'ui Tzu-yü again thought to himself, 'I've allowed him five years, and this has only led to his giving me money and precious things. If I were to allow him another five years, I should surely get a government post out of him.' 'I have already marked you as returning to the Living World for five years', he said. 'Li Ch'ien-feng is, as you know, a great friend of mine and he gave you a letter to bring to me, urgently requesting me to do what I could for you. For his sake I will give you another five years, making ten in all, which you will be able to spend in Ch'ang-an city.' The Emperor, hearing this, said to Ts'ui Tzu-yü, 'I really feel ashamed that you should have the trouble of keeping on making these alterations. If I get to Ch'ang-an city, I assure you I'll give you all the things that are sent to me as tribute.'

Ts'ui Tzu-yü again thought to himself, 'That's the second time he has only offered me money and precious things. Not a word about any official post! He's evidently very mean about official posts.' For a long time he remained silent. Presently the Emperor said, 'When you were talking to me just now, you spoke of my returning to the Living World. If I return to Ch'ang-an I shall take you with me, and you must come and pay your respects to me at Court.' 'Certainly I will do so', said Ts'ui Tzu-yü. 'When are you going to let me start?' asked the Emperor. 'Your Majesty will first have to draw up a document to be kept in the files', said Ts'ui Tzu-yü. 'When I was alive', said the Emperor, 'I never learnt how to draw up documents. How does one do it?' Ts'ui Tzu-yü thought to himself, 'If I don't bully him a bit, I shall never be able to get an official post out of him.' 'If your Majesty does not know how to draw up official documents, I've got a written question here. If you

can answer it, there is no reason you shouldn't start for
Ch'ang-an at once; but if you can't answer it, it won't be
possible to send you back to the World of the Living.' When
the Emperor heard this he was very frightened, and he
entreated Ts'ui Tzu-yü to give him an easy question. 'I won't
forget your kindness, if you do', he said.

Ts'ui Tzu-yü, his heart set on getting a job, asked for
paper and when he had dutifully bowed to the Emperor he
set to work to write out the following question: 'His
Majesty T'ai Tsung, Emperor of T'ang, is asked why, in the
seventh year of Wu-te, he slew his brothers in front of the
Palace and imprisoned his loving father in the women's
apartments? An answer is requested!' He handed the paper
to the Emperor who took it and read it. He was very much
upset and his heart pounded as though hammered with a
pestle. He threw the question-paper to the ground saying,
'This question that you have set me is one I can't possibly
answer!' Seeing how upset he was Ts'ui Tzu-yü took the
question-paper back and said, 'If your Majesty can't answer
it, would you perhaps allow me to answer it for you?' On
hearing this the Emperor was much relieved. Great joy
spread over the dragon-countenance. 'Pray do as you
suggest', he said. 'If I answer this for you', said Ts'ui Tzu-yü,
'I shall certainly expect your Majesty to open your mouth
wide.' 'You promise to answer for me and also tell me to
open my mouth wide', said the Emperor. 'What are you
going to put into it?' 'Not *that* kind(III) of opening the mouth
wide', said Ts'ui. 'What I mean is that in the living world
my rank is low; I am only Clerk at Fu-yang. What I hoped
was that your Majesty would bestow on me "enough land
for one foot to tread upon", and I shall be eternally grateful.'
'What government post is it that you want?', asked the
Emperor. 'I do wish you had mentioned this before! Where
does your family come from?' he continued. 'I am a
P'u-chou man', said Ts'ui Tzu-yü. 'Very well then', said
the Emperor. 'I appoint you Governor of P'u-chou and
concurrently Investigating Commissioner of the twenty-four

districts of Ho-pei, with the rank of Senior Censor and the right to wear the purple and gold fish-bag. In addition to this I bestow upon you twenty thousand strings of cash, to be paid by the treasury at Fu-yang to provide for your household.' Having at last been promised official rank Ts'ui Tzu-yü did the dance of homage below the dais of the office in order to express his thanks to the Emperor, and then coming up on to the dais, took a seat there. While he was conversing with the Emperor, it was announced that an envoy from the office of the Heavenly Tally had arrived from Ch'ang-an. 'What have you come for?' asked Ts'ui Tzu-yü. 'I have come to inform you', said the envoy, 'that you are appointed Governor of P'u-chou and concurrently Investigating Commissioner of the twenty-four districts of Ho-pei, with the rank of Senior Censor and the right to wear the purple and gold fish-bag. In addition to this you are to receive twenty thousand strings of cash, to be paid by the treasury at Fu-yang, to provide for your household. Issued today by the office of the Heavenly Tally, for the attention of Ts'ui Tzu-yü.' 'Well, they didn't take long hearing about it at the office of the Heavenly Tally', said the Emperor. 'I have always heard that "appointments made in the Realm of the Dead take effect in the Land of the Living". It seems it really is so.'

The answer that Ts'ui Tzu-yü framed for the Emperor consisted only of these words: 'A great Sage will exterminate a family in order to save a kingdom.' When Ts'ui Tzu-yü had written this out the Emperor was uncommonly pleased. Having shown his answer to the Emperor, Ts'ui Tzu-yü took it back, and then said, 'When you get to Ch'ang-an you must do good works; for example send out envoys galloping to every quarter of the Empire announcing an amnesty, and also order the director of the monasteries in the quarter to the west of the high road leading to the Red Sparrow Gate to have the *Great Cloud Sūtra* expounded in public. And your Majesty should at your own expense have copies of this *sūtra* made.'

Ts'ui Tzu-yü then, at the Emperor's request, fetched paper and wrote out a list of the good works the Emperor was to perform. When it was ready, the Emperor took the list and put it into the folds of his dress. Then he said to Ts'ui Tzu-yü, 'I feel absolutely famished. How could I get something to eat?' 'If your Majesty is hungry', said Ts'ui Tzu-yü, 'I will get you some food.'

Ts'ui Tzu-yü then gave orders to those about him. . . .

(Here the MS breaks off.)

KUAN LO

There was once a famous magician named Kuan Lo. In the middle of the sixth month he was passing through a plain when he saw a young man who seemed to be about nineteen years old reaping corn to the south of the road. He sighed deeply as he passed, and the young man asked, 'Why do you sigh?' To this he made no reply, but instead he asked the young man's name. 'Chao Yen-tzu', he replied. 'Well then,' said Kuan Lo, 'you must know that I sighed for no other reason but this: it was because I felt sorry that such a fine young man as you is doomed to die suddenly tomorrow precisely at noon.' 'I think I recognize you', said the young man. 'Are you not the famous Kuan Lo?' 'I am.' Chao Yen-tzu then kowtowed to him and begged him to find some means to prolong his life. 'Length of days is decided in Heaven', said Kuan Lo. 'It is not for me to give life. The best thing for you to do is to go home at once and tell your father and mother, so that they may not be taken by surprise.' So Chao Yen-tzu went home and hastened to tell his parents. On hearing what had happened his father galloped off on horseback in pursuit of Kuan Lo and caught him up about ten leagues away. He prostrated himself before him and begged him to help, saying, 'We are sure you must be sorry that our son is going to die at noon tomorrow. Is there no means of saving him?' 'The best thing you can do', said Kuan Lo, 'is to go back home and make ready a casket of venison and a peck of clear wine. I will be at your house tomorrow just at noon, and will try to save him, though I do not know if I shall succeed.'

So the father went home, made ready wine and meat, and waited. Kuan Lo arrived next day at the appointed time and said to the young man, 'To the south of where you were reaping corn yesterday stands a large mulberry tree. Under it two men are playing at dice. Take the venison to them, putting it into a casket; take the wine and pour it out for them, and let them help themselves. If they speak angrily to you, just bow low and remain perfectly silent. If you remember to do this, one of the two will save you. I will stay here and wait for news.'

The young man did as he was told. He took the wine and meat to the big mulberry tree and, sure enough, sitting under it were two men playing dice, . . . each attended by a great number of followers. The young man poured out wine and set the meat in front of them. They took both meat and wine, but were so intent on their game that they did not notice who had brought them. By the time they reached the end of their game the wine and food were finished. Only then did the man sitting to the north look up and see the young man Chao. The sight seemed to make him very angry. 'Young fellow,' he cried, 'you ought to be gone by now. How is it that you are behind time? Instead of starting at noon, you came here and poured out wine for us. How do you account for it?' The young man bowed twice, but did not say a word. Then the man seated to the south said to the man seated to the north, 'You know the saying:[112]

> Accept a cup of wine,
> And it is enough if you show a little embarrassment.
> Accept food as well,
> And something must be done in return.

'This morning we have accepted both wine and food from this man. How can we bear to carry him away?' The man sitting to the north said, 'It is all settled and entered on his papers. It is too late to do anything about it now.' The man sitting to the south said, 'Just let me have a look at his papers. Here it is: "To die at the age of nineteen". That is quite easy to change.' So saying he took a writing-brush, inserted a 'transpose' sign and said to young Chao, 'You were put down as dying at nineteen, but I have altered it to ninety.'(113) This was the origin of the hook-sign in the margin, such as is in use in the world today to indicate that two characters are to be transposed.

When the young man got home, Kuan Lo said to him, 'The man sitting to the north was the spirit of the northern Pole-star, the man sitting to the south was the spirit of the southern Pole-star. All men born from the womb pass through the hands of the southern star and he is overjoyed each time a man is born. But the northern star has charge of death. Every time a man dies, he is delighted. That is why they behaved as they did.'

HOU HAO

Once upon a time there was a man called Hou Hao. Every day when he worked in his fields he heard the sound of sobbing, but could not see where it came from. This went on for sixty days. It was now autumn and, finding the path to his fields so wet with dew that it was difficult to get there that way, he walked along the raised bank of the field, holding up his skirts, and so got to his plot. Near the side of the raised bank was a man's skull, in two parts. Half was lying above the plot and half in the plot. Through one eye-socket a stalk of corn was growing and was about to sprout. Hou Hao was distressed by this sight and plucked away the corn-sprout. Then he piled up earth round the skull and made a small tomb. After that the sound of sobbing ceased.

In the eighth month he had been reaping in his field and was going home in the evening, when he became aware that someone was following him. He walked faster and so did the man behind. He walked more slowly and so did the man behind. At last he turned round and asked, 'Who are you, and why are you following me?' 'I am a ghost', said the other. 'I am a live man', said Hou Hao. 'If you are a ghost you should go by a separate path, a different way. Why are you following me?' 'It was from my socket', said the ghost, 'that you plucked the corn-stalk. I feel I ought to make some return for your kindness. I have nothing to give you; but I know you are unmarried, and I can at any rate arrange for you to have a wife. The wedding will take place on the first day of the eleventh month next year. The bride will be a living woman, not a ghost, and you must receive her with the usual ceremonies.'

Hou Hao kept this news to himself. Only when the first day of the eleventh month came did he collect all his friends and relations, and pound beef and brew wine. He explained that he was going to be married, but did not know where his wife was to be fetched from. His father and mother, brothers and friends were perplexed by this and questioned him. But he refused to give any further explanation and merely went to the south of the village, where he stood, evidently waiting for someone to arrive.

Towards dusk yellow dust, wind, clouds and sudden rain came from the west, making straight for the gates of Hou Hao's house and settling there in so dark and dense a fog that nothing could be seen. He made his way home and on entering his bedroom found a girl of eighteen or nineteen installed there, along with bed-cushions, rugs, coverlets and everything she could need for her toilet, all in the handsomest style. 'Who are you?' she said when he came in. 'And how dare you come into my bedroom.' 'And who are you,' he said, 'and how dare you come to *my* bedroom?' 'I am the daughter of Liang Ho-lung, Governor of Liao-hsi', she replied. 'Today I was to be married to the son of Mao

Po-ta, Governor of Liao-tung. The carriage that had come to fetch me away was already at the door, when a great wind sprang up. I went out of door for a minute to have a look at the weather and then came back into the house and went to my bedroom. How can you say that I am in *your* bedroom?' 'Liao-hsi is five thousand leagues and more away from here', said Hou Hao. 'How can you possibly lay claim to a bedroom in this place? However, if you do not believe me, just go outside and look at the house.' Very much puzzled she went out and saw at once that the house was not in the least like hers. Presently, when she opened a set of nine baskets fitting one into another that was lying behind the bed, she found a jade tablet with an inscription on it written in gold. This cleared matters up, for it said: 'Heaven enjoins you to become Hou Hao's wife.'

This was the origin of the tablet that the bridegroom's party brings when the bride is fetched, and of the wedding announcement, as used in imitation of this for ever afterwards by men of later days.

If ghosts are careful to repay a kindness, surely live men should do the same!

WANG TZU-CHEN

There was once a man of T'ai-yüan called Wang Tzu-chen. His parents were very fond of him and said with a sigh, 'Our son is growing up without ever getting any proper education'. So they sent him to Master Pien Hsiao at Ting-chou, to study with him. Pien Hsiao was a man from Hsin-i, near Ch'en-liu. He was immensely learned, there was no question he could not answer, and indeed since the death of Confucius there had been no one like him. He had three thousand pupils, who showed unparalleled devotion to him. No better teacher was to be found anywhere, so that within the four seas everyone flocked to his school.

When Wang had crossed the borders of the district of

Ting-chou and proceeded for thirty leagues, he rested under a sophora tree[114] that stood by the wayside. Presently a ghost, in the guise of a living man, also came and rested under this tree. Wang, who had no idea that it was a ghost, asked him where he came from. Without replying, the ghost asked Wang the same question. 'My parents,' said Wang, 'regretting that my education is so incomplete, have sent me to Master Pien's place at Ting-chou, to study under him. That is my only reason for being here.' The ghost asked him his name, and he said he was a man of T'ai-yüan, called Wang Tzu-chen. 'I am a man of Po-hai,' said the ghost, 'named Li Hsüan. Both my parents are dead, and I live with my elder brother. As I have had no schooling he sent me to Master Pien's place, to study under him; so we shall be fellow-pupils.' As it was evident that Li Hsüan was older than he, Wang henceforward treated him as an elder brother. They went on together to the town of Ting-chou and lodged in the same house, where they drank wine together and swore eternal friendship; dead or alive, in grandeur or obscurity, neither would ever desert the other.

After Li Hsüan had been at the school for three years his accomplishments exceeded those of Master Pien. 'What are you?' asked the Master. 'You are so much more intelligent than ordinary people that I fancy you must be a Sage. I always regarded myself as fairly able; but I see now that I am nothing compared to you. Have you some magic art? If so, I wish you would tell me.' Li Hsüan prostrated himself twice before the Master, and said, 'Owing to my *karma* in previous existences I have had the good fortune to get you as my teacher. I do not know why you should have such ideas about me.'

From that time onwards Master Pien used Li Hsüan as Assistant Professor and made him instruct all the pupils. They stood in great awe of him, with the result that the rules of the school were never broken; or if by any chance they were broken, Li Hsüan decided on the appropriate punishment. He continued to teach Wang in his private room, and if Wang was inattentive and failed to grasp the meaning of a passage, Li punished him. Wang served him as father and Master, and asked for no special favours. In consequence of this his education was successfully completed.

After some time, the Crown Prince's Chamberlain, Wang Chung-hsiang, who was also a man of T'ai-yüan and had been on fairly familiar terms with Wang Tzu-chen, paid a passing visit to the school and lodged with him and Li Hsüan. He became aware that Li was a ghost, and next morning when he parted from Wang Tzu-chen, before setting out again on his journey, he said, 'I have noticed something strange, and as we are old friends I feel I ought to mention it to you. The person you are now associating with is not at all a suitable friend for you.' 'As regards his education,' said Wang, 'Li Hsüan is a Confucian scholar and perfect gentleman. If it is his appearance you are alluding to, there can surely be few people in the world so good-looking. I don't know what you have against him that makes you think him an unsuitable friend for me.' 'I am not referring to his character or appearance', said the Chamberlain. 'The trouble is that he is a ghost and you are a live man. The living and the dead are separate, and friendship between them is impossible. If you don't believe me, tonight take a bundle of fresh hay and spread half of it under where he lies; then spread the other half in a separate place and lie on it. When you get up in the morning you will see that the hay you lay upon is still there, but the hay on which he lay has disappeared.' He spread the hay as he had been told to, and when he looked next morning, it was exactly as the Chamberlain had said. Wang then knew for certain that Li Hsüan was a ghost. He found occasion to say to him, 'A rumour is going about that you are a ghost. Is that true?' 'It is the case', said Li. 'Last night when the Chamberlain came he saw that I was a ghost, and told you. That is how you found out. The reason that I appeared disguised as a living man[(115)] is that the King of the Dead, seeing that I was young, used me for odd jobs. As I had not had much education, he sent me to study at Master Pien's place, meaning if I made good progress to appoint me as Chief Clerk at Mount T'ai; and if I did not make progress, to send me back to be an ordinary ghost. But, thanks to Master Pien's teaching, in less than a year my education was complete, so that in addition to my work here I have been doing my job as Chief Clerk at Mount T'ai for the last two years. But as you were still at the school and I was so deeply attached to you I could not bring myself to leave you. However, now that you know I am a ghost you will be frightened of consorting with me, and I too feel that I can no longer go about with you; so I had better go away. Do you remember that recently I had a pain in my back? The reason was that someone who had brought an action against your father at the Tribunal of Mount T'ai complained that I had refused to give judgment, being evidently prejudiced in favour of the defendant. The King of the Dead, without looking into the case properly, immediately assumed that I was in the wrong, and condemned me to a hundred strokes with the rod. That is why I had a pain in my back.

'Since then the King has been conducting all the enquiries and giving the decisions himself. Your father is still alive; but he will shortly be sentenced to be entered on the roll of the dead. You had better go home as quickly as possible. If you find him still breathing, you must at once take wine and meat to the cross-roads and make an offering of them to me, calling out my name three times. I will then come to the rescue and shall certainly be able to save his life. But if when you get there he has ceased to breathe, it will be too late for me to save him. Much as I might want to, I could do nothing, absolutely nothing at all! Your education must by now be complete. All that remains is for you to exert yourself so as to get on in life, and act prudently. I am in a position to secure you a long span of life, and I can also ask God on High to make you Chief Magistrate of T'ai-yüan and Governor of Kuang-chou.'

They then parted, and when Wang reached home his

father was still breathing. So he took clear wine and venison, went to the cross-roads and offered them, calling Li Hsüan's name three times. Li arrived at once, riding on a white horse and wearing a red coat and a hat with a bamboo framework, attended by numberless horsemen before and behind and making the bravest show. There were also two boys dressed in blue who went ahead and showed the way.

But the moment he met Wang, Li Hsüan lost all his splendour and appeared once more just as he had been when they were at the school together. He asked Wang whether his father was suffering much, or not. Wang answered, 'It is no longer possible to communicate with him, as he cannot speak. But he is still breathing faintly, and I hope you can do something for him.' 'Shut your eyes for a moment', said Li Hsüan, 'and I will take you to see your father.' He shut his eyes and the next moment found himself standing in front of the gate of the King of Death's office, with Li Hsüan at his side, both of them facing to the north. 'I did speak just now of taking you to see your father', said Li Hsüan, 'but he is held at present in one of the detention cells, in a very distressing condition, and you had better not visit him. Indeed, nothing would be gained by your seeing him. But do you see that man in white trousers, walking barefoot, wearing a purple brocade cap, with a written scroll in his hand? That is your father's enemy. When the evening session opens, he will come before me. I have got a bow and arrows for you. Take them and keep a sharp look-out. When you see him coming, shoot, and if you succeed in killing him, your father will recover. If you do not kill him, your father's name will be entered on the record of the dead, and it won't be possible to save him.' Hardly had Li said this when the man appeared in the distance. 'There is your man', said Li Hsüan pointing to him. 'Take good aim! I must go to the Court and give decisions; I can't stay here any longer, or people will wonder what has become of me.'

After Li Hsüan went to Court the man who was bringing
the accusation against Wang's father passed quite close to
him. He drew his bow and shot, but only wounded his left
eye. The man dropped his scroll and ran off, holding his
hand to his eye. Wang picked up the scroll and looked at it.
He saw that it consisted of two documents, in each of which
his father's name was mentioned. Presently Li Hsüan
returned to him and said, 'The King has smelt the breath of
a living man. You can't stay here any longer; you must go
at once. In what part did you hit your father's enemy?' 'In
the left eye', said Wang. 'That's not a crucial spot', said Li.
'When his eye recovers, he'll come back and do mischief.
It only means that your father will get a short respite. Go
home, find the enemy and kill him. That's the only way to
escape disaster.' 'But I don't know who the enemy is', said
Wang. 'It doesn't matter who he is', said Li Hsüan. 'There
is someone who has been your enemy for a long time, and
you must kill him. You left home in great distress of mind
and naturally did not make enquiries about the enemy's name
and surname. Just go home and reflect about it.'

When Wang got home, he still could not think of any
old enemy. The only unusual thing he found was that the
white cock had not crowed for seven days. No one knew
what had become of it. He looked everywhere and at last
found it lying in a coop, blind in the left eye. 'This is my
enemy', said Wang. 'It was in the left eye that I shot
him. His white trousers were his cock's leg-plumage, his
bare feet were his cock's claws, the purple brocade cap
he wore was his cock's crest. This is my enemy!' He at
once killed the cock and made it into broth, which he gave
to his father to drink, in consequence of which his father
recovered.

Wang did indeed become Chief Magistrate of T'ai-yüan
and in the time of the Emperor Ching of the Han dynasty
he was appointed Governor of Kuang-chou. He died at the
age of 138. No one in the world ever received greater help
from a ghost than did Wang Tzu-chen. There is an old

saying: 'Do not keep a white dog; to keep one bars its master's progress. Do not rear a white cock; to rear one brings harm to the head of the family.' It seems to apply to the present case.

TUAN TZU-CHING

Long ago, in the time of the northern ruler Liu Yüan,[116] there were two men called Liang Yüan-hao and Tuan Tzu-ching, who both lived in P'ing-yang. From their earliest years they loved one another dearly. They lived in opposite houses, always went about together and each had the greatest respect and admiration for the other. They took an oath of eternal friendship, swearing never to forsake each other come what might. When they grew up they both showed great talent, and Liu Yüan took them into his service. Liang became Minister of the Left and Tuan became Chamberlain. But though they were employed in different departments, they remained devoted to one another and were constantly together. Everyone, from the ruler downwards, knew of their great friendship.

After a time Liu Yüan appointed Liang to the Governorship of Ching-chou and Tuan to the Governorship of Ch'in-chou. For the first time in their lives they were parted, and each set out for the place to which he had been appointed.

After three years Liang died at Ching-chou of an illness that deprived him of the power of speech. Before his death he thought much about Tuan and would have liked to entrust him with the arrangements for his funeral; but he had no means of communicating this desire. Ten days after his death his soul appeared in manifest form and ordered that the burial should not take place till Tuan arrived.

His wife was very much upset, and did not know what to do. Meanwhile Liang's soul went to Ch'in-chou and appeared to Tuan in a dream, saying, 'I died of sorrow at being separated from you; but here we are together again! I told my wife not to bury me till you came, but she did not seem to understand and evidently intends to bury me at once. However I was determined that my body should stay in the house till I had said goodbye to you. You must come at once to Ching-chou and bury me.'

When Tuan woke, he sighed and said, 'It is hard to believe that Liang has really died. However, the soul that I saw in my dream was exactly like him (?) and it is certain that what he said was true.' He got up, wrote to the Emperor explaining the case and set out for Ching-chou post haste. When he got there he found that everything was exactly as in his dream. He set up a great wailing, fell senseless to the ground and, on coming to, sat sighing and sobbing in great distress till it was almost dusk. Then he went to the gate and who should he see but Liang, looking just as he looked in life. 'When you have buried me', Liang said, 'death will part us for ever. In a box to the right of my bed you will find seven scrolls of the writings of the Masters, a jade plectrum for playing the zither, and a purple sandalwood wishing-gem staff. Keep these in remembrance of me, and when you think of me, take them and make use of them.'

'I started out in a hurry', said Tuan, 'and have nothing with me that I can give you in return. All I can do is to detach this pair of whip-cords and ask you to accept them as a present.' They then parted affectionately.

Tuan told Liang's wife what had happened. The whip-cord was found tied round Liang's legs; he had tied it there himself, in a same-heart knot. Everyone in the house saw this, and there was great amazement. As soon as the burial was over, Tuan returned to Ch'in-chou.

A year later the Chief Clerkship of the realm of the dead under Mount T'ai fell vacant, and for sixty days the King of the Dead looked in vain for a suitable successor. Liang thought of his friend Tuan, and going to the King of the Dead he said, 'May I mention that the Governor of Ch'in-chou, Tuan Tzu-ching, is a man of great enterprise and energy and thoroughly reliable in his conduct. He would certainly make an excellent Chief Clerk. Perhaps your Majesty might send for him and offer him the post.' 'I shall have to find out at what age he is due to die', said the King, and he ordered one of his ghostly assistants to look up Tuan's record and see what span of life was allotted to him. It appeared that he was due to die at the age of ninety-seven, and was now only thirty-two. 'I dare say he is a very good man', said the King. 'But he is not due to die for a long while. I can't cut him off before his time and force him into my service.' 'I have been very intimate with him since his childhood', said Liang. 'I know him as well as a fish knows the water. If he were not really a good man I would not venture to recommend him for this post. If you will give me an escort I will fetch him myself. I am sure he will be happy to come.' The King accordingly gave Liang an escort of followers, with servants and picked outriders, with whom he went to Ch'in-chou to fetch Tuan. Liang arrived on horseback in the guise of a living man, accompanied by an imposing escort. Everyone he met stood back respectfully to let him pass. On coming to Ch'in-chou he sent a servant to announce his arrival. Tuan was very much taken aback. Liang was dead. How was it that he had turned up here? He hastened out to meet him and brought him back to his office, where after a while wine and meat were served.

All the other local officials and Tuan's sons and other members of the household were convinced that some exceptionally distinguished guest had arrived. None of them had the least idea that it was a ghost. When the wine was finished the two of them went and sat in the inner room and Liang said, 'The King of the Dead has sent me to fetch you. He intends to give you the post of Chief Clerk at Mount T'ai. You must start at once.' The idea was far from agreeable to Tuan and bursting into tears he said, 'I am Governor of Ch'in-chou, the most important official in the district. Surely it would be a great come-down for me to accept the post of Chief Clerk at Mount T'ai?' 'Not at all', said Liang.

'Posts in the World of the Living are of no account. The highest of them can't compare in status with any rank in the Realm of the Dead.' Fearing that Tuan was not convinced Liang drew his sword and made as though about to run it through him, hoping to scare him by this show of force. Tuan saw that there was nothing for it but to consent. He tried, however, to get a year's grace. 'The Great King', said Liang, 'is keeping the appointment open for you, and you must go at once. There cannot be any further delay.' 'Well, if it is as you say', said Tuan, 'I suppose I must do as I am told. But I take it there is no objection to my saying goodbye to my wife and children?' 'As you have now definitely accepted the job', said Liang, 'I can let you stay another three days. But on the third day, precisely at noon, you must be waiting for me with all your packing done, ready to start immediately.'

At this the two of them parted, and Tuan called together all his friends and relations and said goodbye to them. He then gave orders for his coffin to be made, and for everything that would be necessary for his funeral—shroud, pall, cushions and so on, to be ready in good time. His friends and relations and the various local officials were much surprised. 'Everyone in your Excellency's household seems to be in perfect health', they said. 'How comes it that you are making preparations for a funeral?' 'I had a great friend called Liang Yüan-hao', said Tuan. 'But he died before me, and has asked the King of the Dead to let him fetch me. I have promised to go back with him and must not keep him waiting.' Tuan then bathed in perfumed hot water and when all his preparations were complete went out to the gate and waited there. Precisely at the appointed time Liang arrived with a saddled horse and escort. 'I must now die', Tuan said to his wife and friends. 'The messenger is already at the gate and I cannot keep him waiting. You must all of you now bid me farewell, and then take this shroud and cover my face.' Whereupon his life ended.

A year later, however, he was allowed to return to his

house for three months, to put things in order. After which he went back to his duties. All who saw this were amazed, and knew that Tuan Tzu-ching is indeed the Chief Clerk at Mount T'ai, and that this is no idle tale.

There is a saying: 'It was Liang Yüan-hao's early death that gave Tuan Tzu-ching the profit of allotting good fate and bad.' Affairs take many turns. Wang Tzu-chen was aided by a ghost. Tuan Tzu-ching died early owing to a ghost. That is what is meant by the saying: 'Efforts on one's behalf take strangely different forms.'

CHAPTER NINE

MARRIAGE SONGS

IN A.D. 781 the Government forbade the use, at the weddings of women of the Imperial family, of 'the poems about the screened carriage, the getting down (from horseback) of the bridegroom, the removal of the fan, and so on. The wedding night is an emotional occasion; but when it comes to singing and music, it is to be feared that they are contrary to Ritual.'[117]

These customs are said[118] to have been universal, extending from the Imperial family down to ordinary officials and common people. As Tun-huang fell into Tibetan hands shortly after this government regulation, the new rules about marriage ceremonies are unlikely to have been enforced there. By 848, when Tun-huang was recovered by the Chinese, the official effort to suppress dramatized weddings may well have subsided, and wedding songs of this kind certainly continued in other parts of China till much later.

The songs, though here modified to fit in with a Tun-huang wedding, probably originated in central China, i.e. not on the extreme western periphery. They may in general form well date from the seventh or eighth century, or even earlier. The prescribed upper-class form of marriage was for the bride to be brought to the bridegroom's house for the consummation of the marriage. But it is evident that in these songs the marriage is consummated at the bride's house, as in India. I do not think, however, that this was due to foreign influences at Tun-huang. It is likely that this form of marriage existed among the peasants of many parts of China; but the question needs further research.

Among the pieces included in the collection of Sung colloquial literature called *Ch'ing-p'ing-shan-t'ang Hua-pen* there
is an extremely lively account of the wedding of the shrew
Li Ts'ui-lien. The piece is in fact a sort of burlesque cantata
rather than a story. Verses very similar to those in the Tun-
huang manuscript are recited, the bride figuring as the
'Goddess of the Moon', and so on. But the piece is in very
broad colloquial and contains a good deal of slang which is
no longer intelligible.

The bridegroom's party speaks first:

When robbers come they must be smitten;
When guests come they must be entertained.
Tell the aunts and sisters-in-law
To come out and look after us.

The women reply:

Gate is opposite gate,
Door faces door.
Take word to the Governor[119] and ask
In what way we can serve him.

The men reply:

His mind strays beyond the common world,
His thoughts are set upon the Goddess of the Moon.
The sun has reached the farthest west,
Late in the watches he has come here.
We men are tired and our horses worn out;
We entreat the aunts and sisters-in-law
To have us shown in.

The women reply:

The night is far spent, the moon is bright,
The stars of the Pole-star are all shining.
Tell us whence comes the honoured guest
Who at depth of night has come to our gate.

The men reply:

> The phoenix having come here
> Should be welcomed by the hundred birds;
> The aunts and sisters-in-law, unless they mistrust us,
> Ought swift as fire to turn and come our way.[120]

The women reply:

> From what quarter is the gentleman,
> In what place is his talent famous?
> Why should one of soul so eminently bright
> Have chosen to come this way?

The men reply:

> He is a gentleman of the capital
> Who passed his Literary Examinations
> And so was chosen as Governor
> And thus became a person of distinction.

The women reply:

> Seeing that he is a gentleman of distinction,
> Successful and of high rank,
> I do not understand why he came here.
> What is it that he seeks?

The men reply:

> He heard of your high reputation
> And therefore betook himself to you.
> 'Delicately lovely is the fair maiden,
> Fit match for any gentleman.'[121]

The women reply:

> Golden saddle and prancing steeds,
> Embroidered cushions in plenty!
> From what quarter is this gentleman
> Who has come to our gates?

The men reply:

> He is a gentleman of the capital
> Of well-known family, from near the City.
> That he has come on purpose to pay his respects
> Is enough to bring you glory.

The women reply:

> That his Excellence our honoured guest
> Should have come from far across the desert—
> Take word to his companies and ask
> What purpose had he in mind?

The men reply:

> The Governor having, through no merit of his own,
> Managed to reach your noble gate
> Any questions you choose to ask
> He will answer in fear and trembling.

Second question:

> The watches are deep and the night far spent;
> We came on purpose to visit you.
> The aunts and sisters-in-law—
> How would they be disposed towards us, if they came
> down?

The women reply:

> In front of the courtyard the well-water
> Has a railing of wood and gold.
> If the aunts and sisters-in-law came down
> It would be with very peaceful intentions.

The men reply:

> In ancient times Wang Ch'iao
> Practised the arts of immortality;
> And the story of Ching K'o[122]
> Is told in the histories.
> That such or such a gentleman should come to visit you—
> I do not know how you feel about it.

The women reply:

> It is the beginning of spring and already warm;
> That carriage and horse should come forward.
> Your Excellence our honoured guest—
> What does he feel about it?

The men reply:

> This is not an inn,
> We really cannot stay here.
> If you have anything to say, speak at once
> And do not detain us for nothing.

The women reply:

> As it is not an inn
> Of course you cannot stay.
> We send you on your homeward way;
> Do not be late for the next stage of your journey.

The men reply:

> His carriage had gone till its felloes were worn through;
> His horses, till their hoofs were pierced.
> So he had to make the best of it
> And yield to circumstances.

The women reply:

> What quarter does he control,
> What people has he as companions?
> Tell us all that in due order
> And do not mix up your replies.

The men reply:

> He has temporary control over Tun-huang;
> Young noblemen have come with him.
> He is practised in the Three Histories,
> The Nine Classics are his study.

The women reply:

> The night is late, the watches are spent,
> The stars of the Pole-star have waned to the West.
> The Governor on his horse—
> What district is his?

The men reply:

> Gold and snow are equal in beauty;
> Sufficient reason that they should consort.
> The Governor on his horse
> Belongs to Sha-chou.

The women reply:

> Vast is his eminence,
> High stands his renown.
> Take word to the Governor and ask him
> What is his village.

The men reply:

> He is celebrated in the Three Rivers,[123]
> A talented gentleman of the Nine Commanderies.[124]
> The Governor on his horse
> Is of Tun-huang.

The women reply:

> From what quarter is the honoured guest
> Who braving the night has come to us here?
> I venture to ask his companions
> Because I do not know his borough.

The men reply:

> The world is wide,
> Ten thousand lands have their boroughs.
> Politely dealing with your questions
> This is how we have answered them.

The women reply:

>Men should know their ancestry
>Just as a river knows its source.
>The Governor on his horse—
>In what valley is his ancestral home?

The men reply:

>He is a patrol of the Three Rivers,
>A picked worthy of the Eight Waters[125]
>The Governor on his horse—
>His ancestral home was in the Ch'in valley.

The women reply:

>Though his lordship is an honoured guest
>He has been kept at the gate a long time.
>If we were to question him further
>We should be wasting his time.

The men reply:

>He is the fairest in the land,
>With a good understanding of literature.
>But if you are still in doubt, pray question him;
>Why should he think it a waste of time?

The women reply:

>A waiting guest is hard to send away;
>We have spread cushions and stretched brocades across
>   the bed.
>We ask his lordship to dismount and come,
>Then we can talk matters over quietly.
>We have tied our belts and completed our make-up (?),
>We will lead your horse by the rein and bring it this way in.
>In the orb above the Pleiades (?) have begun to rise;
>What reason is there that you should not dismount?

The men reply:

>Only to be kin with the wise and worthy he has at last (?)
>   approached this gate;

Merely for the sake of her outward charms he would not
  get down.
He only needs silk and gauze, a thousand, ten thousand
  pieces;
He does not want foreign goblets—many hundred cups.

The women reply (offering the wine):

This is wine made from the juice of grapes[126]
That we bring out and offer to his lordship the Governor.
If as a favour he condescends to drink it
The springtime of his life will last ten thousand years.

The men reply:

If the wine is indeed made of grapes
Then our hosts should taste it first themselves.
As the aunts and sisters-in-law have not tasted it
This wine we spill against the south wall.

The women reply:

The wine was really made from the juice of grapes,
Every pint was brought for a thousand cash.
We therefore ask his lordship's two companions
'For what reason did you throw away our wine?'

The men reply:

Behind the house is a garden full of leeks;
When one cuts them down, they grow up as before.
What we ask of the aunts and sisters-in-law
Is why they chose to offer us poisoned wine.

The women reply; words of song asking the bridegroom to
  dismount:

Delicate and lovely she comes out of her orchid bower;
Step by step she leaves the sunshine terrace.
Governor, precious as a thousand pieces of gold,
At last you surely must dismount from your horse!

The men reply:

> The Governor rides on golden stirrups,
> In his hand he holds a white jade whip.
> On the ground you must first spread brocade;
> Otherwise he won't be willing to dismount.

The women reply:

> A length of brocade already has been spread;
> The embroidered mattresses have not been taken away.
> The Governor must now make up his mind to dismount
> And lodge paired in the purple upper room.

The men reply:

> The Governor's purpose in coming tonight to this gate
> Was to set eyes on the Goddess of the Moon in the bright
>   autumn moonlight.
> If the aunts and sisters-in-law once more ask him to
>   dismount
> His retinue will not dare again to refuse on his behalf.

Words of the song about the great gate of the girl's family:

> The juniper is a juniper of the Southern Hills
> Taken to make the inscription-board above the gate.
> The inscription board stays there for ever;
> But a girl is only a guest for a little while.[127]

Sung when the middle gate is reached:

> Metal was hammered to make the gate-flaps,
> Jade was worked to make the gate-rings.
> Unfasten the metal hook catch,
> Pull back the purple sandalwood bolt.

Poem on reaching the rubbish-heap:

> There is not there any broken pottery;[128]
> How came this northern heap to rise?
> We will not borrow a spade or pick to use;
> For the moment we borrow a jade lute-plectrum (?).

Poem on reaching the base of the hall:

> Of crystal are made the four walls;
> Jade was worked to form the steps at the base.
> For what reason are you putting pressure upon us,
> Seeing that you are not Ts'ui of the T'ai Shan?[129]

Poem on being confronted with the lock-catch:

> The catch is a silver hook catch;
> Of bronze and iron that have been smelted together.
> Lend us for a little the key, that we may open it
> And the Governor be able to go through.

Sung on reaching the hall gate:

> The hall gate is fenced (?) on its four sides;
> Within there is a four-box couch,
> Surrounded by a twelve-fold screen;
> The brocade coverlet is decorated with patterns.

Request to come down from the couch:[130]

> The water-clock hastens, the sound of the watch-drums
>   is urgent,
> The stars flow away, the light of the moon is hidden.
> This lucky hour must not be missed;
> The time has come at once to leave the couch.

The men reply:

> The moon is sinking, the light of the stars is quenched;
> The watches are spent; I fear that day will break.
> If indeed you intend to fulfil the Great Rite
> Pray at once come down from the couch (?).

Chorus, giving word to start the pelting of the curtains:[131]

> One pair of blue and white doves
> Has flown round the curtains three, five times.
> Say for me to the bridegroom's retinue
> 'Let us see you go three times round the curtains!'

Sending away the virgin boys and girls:
> (This heading seems to have no corresponding song.)

Poem on removing the hangings that screen the bride's seat:
> The night is spent, the watches are late, the moon begins
>> to sink,
> Embroidered curtains, very lovely, hide the silks and
>> satins.[132]
> Give word to the waiting-maids to take them[133] all away
> And let the Imperial son-in-law see her face.

Or again they say:
> Brocade hangings layer on layer hold back
> Every puff of perfume from her gauze dress.
> Give word to the aunts and sisters-in-law:
> 'What harm would it do to take them away?'

Poem on removing the fan:
> Green spring on this night is just making its start;
> The red leaves open and reveal a single cluster of flowers.
> This jewelled tree let him clearly see;
> That she should be hidden by the jade fan now serves no
>> purpose.
> The many layers of the gauze fan must not cover her up;
> Her hundred beauties and charms so many cannot alas be
>> seen!
> The waiting-maids should not try to claim it as a per-
>> quisite;
> It is bound in the end, when the bride goes,[134]
> To belong to another family.

Poem on removing the hood:[135]

> In simple grace her neck clusters with its flowers;
> But all veiled are the tresses at each brow.
> Since she was a child she always had lovely hair;
> It ought not now to be covered by a hood.

Poem on removing the flower:

When we take away one flower, another is revealed;
The first was counterfeit, the second flower is real.
The false flower has also on it a bird with a flower in its
beak,
The real flower again has (?) she who plucked the flower.

Poem on undressing the bride:

On the hill-top a jewelled path shines very fair,
On the back part of her skirt are stitched phoenixes male
and female.
On the two sleeves of her outer mantle are shown a pair
of crows.
Now fold up her gauze clothes and put them in the clothes
box.

Poem on joining the hair:

This is the Palace of the King of Ch'u,
Tonight he has succeeded in meeting his beloved.
On her head is a coiling dragon hairdress;
On her face are dabbed spots of red.

Poem about the comb:

Up in the moon there grows a *sāla* tree;
Its branches are so high they cannot well be pulled.
Lend me for a little that small ivory comb;
When her hair is tidied, you shall have it back.

Poem about tying the finger-tips:

The tying depends on hearts being tied;
When the heart is true, the tying is also true.
Knot it cleverly just above the heart
And entrust it to the pair whose hearts are tied.

Poem; title unintelligible:

Heaven has caused the Weaving Maiden[136] to cross the
Milky Way

And come into the world of men for the sake of a human
 being.
You that stand by on the four sides, you must all retire to
 a distance
And now let this wedded pair begin to be as one.

Poem about letting down the blinds:

The women of the Palace, the Jade Maidens, how slender
 they are!
Our lady, Goddess of the Moon, hides among the crowd.
If you've made up your minds you absolutely must see what
 she looks like
Ask the people who are standing round to let down the
 blinds for a while.

CHAPTER TEN

THE BUDDHIST PIECES

IT is not surprising that there are many more—actually about twice as many—Buddhist pieces than secular ones among the MSS of popular literature from Tun-huang, for the place had long been a byword for the vast number of monasteries crowded into its small area.

When (in about A.D. 545) the famous writer Yü Hsin (A.D. 513–81) was made Governor of Shen-chou in western Honan he wrote that Shen-chou (c. 150,000 inhabitants) had almost as many monasteries as Tun-huang.[137] In the tenth century the proportion of monks to the total population was still abnormally high. In 934 Ts'ao I-chin, the local ruler, on the occasion of an Ordination of new monks, gave a *chai* (banquet for monks) which was enjoyed by 1,600 monks.[138] A few of them may only have been passing through Tun-huang or have come from neighbouring places such as Kua-chou and Hami. But in any case almost one person in ten at Tun-huang must have been a monk or nun. We know of about thirty monasteries there; probably there were others that do not happen to be mentioned. Even at Ch'ang-an, the capital, with its population of about a million, there were in T'ang times only about 120 monasteries.

But I personally find the Buddhist pieces interesting only when they diverge signally from the scriptures upon which they are founded. It is not, for example, of much interest to read timid adaptations of well-known episodes in Buddha's life, such as the Four Encounters (with the old man, the sick man, the dead man, the monk). These, of course, are furnished with plenty of Chinese touches; but little room is left for the play of Chinese creative folk-imagination. I have therefore only translated a few short extracts which differ so much from the standard sources as to give scope to the Chinese legendary style. The one long Buddhist piece I have translated, the 'Story of Mu-lien', owes hardly anything to the Buddhist Canon, and is presumably almost entirely a Chinese invention. The popular expositions of *sūtras*, or 'sermons' as we might call them, are far too technical to tackle in a book chiefly addressed to the average reader rather than to specialists in Chinese popular Buddhism.

The prologue to the Chester Miracle Plays speaks of a monk 'intermingling some things not warranted by Holy Writ. For to glad the hearers he thus did fashion it.' This could well be applied to the spirit and intention of the Tun-huang pieces that set out to enliven Buddhist Canonical legends.

THE LIFE OF BUDDHA

(1) *Buddha's marriage*

The King and his wife talked together about how a marriage could be arranged for Prince Siddhārta. But the Prince, when he heard that his father the King and his mother the Queen intended to choose a bride for him, would not agree to this; for in his heart he had vowed to seek a wife himself. So in the women's apartments he set up an altar and preached the Law, bringing together five hundred ladies of the Palace to hear him. None of them understood his holy teachings. Among them all only the Court lady Yaśodharā recognized the down-sign,[139] and gave the Prince her finger-ring.[140] Prince Siddhārta accepted it and put it in the folds of his dress.

After the audience had scattered, he announced to his father the King and to the Queen: 'Only this lady Yaśodharā will I accept in union.'

After that the Prince day and night carried out the rules of abstinence even more strictly than before. Although he had desired to get lady Yaśodharā, it was now just as though he had no wife. He never once shared a bed with her, but every day four times he took strenuous exercise,(141) and at night always took his rug and cushion to a separate place, and had no longing for ordinary things. His father the King said to the Queen: 'This Prince of ours is not like other people in the world. He has a double light shining from the down between his brows and is always practising austerities, never slackening for an instant.' After that a very strict watch was kept upon him in the Palace, lest he should escape and go off on his own. The Prince, seeing that his parents had recognized his tuft-sign, wanted at once to take flight, in order better to pursue his austerities. But his father the King increased his precautions, fearing that the Prince might slip away. He ordered thirty courtiers to keep perpetual watch, during daylight always sitting beside him on his left and right. At night the door of his room was bolted.

The Prince sat upright and continued his observances, his magic signs brighter than ever. He saw that in this world there were poor and rich, that there was old age and death, and he wanted to go to the Snow Mountains and practise austerities. He had no love for the ways of the world. As the Prince had the Eye of Wisdom, he gradually began to discover a means to escape.

Brought up thus till he was getting on for nineteen he now knew that there were heavenly saints and divinities of the earth that would help him. Later, once when he went into the back garden to divert his sadness, he suddenly saw the hundreds and thousands of dragon steeds in the stables. Among them was a white horse with a tawny mane. And among the grooms who were feeding horses in the back stables he noticed one in particular. The Prince thought to himself, 'This man and no other, this horse and no other can help me to go and practise austerities.' He sighed in great longing and went back to his room in the Front Palace. At last on the seventh day of the second month at the third watch of the night suddenly he saw four divinities who spoke to him out of the sky, saying: 'We have come to fetch the Prince.' The Prince was startled out of his sleep. He sat upright, his whole body bathed in sweat. The courtiers who were guarding him were all awake. The Prince, seeing the divinities with his Eye of Wisdom, said: 'I count on your holy powers to fetch me away. But the doors of the room are bolted and the courtiers are all awake. To meet such a case, what plan have you devised?' He had not finished speaking when one of the divinities pointed with his finger at the courtiers and they all fell fast asleep, and at the same time the bolt and catch of the door opened. Then the divinities at once took the Prince into the back garden. . . .

(Text breaks off.)

(2) *Buddha's son*

He called his wife to him and gave her these last instructions: 'I have no other parting present to give you except this piece of fine incense. If you are in trouble, you have only to burn this incense, looking towards the Snow Mountains, and tell me about it.' Then the Heavenly Kings of the Four Quarters supported the hoofs of his horse, and away he went, over the city walls. As he passed, he pointed at his wife Yaśodharā's belly with his jade whip, and she became with child. . . . So the Prince and the Four Heavenly Kings went off to the Snow Mountains to pursue the way of Enlightenment.

It was already more than ten months after her husband left her that she bore a son. When the King (the Prince's father) heard of this, he smote his desk in great anger. 'My son', he said, 'has already been pursuing the way of Enlightenment on the Snow Mountains for more than a year. How comes it that my daughter-in-law has now born a child?' Then he ordered soldiers to dig a fire-pit ten feet square in front of the Palace. The pit was filled with fire, and the daughter-in-law was to be pushed into it, along with her child. The King

then prayed that if the child was really his grandson the fiery
pit might be changed into a tank of cold water. Having prayed
thus he told the soldiers to push his daughter-in-law and her
child into the pit. The daughter-in-law asked for an incense-
burner and prayed. What did she say?

> I call upon you, for of all perils I face the greatest peril,
> As you at your retreat on the Snow Mountains certainly
>   ought to know.
> It would not matter if only I were suffering this cruel
>   fate;
> But do not allow it to overtake the one child I have born.

So soon as she had uttered this prayer the soldiers pushed
the daughter-in-law and her child into the fiery pit. But the
World Honoured One . . . changed it into a tank of cold
water. In the tank were two lotus flowers, and the mother
and child each sat on a flower. The soldiers went and told the
King, 'We pushed the daughter-in-law and child into the
fiery pit, but they were not burnt to death'. When the King
heard this he knew that the boy was his grandchild. He called
his daughter-in-law to him and said, 'Now I know that you
were not deceiving me'.

The daughter-in-law then bade farewell to the King meaning, she too, to go to the Snow Mountains and pursue the
way to Illumination. The King did not dare oppose this, but
gave her certain instructions. What did he say?

> You, a wife, have now determined to quit your sunny
>   bower;
> You have bloomed like a lotus amid the flames of the
>   pit.
> In your mirror at dawn you will gaze no more at your
>   peach-blossom face;
> No longer will you fix in your dark tresses the phoenix-
>   headed pin.
> The waters of the sea of ignorance will now cease to flow;

The thick forest of defiling passion you can lay low at
  will,
At the Vulture Peak do your best to follow the holy way.
Daughter-in-law, do not having failed to check
Laziness and greed,(142) give up and come home!

When he had given her these instructions, she bade farewell to the great King, went to the Snow Mountains and
pursued the way of Illumination. She was given the name
Shan-lai (Well Come), was changed into a man and following
Buddha became a monk and achieved Arhatship. Her son was
called 'Rāhula of the Mystic Practices'.

(Here the text breaks off.)

(3) *Ānanda*

The World-honoured One tried every kind of expedient,
but he could not manage to convert Ānanda. One day when
Ānanda and his wife were drinking together, the World-
honoured One, through his power of discerning the state of
mind of others, knew from afar that Ānanda's nature was ripe
for conversion:

Our Buddha, Śākyamuni, the great King of the Law,
Looked at Ānanda and felt pity for him.
The tender feelings of brotherhood were still strong
  within him;
From his whole body these feelings gleamed in a mighty
  light.
From the begging-bowl that he held in his hand a light also
  blazed;
The auspicious clouds on which he trod sent out a strange
  perfume.(143)
In the time it takes to snap one's fingers he had come in
  person to the house;
In a loud voice outside the gate he shouted 'Pot luck!'(144)

When the World-honoured One had reached Ānanda's
gate and had shouted 'Pot luck!' two or three times, Ānanda,
who was urging his wife to drink, suddenly heard the World-
honoured One's voice outside the gate and said to his wife,
'Lady! Lady!

There is something about which I must inform my lady,
I must ask you to forgive me if I leave you for a while and
    then come back.
What has happened is that my teacher-brother has arrived;
At this very minute he is at the gate begging for rice.
I would have much preferred at this minute not to go out;
But that is difficult, as he knows that I'm at home.
I'll just run out to the gate and have a look
And then come back at once and drink with you.
When we were happily conversing together and just drink-
    ing a cup
I much feared that my teacher-brother would come beg-
    ging for rice.
Let us each wish ourselves long life and then I'll be off for
    a minute;
As soon as I've seen my teacher-brother I'll come in again.
While I am away pass round one or two cups,
And keep up in gentle time the music of flutes and
    strings.
I leave it to you to make sure that everyone gets his turn;
Directly I have seen him, I'll whisk round and come
    straight back.'

Ānanda went to the gate to see Buddha,
Pretending of course to be delighted he had come.
He pressed together his palms and saluting him asked about
    his health:
'I should like news about my brother's person and fortunes,
To what do I owe this morning's condescension
In coming in person into our poor house?
A personal visit from the World-honoured One

Will certainly cause my whole family to receive great
    blessings.
The Tathāgata has come at his hour of repast;
For I see that the sun by now is high in its course.
I notice that even now my teacher-brother
Has some rice that smells good in his begging-bowl.
But if it is a question of preparing food for him in our house
There will be no difficulty in supplying hundreds of delicacies.
All I ask is that you should not stand on ceremony.
Please ask at once for whatever you want.'

The World-honoured One said, 'I only ask for rice enough
to fill my begging-bowl. I do not want anything else.' Ānanda
took the begging-bowl and went into the kitchen to get rice.
In Ānanda's house there were always on the hob seven pots
of fragrant rice. But Buddha by his magic caused him to scoop
in them till all was gone and yet the whole contents of the
seven pots only half-filled the begging-bowl! (The same,
repeated in verse.)
    When Ānanda had got his half-bowl of rice he came back
and gave it to the World-honoured One, intending then to
rejoin his wife, but Buddha said, 'Just accompany me to my
monastery, and then you can go back'.

Ānanda did not at all want to go,
But when his brother Buddha had repeated the order
    several times
He thought at first of going, as Buddha had said,
But then was afraid that his wife at home would be cross.
The difficulty of making up his mind was unendurable;
He debated with himself, should he go or stay?
But in the end it seemed best to go quickly with Buddha,
And having escorted him, come straight home.
So he at once accompanied the Tathāgata,
Still sorely afraid that his wife would be cross.
It did not take them long to get to the monastery;
Ānanda said goodbye to Buddha and turned to go home.

Ānanda, having escorted Buddha to the monastery, intended
to go straight home, but Buddha said, 'I have got to go today
to a Fast (an entertainment given to monks) and you must
look after the courtyard for me while I am away. There are
four water-jars to fill and the floor of the courtyard will have
to be swept. Wait here till I come back, and then you can
go home.' So saying the World-honoured One went off to
his Fast.

Ānanda, left there in the courtyard, was very depressed.
He said to himself, 'Catch me waiting till the World-
honoured One comes back!' But he was afraid that if he did
not, the World-honoured One would be angry, and he hastened to fetch four jars and set about filling them. But when
three were full, he upset two, and when all four were full,
he upset three. This happened over and over again, and he
was never able to get the whole lot full. In the end he was so
annoyed at not being able to fill them that he smashed them all.

He then started to sweep the ground. He swept from east
to west, but there came a west wind and blew the dust back
at him. He tried sweeping in circles, but there came a whirl-
wind and blew the dust back to the four faces of the yard.
Sweeping was evidently no good; moreover he was afraid his
wife would scold him for being away so long. He got into
a rage and cursed(145) the World-honoured One: 'Give up
your succession to the throne if you like and become a monk,
but don't expect other people to do your work for you!'

(Ānanda then begins to run home. But just at that minute
Buddha arrives at the monastery. Ānanda hides under a tree;
but Buddha 'sees him with his heavenly eye', and orders a
dragon-king to uproot the tree and set fire to it. Ānanda, in
imminent danger of being roasted, is obliged to come into
the open and beg for forgiveness. He asks to be allowed to
go home, but Buddha, a very busy person, explains that he
has an appointment to expound the Law to Indra, chief of the
gods, and is going to take Ānanda up to heaven with him.
While Buddha is preaching, Ānanda has a look-round in

heaven and finds a number of apartments, each containing a god and goddess. In one apartment, however, there is only a goddess and no god. Ānanda becomes interested in her and, stepping forward, asks if she has not a husband. To his delight she replies that she is destined to marry Ānanda, the brother of the Buddha. But when he announces that *he* is Ānanda the goddess refuses to believe him. 'Be off with you', she says, 'and do not wait till you have the humiliation of being driven away. My husband would not be wearing lay dress, as you do, but would have a shaven head and would be dressed as a monk.' Ānanda, now completely captivated by the goddess, rushes off to Buddha and says he has decided to become a monk. Buddha knew quite well what was the reason for this sudden change of front. 'Your heart', he said, 'is not pure. What good would it do you to shave your head? I am going to take you to Hell, and when you have seen what goes on there, it won't be too late to shave your head!'

After witnessing the usual spectacle of boiling caldrons, one of which he learns is intended for himself, Ānanda is of course completely converted, and is received into the Order by Maudgalyāyana, one of the Ten Disciples.)

(4) *The Devil*

The Devil, seeing that his army looked like being beaten, withdrew his forces and went back to Heaven.[146] But though he was clearly the weaker he still hoped to disturb the Tathāgata's meditations; his anger was unabated. After his defeat he sat solemnly in his main hall or ensconced himself in his fragrant woods, clasping his arms about him, raising his eyebrows, pouting his lips, unable to endure his rage. He had three daughters who, suddenly seeing that their father was disconsolate, came to him and said:

'We note that nowadays our father's looks seem quite changed.
Why, Father, are you so gloomy, taking pleasure in nothing?

Is it perhaps that the other gods are being a nuisance to you
Or is it again that within your Palace something has gone
   wrong?
Is it that on the borders of your realm some disturbance
   has happened,
Or is it perhaps that you are worrying about us, your three
   daughters?
We do implore our father and King to take pity on us
And at once inform us your daughters what has happened
   to you.'

Their father the King said:

'No, it certainly is not that I am worried about my three
   daughters;
All of you have grown up without giving trouble,
Nor is it that on the borders of my realm any disturbance
   has happened;
In the halls of Heaven all is joy, nothing can go wrong.
The trouble is that this Siddhārta, son of Śuddhodana,
At this very moment is on the point of achieving Illumina-
   tion.
It is unendurable to stand by and let him come out into
   the world.
If that happens all my followers are sure to get converted.
Once he begins to preach his religion, of this much I am
   certain,
I shall very soon not have left a single pupil or disciple.
Do tell me of some plan that I could now adopt
To dispose of him and make sure that he does not come
   out into the world.'

Upon this the three daughters stepped forward and said to
their father and King:

'Gautama, when he was young, grew up in his father's
   Palace;

How can he now have cut himself off from all joys of the flesh?
Is he not still a young man of very good appearance?
Surely he must at his age need carnal pleasures?
We all of us now desire to go down into the world of men
And upset him so that he won't be able to achieve
   Illumination.
All we need do is to stand before him and his meditations
   will cease;
He will not have a chance of reaching the Higher Under-
   standing.'

This plan pleased the Devil very much. He made his slaves
get ready the finest silks and gauzes and bring them from his
treasury. He drew aside his daughters' cicada tresses and
thrust phoenix hairpins aslant them. He clothed them in silks
and satins and put bracelets on their arms. . . . Only to see
them set in motion the wind and rain;[147] they were such
as to overthrow a kingdom or a city. They flaunted their
five-coloured dresses; the sun shone on their triple-jewelled
garments. Fairy maidens followed behind them holding
jewelled umbrellas to cover them; the Weaving Maiden led
the way, fanning a perfumed breeze that filled their path. All
the ladies of the six Palaces were summoned and deployed
to their left; all the dames of the land were placed separately
on their right. All these came down straight from the upper
world into the presence of the Buddha, with singing and
dancing in a great consort, flutes and strings competing in
their music. . . .

The first daughter said:

'World-honoured One, World-honoured One, a man born
into the world—how short a time he has! If he does nothing
splendid, he spends his days of life in vain. I am very beautiful;
there is none like me. I ought not to praise myself; but in
all the world there are certainly not many. I have come on
purpose to serve you and swear to be true for a thousand
years. If you can bring yourself not to scorn me, you and I
will be for ever as twin zithers!

I exhort you not to achieve the Great Illumination;
Why need you let your heart persist in clinging to this
    mistake?
I have left behind my kind parents and come to the world
    below
In the one desire that you and I may be husband and
    wife.'

The Buddha said:

'I am now fully determined to achieve Illumination,
To preach the Law and devote my thoughts to converting
    all who are astray,
In the Sea of Sorrow to be to them like a ship or raft.
What need can I have of you, that we should be husband
    and wife?'

The second daughter said:
'World-honoured One, World-honoured One, scion of
golden-wheeled Kings, descendant of Emperors, who have
disclaimed the throne to dwell in solitude among the hills!
I have now come to you with no other intent but this: to
sweep your floor, burn incense, fetch water; and when you
are not at home I will look after your house for you.

I am chary of putting on skirts of fine gauze;
I do not scent myself with musk, the perfume that comes
    from me is my own.
I have left behind my kind parents and come to the world
    below
Swearing that with my slender hands I will sweep your
    golden bed.'

The Buddha said:

'At present every thought of mine is centred on Imper-
    manence;

How is it possible that even for a moment I should stop
 burning incense?
A Buddha practising the Four Dhyānas is pure and without
 stain;
What need can he have of you to sweep his golden bed?'

The third daughter said:

'Your humble servant's present age is fifteen springs;
I am like a young lotus bud springing at the water's edge.
The god Indra and King Brahma have often sought my hand;
But my father and mother did not regard them as good
 enough for me.
You, however, I see to be perfect in the arts of war and
 peace;   .
In the Six Accomplishments and the Three Points you far
 exceed the throng.
Now that I have left my kind parents and come to the
 world below
You really must not turn yourself into a teacher or monk.'

Buddha said:

'The thing for you is as soon as you can to discard your
 present body
Which up to now has hindered you from achieving
 Buddhahood.
Be off without losing a moment back to the world above
And never again let me catch you disturbing people's
 thoughts.'

CHAPTER ELEVEN

MU-LIEN RESCUES HIS MOTHER

INTRODUCTION

A STORY linking a visit to a parent in Hell with the upkeep of proper sacrifices to the dead occurs in the Indian epic *Mahābhārata*.[148] The ascetic Jaratkaru sees his ancestors hanging upside down, that is, in a kind of limbo, owing to his failure to marry and provide a line of successors to keep up the sacrifices to the dead. In Buddhism the hero of the corresponding story is Maudgalyāyana (in Chinese, Mu-lien), one of Buddha's chief disciples, who rescues from Hell not his father but his mother. The Buddhist legend explains the origin of the Avalambana ('Hanging down') Festival, which began on the fifteenth day of the eighth month, when the monks came out of their rainy-season retreat. The merit acquired by the offerings made at this time and by the united prayers of the monks repeated Mu-lien's performance and rescued sinners from Hell.

Two extremely short scriptures[149] deal with the Mu-lien story; but the Tun-huang pieces (of which there are several apart from the one I have translated) are chiefly based on monkish folklore. Themes are also taken from stories in the Canon about other people. For example the misdeeds of Mu-lien's mother are modelled on those attributed in the Hundred Legends (*Avadāna Śataka*) to the mother of Uttara.[150] In later times popular Mu-lien plays, lasting several days, were performed at the Avalambana season. They were enlivened by boisterous and often scurrilous *intermezzi*. I give an account of one of these plays below, p. 234. They were also performed at other times of year to avert pests.

Locusts, if a play were given in their honour, could be seen swarming on beams and door-heads to witness it.[151] Then, appeased by the attention that had been shown to them, they would spare that district and depart to another.

After a few lines of preface, founded on the *Avalambana Sūtra*,[152] the story begins: Once upon a time when Buddha was in the world he had a disciple called Mu-lien. This disciple, before he was ordained, was called the Radish. He had a deep faith in the Three Treasures and a great reverence for the Mahāyāna. The time came when he was about to go trading in another land. He handed over part of his property to his mother, telling her to use it, after he was gone, in entertaining monks and anyone that came to the house to beg. But after he was gone his mother coveted the wealth that he had left in her charge and hid it away. Before very long, having completed his business, her son came home. 'I did as you told me', she said. 'I entertained monks and so brought blessings upon us.' Because of this deception, when she died, she dropped down into the Avīci Hell and suffered terrible torment. But Radish, having completed the three years' mourning, put himself at Buddha's disposal and was accepted as a monk. Enjoying the good effect of piety in previous existences, when he heard the Law preached he obtained the fruits of Arhatship. Endowed now with supernatural sight he was able to scan all the six ways of Life and Death; but in none of them could he see his mother. He therefore rose sadly from meditation, and said to the World-honoured One, 'Tell me, where is my mother enjoying bliss?' 'She is in the Avīci Hell', Buddha replied, 'suffering terrible torments. But although you have achieved the fruits of Arhatship, with the best will in the world there is nothing you can do about her. Only the united strength of all the monks of the Ten Quarters, used in concert on the day after the Summer Retreat, can save her.' It was for this that Buddha in his mercy, by a happy device, founded the Avalambana.

(The same story is then told in greater detail in verse; p. 717, l. 12. Mu-lien, in meditation, is transported to Heaven):

With his monk's staff he knocked on the gate three times
    or five,
Scarcely conscious that down his breast the tears were
    flowing fast.
A worthy elder came out and engaged him in conversation;
He pressed together the palms of his hands and spoke of
    his filial feelings.
He said, addressing the worthy elder, 'Do you know me
    or not?
I, a humble monk, am a man of southern Jambudvīpa.[153]
When I was young I had the misfortune to lose both father
    and mother.
The family was well off, but lacked sons and grandsons;
I found myself left all alone without anyone to back me.
This humble monk's kind mother's name was Leek Stem;
My good father was called Axle Box.[154]
His whole life was spent in deeds calculated to bring him
    blessings;
After his death he must have been born somewhere here
    in Heaven.
What a wonderful place this is, so rich in blessings and
    glories!
Merely to gaze on such splendours is a comfort to the
    heart.
Gongs and drums for ever blending their din with noble
    tunes,
The music of lutes also joining with tones so loud and
    clear.
But there is one who toiled and strove with never-ceasing
    care—
The mother who fed me at her breast, her I cannot forget!
After she left us would that I might know if she fares well
    or not;

I have come now to this place to look for her and pay her
    a visit.'
When the worthy elder heard this he felt very sad,
Troubled and anxious was his heart within, and his words
    came slow:
'I, your disciple, in the world of men did have a son;
But I was not aware that I had a son who was ordained as
    a monk.
Your Reverence must not take it ill if I ask a few questions;
In the world human relations are of many different kinds.
When I suddenly heard what you have told me I was very
    much surprised;
And now calmly thinking it over, I find it hard to believe.
It is not uncommon for different people to have the same
    name,
And as for appearance, hundreds of people look just alike.
I have the impression that you *do* resemble someone I once
    knew;
However, thinking it over again, I am not at all sure.
If your Reverence is dead set on being recognized
Try to tell me something more about your family affairs.'

'When I was young', Mu-lien replied, 'I was called Radish.
After both my parents died, I took refuge with Buddha and
became a monk. After I had received the tonsure, I was given
the name Great Maudgalyāyana Supreme in Magic Power.'
When the worthy elder heard him give his childhood name,
he knew that it must be his son. 'It's a long time since we
parted', he said. 'Have you been all right?' Radish-Mu-lien,
having thus been accepted by his kind father and having
questioned him about his present condition, went on to ask,
'And my kind mother, where is she enjoying bliss?' 'When
your mother was alive', replied the father, 'the *karma* she
made for herself was very different from mine. I performed
the Ten Sorts of Good Deed and observed the Five
Abstinences, and when I died my soul was reborn in Heaven.
Your mother during her lifetime committed many sins, and

when she died she dropped into Hell. Go to the Dark Ways
of Jambudvīpa and enquire there. Then you will be able to
find where your mother has gone to.'

When Mu-lien heard this he left his father and returned
to southern Jambudvīpa, where he looked for his mother
everywhere amid the Dark Ways, but could not find her.
Presently, however, he saw eight or nine men and women,
all completely unemployed. Now comes the passage[155] in
which Mu-lien questions them about their plight:

'Good people, do not bow down before me
But tell me who and what you are.
For what reason are you all collected here
Unemployed, doing nothing at all,
Wandering about on the outskirts of the town?
It was only this morning that I reached the Land of Death
And the first sights that met my eyes have very much
    surprised me.'
Thus questioned the unemployed replied to the Reverend
    Man,
'It all happened on account of our having the same names
    and surnames;[156]
Simply owing to an error in names we were brought to the
    Courts of Death.
Since our case was heard there must have passed three
    days or five;
The charge was dismissed and we were told we could go
    back to our homes.
But we got back only to find the funeral already over
And we were cast into these outskirts, left all to ourselves,
Cut off on every side from former kinsmen and friends.
Foxes and wolves, crows and jackdaws race to swoop upon
    us;
The houses we lived in have fallen to bits and we have
    nowhere to go.
We have put our case to the King of Death in most piteous
    tones;

His verdict was, we must all be ghosts, idle and unem-
ployed.
If further retribution awaits us we still do not know.
The barriers between Death and Life have closed on us
for ever,
The Gate of the Springs,[157] once shut, never opens again.
Though on our tombs are piled high a hundred kinds of
food,
What comfort can that bring to the hunger in our bellies?
The mourners' noisy lamentations do us no good;
In making paper into cash[158] they trouble themselves in
vain.
When you go back take this message to the men and
women at home:
Only by doing good works can they ease the torment of
the dead.'

Mu-lien remained silent for a long while. At last he said,
'Do you or do you not know a certain Lady Leek Stem?'
'None of us know her', they all said. 'Where does the Great
King Yama live?' he then asked. 'Your Reverence', they
answered, 'must go a few steps to the north. You will then
see a triple gate-tower, and fierce lictors driving countless
sinners through the gates.'

(Mu-lien is then brought before King Yama.)

The Great King when he saw Mu-lien come in
Pressed together his palms for a while and made to rise to
his feet:
'Your Reverence, what can be the business that has brought
you to this place?'
And hastily from behind his desk he bowed to the holy man:
'Really I am overcome with shame that you do us such an
honour.
Living as I do here in the Ways of Darkness
And busy giving rulings about sinners' fates

I have not had the chance to make your acquaintance,
Although, of course, I have long known your name.
Have you come here as an envoy of the Buddha
Or perhaps on some private business of your own?
Sentences decreed at the T'ai-shan are not easily reversed;
All were first drafted in Heaven and then endorsed by Hell.
The retribution that sinners meet arises from their past
deeds;
It does not lie in the power of others to do anything to
save them.
Here throughout the Endless Night the stench of stale
blood
And clotted grease will soon foul your Reverence's spot-
less clothes.
You cannot possibly stay long in the dark Ways of Death;
I humbly desire your Reverence to go quickly home.'
Mu-lien tried to speak, but at first no words came.
'Great King,' he said at last, 'it may have come to your
knowledge
That I, the poor monk, in life was blessed with a father
and mother
Who day and night kept fast in strict obedience to the
rules.
It would seem that, in accordance with what they did
while still in the World of Men,
After their deaths they ought to be born in the Western
Paradise.
But the Halls of Heaven seem only to harbour my late
father;
I have looked everywhere for my kind mother, and she is
not in any of the heavens.
I cannot think that she deserved to be sent down to Hell
And can only suppose that Mighty Heaven has punished
her unjustly. . . .
If as reward for her past deeds she has come to these regions
I take it that you, the Great King, would surely have been
informed?'

When Mu-lien had finished speaking, the Great King called him up into the hall where he met the Bodhisattva Kshitigarbha[159] who at once bowed down before him. 'You have come to look for your mother?' 'Yes, I am looking for my mother', said Mu-lien. 'Your mother during her lifetime committed many sins—sins countless and boundless. She must have dropped into Hell. . . .'

The Great King then summoned the officials concerned with past deeds—the Guardian of Destinies and the Keeper of Records—who came at once. 'This reverend gentleman's mother is called Lady Leek Stem. How long is it since she died?' The officials replied, 'Great King, it is three years since Lady Leek Stem died. There is a copy of the papers concerning the expiation of her sins at the office of the Recorder of the Heavenly Court, and another with the Commandant of Mount T'ai.' The King then summoned the Two Boys,[160] recorders of good and evil deeds, and bade them discover from the Mount T'ai authorities what Hell Lady Leek Stem was in. He then said, 'Your Reverence had better go with these boys and ask the General of the Five Ways. He will know where she is.' When Mu-lien heard this he at once took leave of the Great King and set out. He had not gone far when he reached the No Hope River. Here he saw countless sinners who had taken off their clothes and hung them on the branches of the trees. They were lamenting loudly, because they wanted to cross the river and could not cross. Again and again turning back in their alarm, five by five and three by three, they clasped their heads, crying and wailing.

Now comes the place where Mu-lien questions them about what had happened to them.

(In the verses that follow, after some repetition of what we know already, the dead, wailing piteously, say):

'In vain (p. 722, l. 5) you buried our white bones and piled a high tomb.

Our dragon steeds from the stable to the south our sons
and grandsons ride,
The perfumed litter by the northern window our wives
and concubines use.'

(Mu-lien can bear the sight of their wretchedness no
longer).

He turned away his head, wiping his tears; he could look
at them no longer.
But in his ears there still dinned the cries of their pursuers.
Who in countless hosts and myriad throngs were driving
them ahead.
There were bull's-head demons with staves in their hands
massed on the southern bank,
And lictors of Hell with forked prongs gathered on the
northern shore.
The eyes of the dead, struggling in the water, were wide
open with fear;
Those who were still on the river bank were weeping
piteously:
'Had we known what land of torment awaited us after we
left you
How we should have striven, while still alive, to win the
fields of blessing!'

Mu-lien then said to one of those who were under the trees
at the side of the river:

'So the Halls of Heaven and the Pits of Hells are no idle tale!
Those who do evil are not merely guilty in the eyes of
Heaven;
All the gods (?) of the Dark World join in their punish-
ment.
This poor monk's kind parent piled up no store of good,
And when she died her soul like yours fell into the Three
Ways.(161)

I hear it said that she was carried off into the Pits of Hell;
All I would know is if any of you have news of her or not?'
The sinners at this with one accord gazed at Mu-lien
All of them sobbing and weeping and with puckered brows.
'We, your disciples, have only been dead for a very short
  time
And about your Reverence's kind parent we know nothing
  at all.
All of us, while we were alive, committed many sins
Of which today, tormented as we are, we now begin to
  repent.
You may have concubines and wives enough to fill the
  mountains and vales;
But which of them, when it comes to dying, would be
  willing to take your place?
If at any time you are ever able to leave the Gates of Death
Take word to our sons and grandsons, to our families at
  home,
Tell them they need not have bothered to face our coffins
  with white jade,
Mere waste was the yellow gold they buried in our tombs.
Their long mourning, their doleful sighs did us no good;
The dirges, the music of strings and drums never reached
  our ears.
The only way, if they want to end the torments of the
  damned,
Is to do such pious works as succour a soul in the Dark
  Land.'

(Mu-lien is then brought to the General of the Five Ways,
the fiercest and most cruel of all the Regents of Hell:)

'Should (p. 724, l. 10) you ask, "In the Three Paths which
  is the cruellest place?"
All will tell you, "It is at the gate of the Demon of the Five
  Ways."
Evil births in animal form seem to be the commonest of all;

True is the saying: "In the Halls of Heaven things are very quiet!"

Since it seems that sinners one and all must pass through these gates

I humbly ask your Worship the General to look through the records.'

The General pressed his palms together and said to the Reverend Teacher,

'You must not howl and cry like this; you are spoiling your appearance.

Those that daily come this way are many as the Ganges sands.

I fear if we ask for Leek Stem, no one is likely to know.

At T'ai Mountain, all told, there are many "identity departments";

It would mean a joint investigation by the Heavenly Court and Hell.

Every official in charge of documents has his list of names,

The relevant tallies, on their way down, have to pass this way.

It happens that this morning I, your disciple, am the officer in charge of names,

And will certainly devote a few minutes to a search on your behalf.

It may be my *karma*, who can tell, to meet the name you want;

In which case it ought to be easy to get on to the right track.'

The General then asked those about him, 'Have any of you seen the name "Lady Leek Stem?"' An officer on his left replied, 'General, three years ago a person of that name was claimed by the Avīci Hell as being on their list, and she is presumably now being tortured in that hell.'

'I was told', said Mu-lien, 'that the cases of all sinners come up first before King Yama and they do not go down to their punishment till he has given a decision. Why was my mother not brought into the presence of the King?' 'There are two kinds of people', said the General, 'who do not see the King face to face. First, those who when alive did the Ten Good Deeds and observed the Five Abstinences. They are at once reborn in Heaven. Secondly, those who established no good *karma* and committed many very grave sins. They go straight down to Hell, without first seeing the King. It is only the half-good, half-bad who are brought before the King for trial and are then reborn according to their deserts.'

Despite the fact that he has been told his mother is in the Avīci Hell, Mu-lien makes enquiries in a number of other hells. In the first, enquiry is useless, as it turns out that this particular hell is 'for men only'. He is directed to another hell, where he is told there are plenty of women. This turns out to be the Hell of the Copper Pillar and Iron Bed. It is the hell where lust is punished. Here are to be found those who 'the woman taking the man, or the man taking the woman, fulfilled their desires on their parents' bed; disciples that used thus their teacher's bed, men slaves and women slaves that used their master's bed'. But Leek Stem's sins had been of another kind.

In the next hell Mu-lien was more successful. 'We had a Lady Leek Stem here three years ago', one of the gaolers says. 'But she was claimed by the Avīci Hell, as being on their list, and that is where she is now.' When at last he reaches the walls of the Avīci Hell, a sympathetic demon tells him that his mother is probably there, but strongly advises him against trying to get in:

'Of (p. 729, l. 6) molten iron are the outer walls, the
   inner walls of copper.
Day and night with shattering blast the wind of *karma*
   blows
Rending and scattering pell-mell the limbs of all that
   come.

I cannot but urge my Reverend Master to go back to his
  home;
To search for someone in such a place is an unrewarding
  task.
To brood about it, beating your breast, will get you nowhere at all;
Far better go back at once and get Buddha's help.'

(Mu-lien then rides through space on his magic begging-
bowl and in a twinkling is sitting at Buddha's feet. Buddha
lends him his own monk's staff, which will protect him from
every peril and enable him to beat down the gates of the
Avīci Hell. On his way there Mu-lien meets in the air fifty
demons 'bull-headed or horse-headed, with fangs like a
forest of swords, mouths like blood-bowls,(162) voices like
the roll of thunder, eyes like forked lightning'. 'Monk,' they
call to him, 'don't come this way. Here is no good road; this
is the way to Hell. Look at that black smoke to the west! It
is thick with the poisoned vapours of Hell. Should you be
caught up in it, your Reverence would turn to ashes and
dust.' But Mu-lien, reciting Buddha's name countless times,)

Wiped (p. 730, l. 12) away his tears and in the air shook
  the Buddha's staff.
At once the demons and evil spirits toppled down like
  hemp . . .
The three-pronged cudgels they held in their hands slipped
  out of their grasp;
The six-tongued forks they carried over their arms were
  flung far away.

(At the first flourish of Buddha's magical staff the bolts and
bars dropped to the ground; at the second flourish the gates
of Hell opened wide.)

'For (p. 732, l. 12) what reason has your Reverence
opened the gates of Hell?' one of the gaolers asked. 'If I did

not open them', said Mu-lien, 'who should open them? Buddha gave me the means to open them.' 'What was it that he gave you?' asked the gaoler. 'He gave me a monk's staff with twelve rings at its head', said Mu-lien. 'But what have you come here for?' 'I have a mother called Lady Leek Stem, and I have come to look for her.' When the gaoler heard this he went up on to a high tower in Hell, waved a white banner and beat upon an iron drum. 'Is there a Lady Leek Stem in the first compound?' he shouted. In the first compound there was none. He went on to the second compound, waved a black banner and beat on an iron drum. 'Is there a Lady Leek Stem in the second compound?' In the second compound there was none. He went on to the third compound, waved a yellow banner and beat on an iron drum. 'Is there a Lady Leek Stem in the third compound?' In the third compound there was none. In the fourth, fifth and sixth compounds it was also said that there was no one of that name. The gaoler went on to the seventh compound. He waved a grey banner and beat on an iron drum. 'Is there a Lady Leek Stem in the seventh compound?' Now Lady Leek Stem *was* in the seventh compound, her body clamped down on to a bed of iron by forty-nine long nails. She dared not answer. The gaoler asked again, 'Is there a Lady Leek Stem in the seventh compound or not?' Then at last came the answer, 'If you are looking for Leek Stem, I, wicked sinner, am she.' 'Why didn't you say so before?' 'Gaoler, I was afraid that you were going to take me to fresh torments in another place. That is why I did not dare to answer.' 'There is a monk outside the gate,' said the gaoler, 'his hair all shaven off and wearing the robe of religion. He says he is your son, and that is why he has come.' Lady Leek Stem, when she heard this, reflected a long while. 'Gaoler,' she said at last, 'I have no son who became a monk. There must be some mistake.' When the gaoler heard this, he went up on to the high tower and called, 'Monk, why are you falsely claiming this sinner in Hell as your mother? What can have made you tell such a lie?'

(Mu-lien then explains that his original name was Radish. Only after the death of his parents did he become a monk, with the name Mu-lien.)

When (p. 733, l. 9) Lady Leek Stem heard this, she said, 'If the monk at the gate was called Radish when he was young, then indeed he is my son, the darling child of this sinner's bosom!' When the gaoler heard this, he raised up Lady Leek Stem, drew out the forty-nine long nails, chained her with iron chains about the waist and with rough truncheons menacing her on every side she was driven out to the gate.

(Mu-lien is appalled at the condition she is in—blood gushing from every pore, flames darting out of her mouth—and cannot understand why she looks so starved. 'Every day', he says, 'I have made offerings at your tomb. Were you not able to eat them?' 'By your diligence in bringing offerings to my tomb', the mother replies, 'you got yourself a reputation for filial devotion, but to me it would have done more good if you had copied out in my name a single line of scripture. This would have helped me far more than torrents of wine poured out at my tomb.' Mu-lien then turns to the gaoler and offers, if only he will release his mother, to go into Hell and suffer there in her place. But the gaoler explains that he is a gaoler and nothing more:)

'All (p. 735, l. 7) decisions of this kind proceed from the
    King of Justice.
For sin that she herself committed only your mother can
    be punished,
You, my Master, cannot suffer for sins you did not
    commit.
From the golden and the jade slabs nothing can be wiped
    away
Nor has anyone the power to change what once has been
    inscribed.'

(The mother, with one hand resting on the doors of Hell, turns her head and bids him farewell. 'If one day you should achieve Illumination', she says, 'do not forget your mother, still suffering the torments of the damned.' When he saw his mother go back into Hell, his heart was cut to the quick, he sobbed and sighed and beat his breast with a violence like that of Mount T'ai crumbling. Blood gushed from all his pores and for a good while he was dead. Then, coming to life again, by pressing his two hands upon the ground he raised himself to his feet, tidied his clothing and, soaring into the air, came once more into Buddha's presence. When he described his mother's sufferings, the World-honoured One decided to go himself and deal with the matter:)

'After (p. 738, l. 1) such sins, though aeons passed she
  still would not be released;
Only a Buddha, no common mortal, can deal with such
  a case'.
The Buddha then called out to Ānanda and the other disciples
'I shall have to go to the Way of Darkness and rescue her
  myself'.

(Buddha then sets out, accompanied by hosts of divinities. As soon as he arrives, the magic radiance that shines from the down between his eyebrows dissolves Hell. The Tree of Swords and the Forest of Knives turn to dust, and all the demon-gaolers fall on their knees, and do homage to Buddha. The damned are all transferred to Heaven. Not, however, Lady Leek Stem; she becomes a Preta, a Hungry Ghost. If in the distance she hears the sound of water, by the time she gets near it has turned into a river of revolting pus. Food the moment it touches her lips turns into fire. She implores Mu-lien to take his begging-bowl and collect some rice for her, thinking apparently that rice given as alms to a monk will not be subject to the laws of the Preta world. And he must be quick about it, she says, for she is in desperate need of nourishment.

Mu-lien goes off to the city of Rājagriha and begs from a man of substance, who is at first shocked at a monk begging at so late an hour in the day. 'Monk,' he says, 'you must already have had your early meal. The time for eating is over. What are you going to do with this rice?' Mu-lien explains, and the man of substance tells his servants to bring rice immediately. Mu-lien hurries back to his mother and begins to feed her 'with a golden spoon'. But all the torments of Hell have not cured her of her inveterate covetousness and greed. She is terrified that the other Hungry Ghosts will snatch away the food. 'The monk who has come', she says to them, 'is my son. It is for me that he has brought this rice from the world of men. Just calm yourselves, and perhaps when I am feeling better I will do something for you. . . .' Looking round anxiously in every direction she protected the bowl with her left hand, while with her right she rolled the rice into balls. But before it entered her mouth, it turned into fire (p. 742, l. 16). She then implored him to get water to put the fire out, and he took her to the great river to the south of Rājagriha. When the people of the common world see this river, it is as pure, clear water that they see it. When gods see this river, it is as a stream of crystal that they see it. When fish see this river, to them it is a mountain brook. But when Lady Leek Stem saw it, to her it was a river of foul pus.)

Mu-lien was obliged to go back once more to Buddha who explained that not till the Avalambana Festival had been celebrated could his mother eat. On the fifteenth day of the seventh month he held the first celebration of this festival and out of the Avalambana bowl of offerings his mother was at last able to eat her fill. After this, however, he lost sight of her and on making enquiries was told by Buddha to go through the city begging at random, not choosing one house rather than another. In this way he would come to the house of a certain man of substance. A black dog would run out at the gate, tug at his cassock, and begin to speak in human language. 'That dog', Buddha said, 'is your mother.'

It turned out as he had predicted. 'As you saved me from the dark ways of Hell,' the dog said, 'why do you not save me from the misery of living in a dog's form?' 'Kind mother,' said Mu-lien, 'it was entirely owing to my lack of filial piety that you got into trouble and dropped into Hell. Surely, however, you are better off as a dog here than you were in the world of Hungry Ghosts?' 'Filial son,' the dog said, 'it is true that in this form of existence I can go or stay, sit or lie as I choose. If I am hungry I can always eat human excrements in the privy; if I am thirsty, I can always quench my thirst in the gutter. In the morning I hear my master invoking the protection of the Three Treasures (Buddha, the Religion and the Community); in the evening I hear his wife reciting the noble scriptures. To be a dog and have to accept the whole realm of impurities is a small price to pay for never so much as hearing the word "Hell" said in my ear.'

Mu-lien then took his mother to Rājagriha and before Buddha's pagoda for seven days and seven nights recited the Mahāyāna scriptures, confessed, prayed and observed abstinence. In consequence of these good works his mother escaped from her dog-form. Her dog-skin dropped off, and she hung it on a tree. There was then revealed a woman's body, perfectly and completely human. 'Mother,' said Mu-lien, 'incarnation as a human being is hard to get, nor is it easy to be born in the Middle Kingdom. It is difficult to hear Buddha's Law and be converted to good thoughts. I call upon you, now that you again have human form, at once to lay up a store of blessing.'

He then took her to the forest of *sāla* trees, walked round Buddha three times and then faced him saying, 'World-honoured One, pray inspect for me the course of my mother's *karma*, examining it from start to finish, and tell me if there are still sins that she has not expiated.' The World-honoured One did as Mu-lien asked. 'Contemplating the three sorts of *karma*,'[163] he said, 'I do not find a scrap[164] of sin left.' Mu-lien, knowing that his mother's sins were obliterated, said to her in delight, 'Mother, go where you belong. The common world of men is no place in which to linger. There is nothing in it but endless birth and death. Far better is the land of the Buddha of the West.'

Then *devas* and dragons leading the way, Heavenly Maidens coming down to meet her, she was brought to the Trāyastrimśa Heaven, there to enjoy bliss.

The stanzas that Buddha uttered after his Enlightenment led to the conversation of Kaundinya and his four companions. That was the time when this *Avalambana Sūtra* was preached. Eighty thousand Bodhisattvas, eighty thousand monks, eighty thousand male lay disciples and eighty thousand women lay disciples paraded round the Buddha, doing homage to him, joyfully accepting his teaching and obeying it.

(There follows a colophon indicating that the text was copied in A.D. 921.)

I append an account of a sixteenth-century Mu-lien play.[165]

Mu-lien has been told at the Tenth Tribunal of Hell that his mother has been reborn as a dog. But thousands of families have dogs, and the trouble is, where to look for her. In despair, Mu-lien applies to the Bodhisattva Kuan-yin, who tells him to go to such and such a place outside the western walls. 'Your mother', she says, 'has been reborn as a dog in the household of Chancellor Cheng's son. Tomorrow he will go hunting with his hounds and one dog will leave the pack and run up to you. This will be your mother.' Mu-lien goes to the appointed place, the hunt arrives, and one dog comes up to him and tugs at his skirts with its teeth. Mu-lien is sure the dog is his mother and, fearing that the huntsmen will reclaim it, hides the dog under his cassock. The huntsmen come up and ask what he has got under his cassock. 'My mother', he replies. 'Nonsense', they say. 'It's our puppy. Someone must go and tell our master that a monk is hiding one of our dogs under his cassock.' Young Mr Cheng gives orders that Mu-lien is to be bound and brought to him for punishment. But Mu-lien pronounces a spell that unties the knots. Mr Cheng is very much impressed, dismounts from his horse and, doing obeisance to Mu-lien, asks him how he acquired his magic arts and why he wants the dog. Mu-lien tells his whole story and, to clinch matters, Cheng asks the the dog, if it is really Mu-lien's mother, to give three loud barks. This it duly does, and after Mu-lien has promised to do what he can to secure a good reincarnation for Cheng's mother, he is allowed to take the dog away.

The next scene is in a nunnery. Sai-ying, who was Mu-lien's fiancée before he became a monk, has refused to marry anyone else and has become a nun. A dog runs into the nunnery, bows to the figure of Buddha and then comes and tugs at Sai-ying's dress. A moment later Mu-lien appears, apologizing for intruding into a nunnery, but explaining that he has come to look for his dog. A scene of recognition follows and, with the permission of the Abbess, Mu-lien and Sai-ying agree to go off to celebrate the newly instituted rites of the Avalambana Festival. At the Festival, a Heavenly Herald announces that Mu-lien, as a reward for his filial piety, has been made a Bodhisattva; his fiancée, an attendant on the Jade Emperor in Heaven; and an Immortal Dog is heard barking among the clouds.

AFTERWORD

(1) THE DISCOVERY AND NATURE OF THE MSS

THE manuscripts translated above come from a hidden library found by the Taoist Wang Yüan-lu in 1900. Wang was a discharged soldier who, finding himself at a loose end, settled in one of the famous 'Caves of the Thousand Buddhas' at Tun-huang in the extreme north-west of China and made a living by selling Taoist spells. These were in demand because the spell-trade was in the hands of Mongolian lamas who catered for Buddhists, and the considerable Chinese population had, at the time of Wang's arrival, nowhere to go for native Chinese spells.

The exact circumstances of the find are unknown. One version of the story is that Wang was removing sand from a cave when he discovered the walled-up library. Nor is it known when the library-cave was walled up nor for what reason. The dated documents found in it are said to range from A.D. 406 to A.D. 996.[166] At least three-quarters of the texts are copies of well-known Buddhist scriptures in Chinese, almost word for word as we have them in the printed Canon today, and therefore of no interest in them-selves, though they sometimes have interesting colophons. Of greater interest, at any rate to specialists in Buddhist history, are a number of apocryphal works, lost commen-taries, and so on. There are also some Taoist texts and a few Manichean and Nestorian Christian ones in Chinese. The Chinese documents further include letters, wills, deeds and administrative papers of all kinds. There are, too, texts in Tibetan, Uighur Turkish and several other languages. I will not dwell on these, as I cannot read the languages concerned. I will deal here only with what is to me the most interesting part of the collection, the eighty or so specimens of popular

236

literature—ballads, stories and legendary expansions and expositions of Buddhist scriptures.

But to return to the history of the finds. In 1907 Sir Aurel Stein, acting on behalf of the British Museum and the Government of India, induced the Taoist Wang Yüan-lu in return for small sums of money to hand over large numbers of MSS and paintings on silk. All the MSS in Chinese and half of the paintings on silk are now at the British Museum. In 1908 Professor Pelliot made a similar haul, not so large as Stein's but more discriminating, since he could read Chinese and Stein could not.

I have given only a brief outline of these proceedings, as they have been described in great detail by the two explorers in books and articles.

The Chinese regard Stein and Pelliot as robbers. I think the best way to understand their feelings on the subject is to imagine how we should feel if a Chinese archaeologist were to come to England, discover a *cache* of medieval MSS at a ruined monastery, bribe the custodian to part with them, and carry them off to Peking. To account historically for the conviction of both Stein and Pelliot that they were behaving in a normal and indeed absolutely irreproachable way, we have to remember that in the nineteenth century archaeology combined with a mild kind of espionage (consisting in little more than map-making) had been carried on extensively in Moslem countries where conversion to Islam had long ago completely divorced the inhabitants from their remote past. It was assumed that in lands of the Near and Middle East no one was capable of understanding or appreciating relics of pre-Mohammedan culture and that their removal to Europe for conservation and study could not reasonably be resented. The continuity of Chinese culture and the existence, even during the twilight of the Manchu empire, of scholars such as Lo Chen-yü and Wang Kuo-wei made the adoption of a similar attitude towards Chinese treasure-trove quite inapplicable. Stein was of course aware that the Chinese were more interested in their own remote past than were, for example, the Bedouins. But I was never able to convince him that the Chinese scholars who in the eighteenth and nineteenth centuries wrote about the geography and antiquities of Central Asia were anything more than what he called 'arm-chair archaeologists'; though they had in fact, as Generals or administrators, spent far more time in Central Asia and travelled far more widely than Stein himself. Pelliot did, of course, after his return from Tun-huang, get into touch with Chinese scholars; but he had inherited so much of the nineteenth-century attitude about the right of Europeans to carry off 'finds' made in non-European lands that, like Stein, he seems never from first to last to have had any qualms about the sacking of the Tun-huang library.

In 1910 the Chinese Government was still able to bring to Peking some ten thousand MSS, despite the fact that a good many found their way into private hands *en route*. Finally, in 1911, a Japanese mission procured six hundred MSS kept back by Wang Yüan-lu, who had concealed them inside stucco Buddha images that (precious old humbug) he had piously dedicated at the caves. The Tun-huang MSS, then, are now scattered over two continents, in London, Paris, Peking and Japan. This has greatly handicapped and delayed the study of them, though the situation has now been to some extent remedied by the existence of microfilms.

Partly owing to the two wars relatively little work has been done on the MSS in the fifty years that they have been in London and Paris. For example, of the twenty or so pieces of popular literature translated above only one[167] has been translated before.

This book is a literary anthology, intended for the general reader. I have therefore to a large extent avoided discussion of linguistic and textual problems, reserving them for separate treatment in the *Karlgren Festschrift*, Copenhagen, 1960. A few such points, however, for which there was not room in the *Festschrift* article, are discussed in the Notes (pp. 252 seq.).

The popular literature of Tun-huang is not of the kind

(such as the Ainu epics) that was only written down after centuries of transmission from mouth to mouth. It was composed, on well-known themes, by people of the scribe or village-schoolmaster class who could read and write, but had not the sort of higher literary education that would have enabled them to join the regular Civil Service. Many of the characteristics of this literature are similar to those of the folk literature of peasant Europe and of folk-tales in many parts of Asia. Some of these characteristics are, (1) Constant repetition of stock passages, (2) Asides in which the story is related to the origin of place-names, or of rites and customs, (3) Disregard of real chronology and topography. Indeed, because of the geographical vagueness of the texts I have generally not tried to relate the places-names to modern maps, (4) The name of the author is hardly ever known. No doubt other features could be listed by anyone making a complete analysis of the pieces. I have only mentioned such characteristics as immediately occur to me.

But in all the pieces there is, in varying degrees, a considerable influence of upper-class, ornamental literature. This is particularly the case in descriptive passages and is least so in dialogue, which always figures very prominently. The dialogue, indeed, probably approximates fairly closely to the current spoken language. One mark of this ornamental style, which was at its zenith from the fifth to the seventh century, is the continual use of parallel phrases, which often amount to little more than saying the same thing twice over in different words. For example, 'Monkeys twittered in the dark valleys, tigers roared in the deep ravines', is parallelism; whereas 'The high peaks were precipitous and bare; the lofty ridges were cleft and rugged'[168] comes fairly near to being merely a repetition.

The sung portions are nearly always in seven-syllable lines. The even lines rhyme, and occasionally there are rhymed couplets. Seven-syllable verse has been the usual Chinese ballad metre down till modern times. It gives the poet more freedom than verse of five syllables to the line, in that he only has to find a rhyme at every fourteenth character. But there is no running over of the sense from one line to another, and Chinese does not run very easily or naturally into hundreds of clauses each consisting of seven syllables. Consequently except in very skilful hands seven-syllable verse is apt to contain a great deal of padding. This tendency is very marked in Tun-huang ballads, and inevitably also in my translations.

Despite the mixed character of the population and its nearness to foreign countries, Tun-huang remained stubbornly Chinese.

In the K'ai-yüan period (A.D. 713–41) the Emperor ordered that monasteries bearing the name K'ai-yüan should be set up in all the principal towns of China. When envoys from the capital arrived at Tun-huang *c.* A.D. 876 they found that, despite nearly seventy years of Tibetan occupation, the K'ai-yüan Monastery there was intact, as was also the image of the Emperor Hsüan Tsung, who had ordered its foundation; for Tun-huang, 'although it had been cut off from China for a hundred years and had eventually fallen into the hands of the Tibetans, continued to hold the T'ang dynasty in awe and had preserved the Emperor's image, a thing which had not happened in any of the four neighbouring commanderies of Kan-chou, Liang-chou, Kua-chou and Su-chou, where the battlements were in ruin and the inhabitants mingled promiscuously with the foreigners and even adopted foreign dress. Only at Sha-chou (Tun-huang) did the people and their customs remain exactly as in China proper.'(169)

But a monk preaching at Pei-t'ing(170) in northern Turkestan in the tenth century found it necessary to remind his hearers that when he said Buddha he did not mean the Buddha of the Manicheans or the Buddha of the Persians (i.e. Christ; for Christianity was still common in Persia), nor yet the Buddha of the Fire-worshippers (Zoroaster). What he meant exclusively was the Buddha Śākyamuni. The same warning might well have been necessary at Tun-huang where there were also Manicheans, Christians and followers of Iranian cults.[171]

One might, then, have expected to find a good deal of foreign influence in the popular literature of Tun-huang. But the secular literature remained faithful to standard Chinese themes, many of which have retained their popularity to the present day. There is, of course, the omnipresent influence of Buddhism; but Buddhism had become an intrinsic part of Chinese culture many centuries before the earliest pieces of Tun-huang popular literature were composed. And here arises the questions whether this popular literature, copied in the tenth century at Tun-huang, originated there or was imported from less outlying parts of China. The number of pieces that bear any mark of local, Tun-huang origin is very small. There are two fragmentary chronicle-ballads dealing with campaigns of local rulers in 856 and c. 876; these were certainly composed in the Tun-huang region. There are prayers for the welfare of local rulers and their families attached to some of the Buddhist pieces; but these may have been added locally to texts that originated elsewhere. The names of two persons[172] in the 'Story of the wizard Yeh Ching-neng' are characteristic of the region and may have been used to give local colour. Otherwise there is no reason to suppose that any of the ballads and stories were composed at Tun-huang and might not equally well (given the right climatic conditions for their preservation) have been found anywhere in China. I do not think there is any linguistic evidence that contradicts this; but that is a technical question into which I will not here enter.

One can roughly divide the texts into five kinds—(1) Ballads, in which I include those in alternate passages of verse and prose, and also those entirely in verse. (2) *Fu*, pieces entirely or largely in rhymed prose. (3) Stories in prose. (4) Buddhist stories told in alternate verse and prose, but closely following Canonic texts. (5) Popular expositions of Buddhist scriptures, the argument being from time to time resumed in song.

About the tunes used in the sung portions of these forms we know nothing. Some MSS have musical indications above the verses; but these have not been satisfactorily explained. Only one piece of formal musical notation was found at Tun-huang (Pelliot 3808), and this gives the string accompaniment to lyric songs (*ch'ü-tzu*) and has no relevance to the ballad tunes. We also have two specimens of dance-script (Pelliot 3501 and Stein 5643, No. 5). The latter is wrongly called musical notation in the British Museum Catalogue.

(2) THE CONNECTION WITH PAINTING

This is a large and speculative subject into which I shall not enter deeply here. My friend Terukazu Akiyama[173] has dealt with it admirably in his article on the illustrated *pien-wen* of 'Śāriputra and the Heretics' (Pelliot 4524). I would suggest, in the light of his studies and my own, that three kinds of painting were probably used to illustrate popular recitations:

(1) Small illustrations inserted between sections of writing, either in scrolls or booklets, intended to inspire the singer or reciter with a vivid sense of the scene he (or she) was describing; used in fact as aids to visualization much as were the pictures of Buddhist divinities in religious meditation. Of this kind must have been the illustrated scroll of the Wang Chao-chün *pien-wen*[174] which a singing-girl from Szechwan held while she sang, with the result that her mind was carried to the steppe-land scene of Wang Chao-chün's exile. We know about her performance from a poem by the eighth- or ninth-century poet Chi Shih-lao,[175] the sense of which is: 'Before she adopted the singing-girl's pomegranate skirt she lived, as she tells us, on the banks of the Brocade River at Ch'eng-tu. Her red lips can recite the history of ten thousand years, her moving text expresses all the sadness of autumn's ninety days. When she lowers her head, she thinks of the moonlight of her youth in Szechwan; but the moment she opens the painted scroll, she is amid the clouds of the north-west frontier. . . .'

(2) Larger paintings in a broad style which could be seen clearly at a distance of twenty feet or so. These were held up to the audience (necessarily a rather small one) while the singer chanted from the text on the other side of the scroll. Of this kind, if I am right, is the illustrated scroll of the contest between 'Śāriputra and the Heretics' published by Madame Vandier-Nicolas (Paris, 1954) and discussed, as I have said, by Akiyama.

(3) Larger paintings, more on the scale of stage scenery, that could be seen at a considerable distance and consequently by a large audience. These were 'set up' (*li*) and 'spread out' (*fu*) successively.[176]

From time to time the formula 'Look how such and such a passage (or scene) goes!' occurs before a verse description. The word 'look' has been interpreted[177] as meaning that a picture was being displayed to the audience. But in Chinese stories the listener (or reader) is constantly referred to as *kan-kuan*, 'looker-on', and is invited to 'look' at what is happening in the story. For example in the *Hsi Yu Chi* (*Monkey*) Chapter 1, p. 3: 'All the monkeys were playing in the shade of the pine-trees. Just you look at them one and all!' followed by a verse description. When, therefore, for example in the ballad of 'Śāriputra and the Heretics' (not translated in this book) Sudatta is paying for the Crown Prince's garden by covering every inch of it with gold pieces and it is said before a verse description of the scene 'Look[178] how the passage about the spreading of the gold pieces goes!' I do not think this necessarily means that the audience is being invited to look at a painted illustration of the scene. They are, perhaps, rather being asked to visualize the scene that the singer is about to describe.

And I say this even though we do happen to possess (Pelliot 5424) an illustrated copy of the sung portions of this piece.

APPENDICES

I

DATED MSS

Eleven MSS of Tun-huang popular literature bear definite dates (as opposed to mere indication of place in the sixty-year cycle). These dates range from A.D. 921 to 981. I refer, of course, to colophons stating when the MSS was copied, not to the date when the piece was composed. The period covered by these dates was that during which Ts'ao I-chin and his successors ruled Tun-huang as practically independent sovereigns. There is some evidence(179) that, like several other Chinese rulers of the period, they set up a Painting Bureau, and they may well have also been patrons of musical performances such as the *pien-wen*, just as later on Chinese Emperors were patrons of the drama.

II

THE MEANING OF 'PIEN-WEN' AND 'FU'

Only six pieces in the surviving popular literature of Tun-huang actually bear the title *pien-wen*. Of these, five are in alternating prose and song. It has therefore been assumed (perhaps rightly) that this is the form to which the term *pien-wen* is normally applied, and modern editors have listed as *pien-wen* many pieces which are in this form, but have lost their titles. There was evidently some looseness in the application of the term in Tun-huang times; for the story of Shun, called a *pien* at the beginning of the MS and *pien-wen* (the fuller term) at the end, is what we should have expected to be called a *fu*, being in prose which frequently rhymes and not containing any portions intended for singing.

On the other hand the second 'Swallow and Sparrow' piece (not translated in my book) is called a *fu*, but is in fact a ballad in five-syllable verse and is described in the very first line as a *ko*, 'song', and is indeed clearly intended for singing; whereas *fu* were recited, not sung. So that not only the term *pien* but also the term *fu* were obviously used with some looseness.

I suggest that *pien-wen* means etymologically 'incident-text', the *pien* being similar to the *pien* of the modern term *pien-shih*, 'incident'. It in any case means 'unusual occurrences', and one could use the stronger term 'marvels', or even 'miracles'. The name, then, stands very close to that of the *miraculum* (miracle play) of Europe, though in form the *pien-wen* bears more resemblance to an oratorio. The term *pien-wen* is parallel to *pien-hsiang*, 'pictures of incidents', which in hundreds of Buddhist temples in China illustrated wondrous happenings in the scriptures.

It is, however, perhaps better not to translate the expression *pien-wen*, but to leave it as a Chinese term with which anyone interested in Chinese literature must become acquainted. An additional advantage of leaving the term untranslated is that Chinese and in many cases also Japanese readers will know what one is talking about.

A number of references to *pien-wen* exist in standard literature; but it was not till long after the discovery of the Tun-huang MSS (the study of which proceeded very slowly) that these references were understood—not, indeed, till about 1930. For example in the *Life of Kao Li-shih*[180] we are told that in A.D. 760 after the abdication of the Emperor Hsüan Tsung the eunuch Kao Li-shih used to divert him from his sorrows by reciting popular expositions of Buddhist texts, by singing *pien* and telling stories. They were 'far from according with the rules of high-class literature'; but he hoped by doing so to cheer up the Ex-Emperor.

The Ex-Emperor was in fact being regaled with popular literature of exactly the same kind as has turned up at Tun-huang. Another reference to *pien-wen* has already been mentioned (p. 242 above) in connection with Chi Shih-lao's poem about the singing-girl from Ch'eng-tu. There is also an anecdote about an exchange of quips[181] between the famous poet Po Chü-i (A.D. 772–846) and the less famous poet Chang Hu. Po laughed at Chang for writing a poem which contained a number of questions, such as 'Where was the inlaid belt thrown?' 'Who did the gauze shirt belong to'?, and said it sounded more like a legal interrogatory[182] than a poem. Chang retorted by saying that 'Above he looked everywhere in Heaven; below, everywhere in the Land of Death, but in neither place was there any trace of her' (a couplet from

Po's *Everlasting Wrong*, about the Emperor Hsüan Tsung's search
for the soul of his mistress Yang Kuei-fei) sounded as though it
came out of the *pien-wen* of Mu-lien and described Mu-lien's
search for his mother.

The fourth reference occurs in a book (183) which reached its
present form in 1237. It says that 'various laws of our ancestors'
forbade the circulation of the *Kua-ti Pien-wen* ('The *pien-wen* about
the compacting of the Earth').(184) It is clear from the context
that this was a Manichean or quasi-Manichean work. After that,
pien-wen (so far as is at present known) were never mentioned
again till actual specimens were found at Tun-huang.

Before the Tun-huang finds, too, hardly anything was known
about popular *fu* partly in colloquial. This may merely have been
because they were not thought worth printing. So far as I know
the only colloquial *fu*, apart from the Tun-huang MSS, that we
know about is the '*fu* about the Hot Springs',(185) by Liu Ch'ao-
hsia, written in the winter of A.D. 743. This was a humorous
work, containing passages in colloquial, for example the lines:

> *Che-mo ni ku-lai ch'ien Ti*
> *Ch'i ju wo chin-tai San-lang?*
> 'Even among a thousand of your vaunted Emperors of the past
> Is there one that equals our own Third Son?'

'Third Son' was the name by which his courtiers jocularly
referred to the Emperor Hsüan Tsung. There is an essay on the
art of love in *fu* form (Pelliot 2539) which is humorous (or so
its Preface claims) and contains a few colloquial terms of lovers'
slang; but it is in the main highly literary.

III

NOTES ON SOME PIECES NOT TRANSLATED

(1) '*The pien of the Han General Wang Ling*'

This long and important piece tells how Wang Ling and his companion, in a surprise raid on the enemy's camp, slay fifty thousand
men in a matter of an hour or so, at the rate, let us say, of two
hundred a minute. When someone who is introduced as a wizard

(for example, Yeh Ching-neng, see above, p. 124) does miraculous things, he is merely living up to his reputation and one accepts the miracles without demur. But it is nowhere said that Wang Ling or his companion had any miraculous powers and when he does what is obviously impossible, the story, for me at any rate, loses interest.

(2) *'Text about the arrest of Chi Pu, in one chapter'*

This is a long ballad, entirely in seven-syllable verse. The theme is the 'cursing' of the King of Han by his enemy Chi Pu, in the presence of the King's Generals and troops. The result of this 'cursing' is that the King of Han crumples up altogether and withdraws his armies. Here is the cursing, which seems to us a very mild affair:

Looking at the King of Han from afar he waved his hand and cursed him, with such words as to shake heaven and earth. In a loud voice he shouted straight at him, 'Liu the Younger, you are a man of Feng-hsien in Hsü-chou. Your mother was a village-woman who lived by twisting hemp; your father was a villager who took out the cattle to graze. At Ssu-shui you were once a headman of ten hamlets; for a long time you haunted the purlieus of the market, poor and hungry. During the troubles that followed the fall of the Ch'in dynasty you called yourself 'King', confounding the false with the true. How can the crow spread the wings of the phoenix or the tortoise wear the scales of the dragon? In a hundred battles you were worsted a hundred times; Heaven failed to help you. Of three parts of your officers and men you lost two parts.

'Why do you not take a rope and, binding yourself, make submission to our King and beg for mercy? If once again, persisting in your folly, you boast that you are a match for us, we shall capture you alive and not let you go!'

Before the drums had sounded or the flags been unfurled he said all this in a loud voice, so that everyone could hear. The King of Han, when he was cursed and his origins brought in, could not look those about him in the face and was ashamed before his army and officials. The phoenix, fearing the parson-crow, shuns a tree that is noisy; the dragon, afraid of common fish, avoids water that is troubled. He (the King) pulled back his horse, waved his whip and galloped off; his marshalled hosts crumbled like a landslide that fills the wilds with dust.

(Two years later the King of Han routs Ch'u, the State to which Chi Pu belongs, and puts a price on Chi Pu's head. Chi Pu becomes an outlaw, pursued by people greedy to gain the reward, and the story follows a course rather similar to that of Wu Tzu-hsü.)

The normal Chinese reaction to being cursed or insulted, in ancient times, was either to return insult for insult or make a physical attack on the insulter. For example when Li K'o-yung, who figures in so many legends and plays, 'was besieging Hua-chou (*c.* A.D. 881) a man suddenly appeared on the walls and began shouting insults at him. Li K'o-yung ordered his cavalry to let fly with their arrows at the man on the walls, but they failed to hit him. Finally, he ordered Chu Yu-yü (eldest son of the future first Emperor of the Liang dynasty) to shoot, and he killed the man at the first discharge of his bow.'(186) There are, however, though it is not a common theme, examples of cursing having a catastrophic effect. In Chapter 93 of the *Romance of the Three Kingdoms*, Wang Lang is cursed by the famous warrior-statesman Chu-ko Liang, and falls dead on the spot. The crucial point in the Chi Pu ballad is, I think, that the King is cursed in the presence of his Generals and troops and so 'loses face'. One is apt to associate insistence on the supreme importance of 'face' in China with books by nineteenth-century Western observers who were fundamentally out of sympathy with the Chinese, and to consider this insistence exaggerated. But I think it is right to regard the Chi Pu story as an extreme example of the catastrophic effects that 'loss of face' could have. It is of interest that, though the early histories give a full account of Chi Pu's career, there is nothing in them about his cursing the King of Han; nor so far as I know was the episode taken up by later ballads and plays.

(3) *The story of Wang Chao-chün*

This fragmentary and very corrupt piece exists only in one MS. It is in two chapters; of the first, only approximately the last third survives. The subject is one of the most popular in the whole repertory of Chinese legend and has been the theme of countless poems, plays and pictures. The usual form of the story is that Wang Chao-chün, a Court lady, *c.* 30 B.C., confident in her own charms, refused to bribe an artist to paint her more beautiful than she was. Consequently when the Emperor was deciding which Court lady to send as a peace-offering to the Huns, he decided upon Wang Chao-chün, whom the painter had, out of spite, deliberately caricatured. In some versions of the story she throws herself into a river on the Hun frontier rather than become a nomad barbarian's mistress. In this piece she dies of homesickness at the Hun encampment. The author speaks of this as having happened 'more than eight hundred years ago'. He may have been a little vague about dates, but we should be safe in assuming that it was written in the ninth century. The subject was then a topical one, for in 821 a Chinese princess was sent as bride to the Uighur Turks. Unlike Wang Chao-chün she did not succumb to the trials of exile but returned (now a middle-aged woman) to China in 843, after the defeat of the Uighurs by the Khirgiz. Though Huns are occasionally mentioned, the people among whom Wang Chao-chün found herself are in this piece generally referred to as Turks. The author shows great knowledge of Turkish customs, particularly hunting and funeral rites, and he may well have been one of the Chinese escort party that brought the Chinese princess to the Uighur Turks in 821. The Turkish-looking plant names at the beginning may, however, be spoof, as my friend Denis Sinor can attach no meaning to them.

The piece shows strong influences of ornate upper-class (as opposed to popular) style.

IV

'AUCASSIN ET NICOLETTE'

There is a striking resemblance between the sort of *pien-wen* that is in alternating prose and verse and the thirteenth-century French romance *Aucassin et Nicolette*. Both are in alternating passages of prose and verse and in both the verse sometimes repeats what has been said in prose but sometimes carries on the narrative. Both are prevailingly in verse of seven syllables to the line. One point of dissimilarity is that in *Aucassin et Nicolette* all the lines of the verse parts rhyme or assonate (except for the short *vers orphelin* at the end of each verse section) whereas in *pien-wen* normally only the even lines rhyme.

It is worth noting that the term *chantefable*, commonly used today by French writers to denote romances in alternate verse and prose, apparently only occurs once in medieval literature: in the last line but one of *Aucassin et Nicolette*, 'no cantefable prend fin'.

Whether there is any question of an indirect Chinese influence on *Aucassin et Nicolette*, with (for example) the Turks or Arabs as intermediaries, I am not competent to discuss.

V

LIST OF DATES

A.D. 111	Inauguration of Tun-huang as a Commandery.
353	Making of first cave-temples.
406	Earliest dated Stein MS (S. 797).
781	Tun-huang, after being cut off from China for about ten years, surrenders to the Tibetans.
848	Chang I-ch'ao drives out Tibetans. Dies, 872; succeeded by Chang Huai-shen.
890	Chang I-ch'ao's son-in-law So Hsün assassinates Chang Huai-shen and usurps the government of Tun-huang.
c. 893	Rebellion against So Hsün, led by Chang I-ch'ao's fourteenth daughter. So Hsün defeated and killed. The Changs return to power.
905	A descendant of Chang I-ch'ao, Chang Ch'eng-feng, calls himself the 'White-clad Emperor of Western Han, Land of the Golden Mountain'. 'White-clad' probably means Manichean.
911	The Uighurs (who were Manicheans) take over Tun-huang and Chang Ch'eng-feng becomes their vassal.
919–920	Ts'ao I-chin wins power at Tun-huang. His second daughter marries the King of Khotan.
c. 935	Accession of Ts'ao Yüan-te.
c. 938	Accession of Ts'ao Yüan-shen.

Appendices

c. 945   Accession of Ts'ao Yüan-chung.

974   Accession of Ts'ao Yen-kung.

c. 980   Accession of Ts'ao Yen-lu, who married a daughter of the King of Khotan.

995   Latest dated Stein MS (S. 4172).

c. 1001   Death of Ts'ao Yen-lu.

1035   Tun-huang falls under the dominance of the Hsi-Hsia (Tanguts), but remains nominally independent.

1227   Tun-huang passed into the hands of the Mongols.

1516   The 1,230 inhabitants of Sha-chou (i.e. Tun-huang) shifted to a point near Su-chou. The old Tun-huang was left unoccupied and in 1524 fell into the hands of the Moslemized Mongol Khan of Turfan (*Ming History*, 330).

1725   The Manchus establish a military post at Tun-huang.

1760   Tun-huang resettled by Chinese and made into a civil district (*hsien*).

1900   The Taoist Wang Yüan-lu discovers the hidden library.

1907   Sir Aurel Stein bribes Wang to let him remove a large number of MSS and paintings on silk.

1908   Professor Pelliot does ditto.

1910   The Peking Government brings some 10,000 remaining MSS to Peking.

1916   A Japanese mission procures some 600 MSS that had been kept back by Wang Yüan-lu who had hidden them inside stucco Buddha images that he had dedicated at the caves.

NOTES AND REFERENCES

CHAPTER ONE: SWALLOW AND SPARROW

Original title: 'The *Fu* of the Swallow.'

Date of composition: not long after A.D. 721.

Date of MSS: Stein 214 has cyclical dates indicating 923 or 983.

Form: In rhymed prose throughout, apart from two poems at the end. I tried translating it as prose, but found it worked better as verse. It does not seem to go back to any legends about swallows and sparrows; but fables about birds have always been a favourite Chinese way of letting off steam about unpopular government measures. Not long ago a Peking daily printed on its front page a fable about a bird-catcher who gained the confidence of birds 'by speaking to them in their own language'. He was then easily able to catch them and pop them into cages. That the fable referred to the Hundred Flowers episode is obvious.

(1) 'The General and the Year Star' . . . Stars portending danger.

(2) 'Would not nest on feather curtains' . . . 'Like a swallow making its nest on the curtain' is a traditional metaphor expressing a precarious situation.

(3) *Nieh*, 'bastard' for *nieh*, 'gnaw'.

(4) 'The Leopard's Tail.' Another name for the Year Star, i.e. the planet Jupiter, mentioned above. There may be a pun on *niao*, 'cursèd', and *niao*, 'bird'.

(5) 'There was a Decree. . . .' In A.D. 721 all strangers were to register within a hundred days or return to the place where they had originally been registered. See Pulleyblank, *Background. . . .*, p. 178.

(6) 'Tan, Yai, Hsiang and Po. . . .' Places in the far south. An allusion to the swallow's winter migration.

(7) 'a guest may be in a hurry . . .' An often-quoted proverb. *Complete T'ang Poems* XII. 8.

(8) 'family meal'. Literally 'house-ordinary'. Cf. p. 207.

(9) 'How he puckered.' Apparently superfluous negatives are common in these MSS.

(10) 'A vile creature. . . .' Literally 'How comes he to be so insufferable?', but the phrase functioned as a strong term of abuse.

(11) 'To five bouts. . . .' Each bout consisted of twenty strokes.

(12) 'When "five beats" is the tune' . . . Pun on 'five musical beats' and 'five bouts' of flogging.

(12b) 'Burst out angrily.' I read *fa ch'en*, following Stein 214.

(13) 'sprinkled urine'. Urine was much used for medical purposes, as also in medieval Europe. 'Old paper' often means paper in which drugs have been wrapped; used by those too poor to buy the drugs themselves.

(14) 'The God of the Stove.' He apportions good and bad luck.

(15) 'That black crone. . . .' *Hei-lao-p'o*, 'the black old woman', was a name for the swallow.

(16) 'The person who comes with my food.' Chinese prisons did not supply food; the prisoners depended on what was brought to them by their families.

(17) 'In the Yellow Sands', i.e. in prison.

(18) 'The *Heart Sūtra*.' This *sūtra* is about half a page long.

(19) 'The Clerk.' Sent to question prisoners and if possible secure a confession of guilt.

(20) 'for humble reception', i.e. of scourging ordered by the King.

(21) 'My famous brain.' Sparrow's brain was valued for its medicinal qualities.

(22) 'The nineteenth year of Chen-kuan', i.e. in A.D. 645.

(23) 'The Book of Hills and Seas.' An early book of mythological topography and other wonders.

(24) 'Sings just at this time.' This line seems to be corrupt.

(25) These last four lines are an adaptation of a passage at the beginning of the Taoist work *Chuang Tzu*, coupled with an allusion to the saying 'What can the swallow or the sparrow know of the heron's ideas?' quoted for example in *Shih Chi* 48, fol. 1.

CHAPTER TWO: WU TZU-HSÜ

Original title missing.

No dated copies.

Form: Alternate prose and song.

(26) 'an Eastern Palace'. The establishment of the Heir Apparent.

(27) 'How does this passage go?' This or a similar formula often occurs before a sung passage or, as here, a passage of prose apparently intended to be given to a fresh voice, begins. I take it to be the cue to a fresh performer to come in. See above, pp. 28 and 243.

(28) Ling Che. About 607 B.C. the enemies of the statesman Chao Tun removed one wheel of his chariot in order to prevent his escape. A strong man rushed to the chariot, propped it up on the wheelless side and, taking the place of the missing wheel, enabled Chao Tun to escape. The strong man explained presently that he was the person, Ling Che by name, to whom Chao Tun had once given a meal when he

lay starving in a mulberry grove. This is one of the episodes in the famous play adapted by Voltaire as *L'Orphelin de la Chine*.

(29) 'the yellow sparrow that was given a salve'. The man who doctored the sparrow was Yang Pao, first century A.D.

(30) 'Swift as Lü Ling.' This phrase constantly occurs at the end of spells, but no one knows if Lü Ling was a spirit or whether it means 'the Law'.

(31) 'Yin-Yang magic.' Something like the Natural Magic of the Renaissance Neo-Platonists. By fully using the two great forces of the universe (Yin and Yang), the 'dark and sunny', 'female and male', 'negative and positive', its exponents sought to control the powers of Nature.

(32) 'Won gratitude by a present of wine.' Some roughs stole a valuable horse belonging to the Duke, and ate it. Instead of punishing them he gave them some wine, saying that horse-flesh caused indigestion unless wine was drunk with it. I omit two further allusions which do not seem to make sense as they stand.

(33) 'If you accept one dish only. . . .' This saying occurs several times in the Tun-huang pieces and elsewhere, in a number of different forms. See pp. 48 and 175.

(34) 'capsized his boat . . .' We are presumably intended to suppose that the fisherman committed suicide in order to set Wu Tzu-hsü's mind at rest, just as the girl had done. Compare the play *Wu Tzu-hsü blows the Pipes* where, before killing himself, the fisherman says, 'I will make sure that you go with your mind at rest'.

(35) 'the three religions'. Confucianism, Buddhism and Taoism. This is, of course, an anachronism, as Wu Tzu-hsü lived in the sixth and fifth centuries B.C. and Buddhism did not come to China till the first century A.D.

(36) 'Ch'eng-fu hsien.' The place still existed in the ninth century A.D., but is not heard of later.

(37) 'I appeal to you not to cast me aside.' These six lines are intentionally cryptic and I may well have misunderstood them.

(38) 'Those who do not repay a kindness. . . .' Quotation from *The Instructions of T'ai-kung*, a book of moral aphorisms popular at Tun-huang. See Wang Chung-min, in *Han Hsüeh*, 1949.

(39) 'means dew like hoar-frost'. The sense is not clear; but in any case P'i's interpretation is probably meant to sound absurd.

CHAPTER THREE: THE CROWN PRINCE

Original title: 'Tradition about the Crown Prince of the House of Liu, in the former Han Dynasty.'

Form: Prose throughout.

Notes

HAN P'ENG

Original title: 'The *Fu* of Han P'eng.'

Form: Prose with a good deal of rhyme.

(40) 'reaches the great Mountain'. *Sheng* ('born') seems to be a mistake for *chih* ('reaches'), due to almost identity of cursive forms.

(41) 'Then she went back to the tomb. . . .' The words in brackets are supplied from other versions of the story; in the present text several words seem to have dropped out. For these other versions, see Jung Chao-tsu in Vol. II of *Studies in honour of the sixty-fifth birthday. of Ts'ai Yüan-p'ei*, Peiping, 1933. On the strength of two rhymes of early type, Jung is inclined to place the Tun-huang version in the fifth or sixth century; but if the words in question are really intended as rhymes it would seem to place the *fu* in Han times, which is very improbable. See the report of papers read at the 1959 conference of Junior Sinologues.

THE STORY OF SHUN

Original title: 'The *pien* of Shun Tzu.' At the end, 'The *pien-wen* of Shun Tzu's extreme filial piety in one chapter'.

Form: Prose and considerable parts in rhymed prose.

(42) 'King Yao.' Mythical monarch of antiquity.

(43) 'he took out his zither'. I have assumed that *pu*, 'step', is a graphic mistake for *ch'u*, 'take out'.

(44) 'This land of Chi . . . dogs.' The text of this sentence is certainly corrupt.

(45) 'Little Elephant.' Ku-sou's son by his second wife.

(46) 'Indra.' The role of Indra in Chinese folk-tales is taken from Buddhist Jātaka stories.

(47) 'A righteous King', i.e. was destined to be.

CHAPTER FOUR: THE STORY OF CATCH-TIGER

Original title: missing. The concluding sentence shows that the copyist used an illustrated text, but omitted the illustrations.

Date of composition: Later than A.D. 843–5, the period of the great persecution of Buddhism.

Form: Prose throughout.

(48) 'The Hui-ch'ang Emperor.' Reigned A.D. 841–6. The author has confused the persecution of 843–5 with that of 574–6.

(49) 'get Heaven's portion . . .', i.e. become Emperor.

(50) 'and that is why I am late'. A few words seem here to have slipped out of the text.

(51) 'the Holy Man', i.e. the Emperor.

(52) 'a white ram'. *Yang*, 'ram', has the same sound as Governor Yang's name.

(53) 'Ch'en Shu-pao', i.e. the King of Ch'en. His name, without any title, is here used contemptuously.

(54) 'Glad to make your acquaintance.' Literally 'If by any chance. . . .', meaning 'I always said to myself, "If by any chance I happened to meet you, how nice it would be!"'

(55) 'the Khan of the Ta-hsia'. The text calls him the *Shan-yü*, but I use the term Khan because it is more familiar to English readers.

(56) 'painted a deer'. The text says, 'two deer', but this is probably a slip.

(57) 'The General of the Five Ways', see p. 225.

CONFUCIUS AND THE BOY

(58) 'the earliest mention of Hsiang T'o'. *Huai-nan Tzu*, Ch. 17, fol. 6.

(59) 'but about a new theme'. Compare the opening of the Tung Chieh-yüan *Western Pavilion*, and also the pedlar's song sequence in the last act of the play *Huo-lan-tan*.

(60) 'Confucius discovered that this rival.' For references see Chavannes, *Mémoires Historiques*, V. 327.

(61) 'dwarf jesters'. See Granet, *Danses et Légendes de la Chine Ancienne*, pp. 171 seq.

(62) 'a child three days . . .' Following Stein 1392.

(63) 'level the world'. *P'ing*, 'level', 'flatten', is here used in its physical and at the same time in its political sense.

(64) 'a saying . . . in the *Analects*'. *Lun Yü*, IX. 22.

(65) 'pricked his legs'. To keep himself awake while he studied at night.

(66) 'to steal the lamplight'. He was too poor to have a lamp, so he 'stole' the neighbour's lamplight.

(67) 'Tzu-lu . . . Tzu-chang.' Pupils of Confucius. The *Songs* is the *Book of Songs*; the *Book* is the *Book of History*, both of them Confucian classics; see above, p. 68.

(68) 'Vajrapāni.' Buddhist temple-guardian.

(69) 'these two people', i.e. Confucius and the boy. This couplet is displaced in the original.

(70) 'mounted warriors'. Compare above, p. 53.

CHAPTER FIVE: THE STORY OF HUI-YÜAN

Original title: 'The Story of Yüan-kung of the Lu Shan.' One MS dated A.D. 972.

Form: Prose with a number of *gāthās* (Buddhist stanzas).

(71) 'The Tathāgata.' Buddha, the King, Sākyamuni, the Tathāgata, are all different aspects of the same person.

(72) 'in the Second Phase'. The second five hundred years after Buddha's death.

(73) 'the end of the dynasty'. The Former Ch'in dynasty actually fell in A.D. 394, thirteen years after Hui-yüan went to the Lu Shan. The usual dates given for Hui-yüan's life are 334 to 417.

(74) 'the *Nirvāna Sūtra*'. The *sūtra* of Buddha's decease.

(75) 'Shou-chou.' About 200 miles north of the Lu Shan.

(76) 'the Gateway into the Void', i.e. Buddhism. Strictly speaking it means the gateway (into Nirvāna) via realization that certain *dharmas* (elements of existence) are void of self-nature.

(77) 'single horse and lonely spear', i.e. unaided.

(78) 'He also gave him the additional name. . . .' I have continued to call him Hui-yüan, as a change of name would have been confusing to the reader.

(79) 'the embodied and the unembodied'. Compare *Pien-wen Chi*, p. 182, lines 3 and 13.

(80) '*Analects* of Confucius.' *Lun Yü*, XI. 25.

(81) 'The Secret Thunderbolt deity.' Guardian of Buddha in Tantric Buddhism.

CHAPTER SIX: THE WIZARD YEH CHING-NENG

Yeh Ching-neng is here, as often, confused with his great-nephew Yeh Fa-shan. The latter was a Taoist master much favoured by the Court in the early part of the eighth century. He was known as a stout opponent of Buddhism, but also of the pretentions of rival Taoists who undertook to prolong the Emperor's life by alchemy. Most of the stories told above, in a less complete form and with considerable variations, occur in the printed collections of marvel-stories. Some of them give the Taoist magician concerned a quite different name.

Original title: Unknown. The words 'Poem about Yeh Ching-neng' which occur at the end seem to refer only to the poem by the Emperor, which I have omitted.

Date of composition must be later than 764, as the Emperor Hsüan Tsung is referred to by his posthumous title. Probably ninth or tenth century. There are marginal additions and corrections in a different hand.

(82) 'said the spirit'. The text reads 'said in writing', but I think this is corrupt.

(83) 'The Great Unity.' Supreme Star-god.

(84) 'Bowing to the hall', i.e. entertaining the bridegroom's relations, on the day after the wedding.

(85) 'mouth-noises'. *Hsiao*, usually translated 'whistle', but it included imitations of bird-cries, and so on.

(86) 'like a blood-bowl'. As used at child-birth.

(87) 'the curfew was abolished'. The curfew compelling everyone to be back in his own ward before night fell and the gates of the ward were locked.

CHAPTER SEVEN: MENG CHIANG-NÜ

Original title: Missing.

Form: Alternate song and prose.

For a translation of an interesting modern Meng Chiang-nü ballad, see Joseph Needham and Liao Hung-ying in *Sinologica*, 1948, pp. 194 seq.

(88) 'A poor soldier . . . will not forget.' These four lines are spoken by the ghost of the husband.

(89) 'Have not the power to move', i.e. to affect Nature.

(90) 'at my wit's end'. For *Ch'ü-tz'u*, see Chiang Li-hung, p. 54.

THE STORY OF T'IEN K'UN-LUN

The Swan Maiden legend is, of course, one of the most widely diffused stories, particularly in the Far East. The present version has a curious ending, not so far as is known found anywhere else, in which the Swan Maiden's son answers conundrums. I do not believe that this addition has any intrinsic connection with the main story. Chinese popular literature teems with scenes in which sages (Confucius, Yen Tzu, Tung Chung, the boy Hsiang T'o) distinguish themselves by answering difficult questions, and it is evident that listeners and readers delighted in and demanded such passages. There are, of course, versions of the Swan Maiden story (compare O. Mänchen-Helfen, *T'oung Pao*, 1936, p. 10) in which her husband is put through his paces by being made to answer a series of questions or riddles, but I do not think the second part of our story is connected with episodes of that kind.

Original title lacking. It is from the series headed *Sou Shen Chi*,

'Record of Enquiry into Spirits'. I will not deal here with the complicated history of the various story-collections bearing this title. There is a short and very jejune version of the Swan Maiden story in Chapter 14 of the twenty-chapter version of the *Sou Shen Chi*.

As regards the wide diffusion of the story, I think the view put forward by Norman Penzer in Vol. VIII of *The Ocean of Story* that it spread along with Buddhism is difficult to maintain. Buddhist texts contain many versions of a story about a divine girl-musician, the Kinnarī, who married a human being. But so far as I know these Buddhist stories lack the stolen feather-robe *motif*, which appears to occur only in Indian non-Buddhist texts. I would tentatively suggest that the stolen robe *motif* is a widely diffused archaic folk-theme and occurs as such in India, China, Japan, South-East and North-East Asia, as also in the Germanic and Celtic worlds, without any influence of Buddhism. In the Buddhist area the robe *motif* tended in folk-legend to be interpolated into the quite independent Kinnarī legend, as happened, for example, in the Siamese folk-play *Nakhon Nora*.

The MS containing our story is now preserved at the Museum of Calligraphy (formerly the Nakamura Fusetsu collection) at Tōkyō. It originally belonged to the Chinese scholar Lo Chen-yü, and there seems to be no doubt that it came from Tun-huang.

The story is in prose throughout.

(91) 'K'un-lun' means 'the Negro'; probably a nickname.

(92) 'made for me a heavenly robe'. Compare the Hymn to the Soul (Apocryphal Acts of Thomas): 'My parents . . . took off the glittering robe that in their love they had made for me.'

(93) 'Master Tung Chung.' Compare below, p. 160. The wizard Tung Chung is popularly identified with the famous Confucian philosopher and scholar Tung Chung-shu (*c.* 179 B.C. to *c.* 93 B.C.).

(94) 'an offence in the Back Palace', i.e. had an intrigue with a Court lady.

(95) 'only T'ien Chang could recognize these things'. There was an obscure historical personage (*c.* 313 B.C.) called T'ien Chang who probably has no connection with this story. T'ien Chang, the answerer of riddles, figures in a fragmentary text discovered by Stein near Tun-huang, dating from about the first century A.D.: 'T'ien Chang replied, "I have heard that the height of Heaven is 19,000 *li*, and that the width of the earth is equal to the height of Heaven".' (Maspero, *Documents Chinois*, No. 28.)

(96) 'He was swallowed by a crane.' This is reminiscent of the story of the pygmies and the cranes which is first found in *Iliad* III. 3. The question of classical influences in Chinese folk-tales was treated by

B. Laufer in *Ethnographischen Sagen der Chinesen*, in *Aufsätzen* . . . E. Kuhn
. . . gewidmet, München, 1916, pp. 198 seq., especially pp. 200 seq.
What is perhaps the earliest Chinese version of the pygmy-crane (in this
case, swan) story is contained in the *Shen I Ching*, a work of perhaps
c. A.D. 300: "Beyond the western ocean there is a country called Swan
Land. The men and women are seven inches high. They have natural
good manners, and are fond of learning, bowing and kneeling. They all
live for three hundred years. They walk as though flying and can go a
thousand leagues a day. No creature dares molest them. Their one fear
is of the lake-swan which, if it meets them, instantly swallows them.
But all the same they live for three hundred years, because they do not
die through being in the swan's belly. However, the swan carries them
far away, a thousand leagues at a stretch.'

(97) 'Hsi Wang Mu.' The Queen of the Fairies.

THE BALLAD OF TUNG YUNG

Original title: Missing. There is no reason to call it a *pien-wen*.

Form: Entirely in verse of seven syllables to the line, with the *-ang*
rhyme running right through.

This is one of the most popular themes, and has been used in countless
stories, ballads, plays, etc. The version that comes nearest to the Tun-
huang ballad is a thirteenth-century (?) story, the fourth in the *Rainy
Window Collection*, preserved in the *Ch'ing-p'ing-shan-t'ang Hua-pen*.

(98) 'a hundred thousand odd'. Normally a string of cash was 1,000
copper coins. This passage seems to imply that there were over 1,200
coins to the string; but I may well have misunderstood it.

(99) 'Here is your son kneeling.' Or 'the father and mother saw
their son kneeling', etc., but that does not seem to make sense.

(100) 'indeed'. This character is not clear; but I read *hsün* with
'heart' on the left.

(101) 'Tung Yung knelt before his master.' This sudden transition
has been taken to mean that the MS only records the sung portion of
the text and that prose links have been omitted. But the transition is
no more abrupt than those in the 'elliptic' ballads of the *Book of Songs*.

(102) 'the goddess Śrī'. Patroness of the arts; if indeed Chi-hsiang
is to be taken as a proper name.

(103) 'Tung Chung.' See above, p. 152.

(104) 'Sun Pin.' Master of war-magic, fourth century B.C.

(105) 'Sixty Cyclical Signs.' Used to denote days and, later,
years.

(106) 'Contract found at Tun-huang.' See *Tun-huang Tsa-lu*, II. 127.

Notes

THE DOCTOR

From the *Sou Shen Chi*. Prose throughout.

CHAPTER EIGHT: THE WORLD OF THE DEAD

T'AI TSUNG IN HELL

Original title: Missing.

Date of composition: Not likely to be earlier than the ninth century. The MS is fragmentary and I have only translated the more intelligible parts of it.

It is in prose.

For T'ai Tsung's visit to Hell compare the novel *Monkey* (*Hsi Yu Chi*), p. 103 seq. T'ai Tsung reigned from A.D. 627 to 649.

(107) 'a short text'. *Taishō Tripitaka*, XXI. 374.

(108) 'Kuan and Pao.' Kuan I-wu and Pao Shu-ya were statesmen of the seventh century B.C., whose deep friendship was famous.

(109) 'Chien-ch'eng and Yüan-chi.' Murdered by T'ai Tsung in 626 in order to clear his path to the throne.

(110) 'Two Boys.' See above, p. 156.

(111) 'Not *that* kind. . . .' For a similar play on words, compare *Monkey*, p. 19.

KUAN LO

This and the three following stories are all from the *Sou Shen Chi*.

(112) 'Accept a cup of wine.' See above, pp. 39 and 48.

(113) 'altered it to ninety', i.e. from 'ten-nine' to 'nine-ten'. Compare the story of T'ai Tsung, above, p. 170.

WANG TZU-CHEN

(114) 'a sophora tree'. Written 'ghost' plus 'tree' and consequently associated with spiritual beings.

(115) 'as a living man'. I follow Stein 525 which is punctuated in red. The punctuation is not visible in photographs. There is a similar story in Chapter 2 of the eight-chapter *Sou Shen Chi*, but the divergences are so great that it seldom throws light on the difficulties of the Tun-huang text.

TUAN TZU-CHING

(116) 'Liu Yüan.' About A.D. 304 to 310. Hun ruler in North China.

CHAPTER NINE: MARRIAGE SONGS

Original title: Hsia nü-fu tz'u, which I take to mean 'words (of songs) about the getting down of the bridegroom (from his horse)'.

The *Pien-wen Chi* collates seven MSS, all undated. There is apparently an eighth at Peking. All in verse, apart from the headings.

(117) 'contrary to ritual'. *T'ang Hui Yao*, 83.

(118) 'These customs are said. . . .' *Feng Shih Wen Chien Chi*, 5 (*c.* A.D. 800).

(119) 'Take word to the Governor.' The bridegroom is said to be a Governor by a ritual fiction, just as the bride is said to be the Goddess of the Moon.

(120) 'come our way'. I read *hsiang*, 'towards', not *hui*, 'return'. The latter does not give the needed rhyme.

(121) 'match for any gentleman'. See *Book of Songs* (*Shih Ching*) first poem.

(122) 'Ching K'o.' Who unsuccessfully attempted to assassinate the First Emperor.

(123) 'Three Rivers.' Usually means the three rivers near the capital.

(124) 'Nine Commanderies.' I do not know what these are.

(125) 'Eight Waters.' Of what is now Shensi.

(126) 'juice of grapes', i.e. it is not rice-wine.

(127) 'a guest for a little while', i.e. in the end she always goes back to live with her husband's family.

(128) 'broken pottery'. In passages like this there may be plays on words, of a kind hard to recognize.

(129) 'Ts'ui of the T'ai Shan.' See above, p. 166 seq.

(130) 'Request to come down. . . .' This song is displaced in the original.

(131) 'pelting of the curtains'. With coins and balls of coloured silk.

(132) 'hide the silks and satins'. Of her dress.

(133) 'take them away', i.e. take the hangings away.

(134) 'when the bride goes', i.e. to the husband's house.

(135) 'on removing the hood'. I omit a quatrain about the sharing of the sacrificial meat, which is obscure and does not fit into the context.

(136) 'Weaving Maiden.' See above, p. 161.

Notes

CHAPTER TEN: THE BUDDHIST PIECES

(137) 'as many monasteries as Tun-huang'. *Wen Yüan Ying Hua*, 850, 1.
(138) 'Ts'ao I-chin gave . . . a banquet.' *Tonkō Isho* (Manuscrits de Touen-houang), Pelliot and Haneda, Kyōto, 1926, p. 3.

BUDDHA'S MARRIAGE

A fragment; beginning and end lost, *Pien-wen Chi*, p. 325.
(139) 'the down-sign'. One of the thirty-two signs of Buddhahood—shining white down between the eyebrows.
(140) 'gave the Prince her finger-ring'. In most versions of the story it is the Prince who gives the ring to her.
(141) 'Took strenuous exercise.' The radical of *mu* should be 'heart', not 'day'.

BUDDHA'S SON

Original title: Sūtra of how the Prince achieved the Way. I give an extract beginning at *Pien-wen Chi*, 295. 5.
Form: Alternating song and prose.

For the fiery pit, etc., see *Tsa Pao Tsang Ching*, end (*Taishō Tripitaka*, IV. 496). For general suspicion about Rāhula's legitimacy, see *Ta Chih Tu Lun*, XVII. (*Taishō Tripitaka*, XXV. 182b.)

(142) *Ch'an* should have the 'food' radical.

ĀNANDA

Original title: Missing. The author takes some hints from the Buddhist Canon, particularly *Taishō Tripitaka*, III. 911; but most of the story seems to be invented.
(143) 'a strange perfume'. 'Sound' in the text seems to be a misprint for 'perfume'.
(144) 'pot-luck', literally 'house-ordinary'. Compare p. 15 l. 16.
(145) 'Cursed the World-honoured One.' A blank in the text makes the curse hard to understand.

THE DEVIL

Original title: 'Pien about the breaking of the Devil.' I begin at *Pien-wen Chi*, 349. 15.
Form: Alternating song and prose.
(146) 'The Devil went back to Heaven.' The Devil, Māra, is a *deva*, a celestial being, like other gods.
(147) 'wind and rain', i.e. caused carnal feelings.

Ballads and Stories from Tun-huang

CHAPTER ELEVEN: MU-LIEN RESCUES HIS MOTHER

Original title: 'The *pien-wen* about Great Maudgalyāyana rescuing his mother from the World of Darkness, with illustrations. One volume.' But the illustrations were not copied and the words 'with illustrations' are partly effaced.

Dated MSS: 921 and one (at Peking) 977.

Form: alternating song and prose.

(148) '*Mahābhārata*', Ādiparva (Book I) 13 and 14; repeated in 45 to 48.

(149) 'Two extremely short scriptures.' See note, 152.

(150) 'Uttara's mother.' See *Taishō Tripitaka*, IV. 224.

(151) 'Locusts.' See Wang Hsiao-ch'uan's *Yüan Ming Ch'ing chin hsi-ch'ü shih-liao* (*Novels and dramas prohibited and burnt*. . . .), p. 107.

(152) *Avalambana Sūtra*. See *Taishō Tripitaka*, XVI. 779. Shorter version, XVI. 780.

(153) 'Jambudvīpa.' The ordinary world of men.

(154) 'Leek Stem', 'Axle Box.' My interpretation of the names is a mere speculation.

(155) 'Now comes the passage. . . .' See above, pp. 28 and 243.

(156) 'the same names', i.e. the same names as certain people due to die.

(157) 'The Gate of the Springs', i.e. the Yellow Springs of Death.

(158) 'paper into cash'. Paper cash was burnt as an offering to the dead.

(159) 'Kshitigarbha.' The harrower of Hell.

(160) 'the Two Boys'. See above, pp. 156 and 170.

(161) 'the Three Ways'. Of fire, blood and sword.

(162) 'blood-bowls'. See above, p. 133.

(163) three sorts of *karma*. Those due to act, thought and word.

(164) 'a scrap of sin'. It is possible to interpret *shuai-ssu* ('follow private') as 'selfishness'. But I think the text is corrupt and that, in any case, *ssu*, 'private', stands for *ssu*, 'thread'.

(165) *Ku Pen Hsi-ch'ü Tsung-k'an* I.82

AFTERWORD

(166) '. . . are said to range from A.D. 406 to A.D. 996.' The colophon of a *Tao Te Ching* MS (see Jao Tsung-i, in *Journal of Oriental Studies*, 1955) bears the date A.D. 270. But though the MS itself is certainly very early,

Notes

there are many reasons for doubting the genuineness of the colophon. The question is too complicated to discuss here.

(167) 'only one translated before', i.e. 'Confucius and the Boy', translated by M. Soymié.

(168) 'ridges were cleft and rugged'. See above, p. 98.

(169) 'exactly as in China proper'. Pelliot MSS, 3451.

(170) 'a monk preaching at Pei-t'ing'. Stein MSS, 6551.

(171) 'Iranian cults.' See my 'Some references to Iranian temples in the Tun-huang region', studies presented to Hu Shih on his sixty-fifth birthday, pp. 123 seq.

(172) 'The names of two persons.' K'ang T'ai-ch'ing (see above, p. 129) and Ti Ch'ang (p. 138). But both surnames were also found in Central China.

(173) Akiyama article. Bijutsu Kenkyū, No. 187 (July 1956).

(174) 'Wang Chao-chün pien-wen.' See p. 248.

(175) Chi Shih-lao poem. See Ts'ai Tiao Chi, VIII. 18, and Complete T'ang Poems, XXVIII. 64b.

(176) ' "set up" and "spread out" '. See Pien-wen Chi, p. 100.

(177) ' "Look" has been interpreted. . . .' For example by H. Kawaguchi, in Nihon Chūgoku Gakkai Hō, VIII. 125.

(178) 'look how the passage . . . goes'. Pien-wen Chi, p. 370.

APPENDIX I

(179) 'There is some evidence. . . .' Inscription at the Yü-lin (Myriad Buddhas) caves; see Yü Chien-hua, Chung Kuo Pi Hua (Chinese Wall-painting), Peking, 1958, p. 263.

APPENDIX II

(180) Life of Kao Li-shih. Shuo Fu, 196.

(181) 'anecdote about an exchange of quips'. See, for example, the collection of anecdotes T'ang chih-yen, Chapter 13.

(182) 'legal interrogatory'. wen-t'ou. For this expression see 'Swallow and Sparrow' (above, p. 21) and 'T'ai Tsung in Hell' (above, p. 172).

(183) 'in a book . . . 1237'. The Shih-men Cheng T'ung, a history of the T'ien-t'ai Sect. Tripitaka Supplement C. 3. 5. fol. 412.

(184) 'The compacting of the Earth.' This was done, according, for example, to St Ephraim (died A.D. 373), by using as material the excrements of the defeated Powers of Darkness.

Listed with this pien-wen is the 'Song of the Five Olives' (?) (Wu *lai-tzu ch'ü*), which must be the same as the *Wu lai-tzu ko* which is said (*Sung History*, 66. 10) to have been immensely popular about A.D. 960. The Manichean *pien-wen* about the compacting of the Earth may also well belong to the tenth century.

(185) '*fu* about the Hot Springs'. *T'ai-p'ing Kuang-chi*, 250. 5.

APPENDIX III

(186) 'at the first discharge of his bow'. See *Old History of the Five Dynasties*, XII. 5.

INDEX

Index

271

Index

SE